LONDON SUBURBS

LONDON SUBURBS

INTRODUCTION BY ANDREW SAINT

MERRELL HOLBERTON
PUBLISHERS LONDON

in association with

ENGLISH HERITAGE

First published 1999 by
Merrell Holberton Publishers Ltd
Willcox House
42 Southwark Street
London
SE1 1UN

ISBN 1 85894 077 X

British Library Cataloguing in Publication Data
London suburbs
1. Architecture - England - London - History 2. Suburbs - England - London
720.9'421

Distributed in the USA and Canada by Rizzoli International Publications, Inc. through St Martin's Press, 175 Fifth Avenue, New York, New York 10010

Editor Julian Honer
Consultant Editor Kit Wedd
Designer Matthew Hervey

Acknowledgements
The authors wish to thank the following for their kind help in the preparation of this book:

Bridget Cherry and the late Sir Nikolaus Pevsner, whose London volumes of The Buildings of England series have proved, as ever, an invaluable resource.

The conservation officers and librarians of all 32 London boroughs, who have tirelessly answered questions and helped with the compilation of the gazetteer.

Julia Brown for her assistance with the picture research.

In addition, the authors wish to thank all their colleagues at English Heritage. Special thanks are owed to Nigel Corrie, Jonathan Bailey and Jeremy Richards of the English Heritage Photographic Section, who have taken a large number of photographs throughout Greater London especially for this book; also to Paul Charlton of the Greater London Sites and Monuments Record (GLSMR) at English Heritage, for his help with the mapping.

Front jacket: Little Gaynes Lane, Upminster (London Borough of Havering)

Back jacket: It's a change you need – move to Osterley: a London Underground poster of 1926 by Victor Hembrow (© London Transport Museum)

Half-title: 'Stockbroker Tudor', from Osbert Lancaster, Pillar to Post, London (John Murray) 1938 (© John Murray/Osbert Lancaster estate)

Frontispiece: Wharton Street, Finsbury, WC1 (London Borough of Islington)

All works of art, photographs and maps are reproduced by kind permission of the following:

B.T. Batsford Ltd: fig. 111

Birmingham Museums and Art Gallery: fig. 2

Eddie Booth: figs. 148–68, 170, 172–74

Christie's: fig. 94

Community Initiative Partnerships: figs. 8, 81, 84

English Heritage: figs. 6, 15, 18, 21–23, 25–29, 31–36, 39, 41–45, 47–48, 50, 53–55, 57–61, 63, 65, 67–69, 80, 82–83, 86, 88, 91–93, 96–97, 106, 109–10, 115, 117–18, 120, 123, 131–39, 142–43, 147, 169, 171 and all gazetteer images

Guildhall Library, Corporation of London/Geremy Butler Photography: fig. 5

Hornsey Central Library, London Borough of Haringey: figs. 51–52

Richard Lea: fig. 37

London Borough of Bexley Museums Service: fig. 40

London Metropolitan Archives, Corporation of London: figs. 10, 13, 16, 20, 30, 38, 56, 62, 64, 70–71, 87, 89–90, 95, 99–100, 104–05, 107, 112, 121–22, 124–30

London Transport Museum: figs. 14, 101

John Murray/Osbert Lancaster estate: fig. 108

National Federation of Builders: figs. 113–14

National Trust/Richard Bond: fig. 19

Orion Publishing Group: London development maps pp. 9, 11, 13, 16, 22

Photographs Collection, British Architectural Library, Royal Institute of British Architects: figs. 49, 72–75, 78–79

Royal Commission on the Historical Monuments of England/Crown Copyright: figs. 4, 7, 24, 66, 76–77, 85, 98, 116, 119

Andrew Saint: figs. 9, 11–12, 17, 46

Shepheard, Epstein and Hunter/Chris Hollick: fig. 146

Wates Estates: figs. 140–41, 144–45

Gazetteer maps
The symbol locating the London Underground stations is © London Transport and is reproduced with their kind permission

Borough boundaries are based on information supplied by the boroughs as set out by the Local Government Commission for England

Maps prepared for Visitmap by Arka Cartographics Ltd are from satellite imaging, aerial photography, AA road classification and original field surveys carried out by Arka Cartographics Ltd © 1999

Printed in China

Contents

Foreword

The suburbs of London have a special place in our imagination and affections. Whether or not we actually live there, we feel we know them. As the inspiration for novels and poetry, the butt of jokes or the setting for sitcoms, they have been part of the cultural landscape for decades. But in this case familiarity has not always bred contempt. Even as we think of cherry blossom billowing across the neat avenues of 'Metroland', or net curtains twitching behind Neighbourhood Watch stickers, we know that the suburbs are more complicated and less cosy than their popular image.

In London in particular, the complex factors involved in suburban growth have long been the focus of statistical research and scholarly analysis. Meanwhile, decoding the social and architectural significance of the suburb is becoming a newly fashionable academic pursuit. I share Andrew Saint's view that London's suburbs form an integral and equal part of the greater metropolis and that they have a crucial part to play in the current debate about regenerating our cities. For all these reasons, the time seems right for a book that places the process of academic enquiry in a context that can be enjoyed by all. Hence English Heritage, in the interests of greater public appreciation, has decided to turn what began as an internal report into a book that we hope will reach a wide audience and help to make a difference to the conservation of our historic suburbs.

For the architectural historian, London's suburbs are infinitely fascinating – each one a snapshot of the times, the civic consciousness or the individual aspirations that made it. Less susceptible than the metropolitan centre to the beguiling promise of renewal through change and more willing than rural England to embrace the unfamiliar, the suburbs preserve town planning, house design and garden layout in a particularly instructive way. This is how most people in London live today. Indeed, among the contributors to this book (all of whom work, or have worked, for English Heritage) are several suburbanites, whose affectionate regard for their home territory flavours their writing.

At their best, London's suburbs are a conscious exercise in romantic place-making, embracing some of the finest and most evocative architecture of their times. The architectural originality and innovation of the early garden suburbs, such as Bedford Park and Hampstead Garden Suburb, have long been applauded as being among England's finest contributions to the art of town planning. But what of London's lesser-known suburbs?

Muswell Hill, that Queen of Suburbs, astride the heights of north London, has an Edwardian exuberance and vitality that is unmatched anywhere in England. Its extraordinary range of Edwardian free-style houses and terraces, carefully aligned to one other and to the undulating landscape beneath, makes our current attempts to create civilized residential areas look laughably banal by comparison.

At Golders Green, the commercial centre was created from green fields in just four years by the architects Welch and Hollis in a series of brilliant, well-articulated terraces in Arts and Crafts, neo-Georgian, Art Nouveau and classical styles, which coalesce to create an urbane environment of real quality.

It is a measure of their success that, be it Acton or Crouch End, Southgate or Petts Wood, Winchmore Hill or Gidea Park, London's suburbs engender fierce local loyalties and intense civic pride. Many, such as Stanmore, Mitcham, Tottenham and Dulwich, are based on older settlements that were subsumed by later development. These urban and suburban villages are a unique aspect of London's polynuclear development. Those who once sneered dismissively at suburban values are now being forced to reappraise their views as new generations move into the older suburbs, captivated by their leafy avenues and generously proportioned houses enriched with carved oak timbers and stained-glass galleons.

Some of the most gifted architects of their generations practised in the London suburbs. While Lutyens, Baillie Scott and Voysey achieved lasting fame, others such as John Sydney Brocklesby, who worked in Merton Park and Wimbledon, or Ernest Trobridge, who produced some wonderfully eccentric fairy-tale houses in Kingsbury and Neasden, have long since been forgotten.

As the government's chief adviser on the historic environment, English Heritage is determined that the special qualities of London's suburbs should be recognized and adequately protected. London's borough councils need to look with fresh eyes at their Edwardian and inter-war shopping centres and residential estates and make Article 4 directions and conservation-area designations to protect them from the cumulative impact of permitted development. In the absence of Article 4 directions, the unthinking replacement of original windows, doors and boundary treatments, crude extensions and other creeping alterations usually lie beyond planning control, yet they destroy the very qualities that make an area special. Studies by English Heritage demonstrate that houses and areas that retain their original features are worth up to 15% more than those which have lost them. Conservation makes real economic sense.

One of the greatest qualities of many London suburbs is their uncluttered streetscape with generous tree-lined avenues creating areas of real environmental quality. Ironically, this very quality is most threatened by those charged with preserving it – London's borough councils – through misguided traffic-calming measures that generate a blizzard of signs and other devices without reference to the wider character of an area. This sort of intervention is rarely needed. With care and sensitivity it is usually possible to design tailor-made solutions that can minimize signs and reinforce rather than diminish local character. In every case detailed consultation is essential with the council's own conservation staff, or, where necessary, with English Heritage. Our forthcoming *London: Streetscape Manual* is intended to provide advice and guidance on just these issues to achieve uncluttered, well-designed streets for all.

This is the first time that London's suburbs have been accorded such a wide and free-ranging treatment, but if they are to be preserved and enhanced for future generations to enjoy, then better public understanding and appreciation are crucial. This book represents an important step in that process.

Philip Davies, *Director, London Region, English Heritage*

Introduction
The Quality of the London Suburb

ANDREW SAINT

This suburb of mine is not a period piece. The old houses hereabouts are part of the gross tissue of London, just as are the pre-war flats which I can see down the road (the marks where the oil-bomb crashed into them in 1941 invisibly mended) or the post-war Council flats beyond them or, indeed, the synagogue which is being built on the site of the old vicarage. It is a most ordinary suburb. But like so many ordinary things it holds a mystery – the mystery of its origins and its first makers and denizens and this is, to some minds, a mystery that rankles and goads. Why did they do it like that, with what ambition and for what rewards? On what precedents and with what illumination of mind – or if with none, why none?

John Summerson (1973)[1]

Everyone has an idea of the suburb, can recognize and feel his or her version of the thing. At that point unanimity ends. The suburb has meant different things at different times to different people. Refuge for the riff-raff beyond the confines of the ancient or medieval city; haven for the family, idyll of comfort, safety, ordinariness and respectability; backdrop for Utopian reconciliation between the classes; picturesque medley of half-grasped building styles and over-foliaged gardens; servile and repetitious creature of the tyrant tram, bus, train or automobile; dump for the isolated, the unwanted and the dispossessed; place and space without definition or feeling, sandwiched between the sincerity of the countryside and the vitality of the city; focus for the independent and private way most people now live and want to live. All these caricatures of the suburb have their legitimacy and tell some part of its story.

On at least two counts there is agreement. The suburb is by definition an appendage to the city. And the ideal of the modern suburb was an Anglo-American invention that began its life in London. The elusive relationship between London and its suburbs set off a revolution that still resonates the world over. This helps explain the assurance and authority palpable in many London suburbs. For here the positive conception of the suburb first saw the light of day. Here, for centuries, the suburb has seemed to a majority of the British metropolitan population a desirable, reasonable and natural place to be.

Robert Fishman has offered the most persuasive account of the suburb's rise to respectability in his book *Bourgeois Utopias* (1987). In England, as elsewhere, he explains, the image of the suburb was always a negative one until the eighteenth century. Even later, the word and the idea could still have pejorative connotations. 'What made you take such a very ugly subject?', asked Ruskin (a suburban dweller) of Ford Madox Brown in 1855, on seeing his picture of the prospect from the back yards

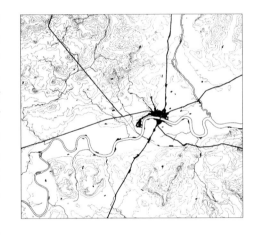

Medieval and Tudor London

1

Alton West, Alton Estate, Roehampton
LONDON BOROUGH OF WANDSWORTH
Le Corbusier confronts the suburb: a formidable image of the newly completed slab blocks built by the LCC in 1954–58 in imitation of the Unité d'Habitation, Marseilles.

2

An English autumn afternoon, Hampstead
by Ford Madox Brown, 1852–55

Oil on canvas, 71.2 × 134.8 cm

Birmingham Museums and Art Gallery

A view looking across Hampstead Heath
towards Highgate, painted from the window of
the artist's lodgings in Hampstead. Brown has
shunned the conventions of Victorian painting
favoured by the public and critics and instead
depicts the ordinary, everyday suburban
landscape of back gardens and rooftops.

of Hampstead, *An English autumn afternoon* (fig. 2). Brown replied: 'Because it lay out of a back window.'[2]

In medieval times, to live outside the walls of a city was to live literally an uncivilized life and often an illicit one – 'beyond the pale'. The Canon's Yeoman in *The Canterbury Tales* speaks of the suburbs of a town as the residence of robbers and thieves, 'lurking in hernès and in lanès blind'.[3] London had various scruffy peripheral concentrations in the form of ribbon developments along major corridors of access, beyond the reach of most urban authority and order. For that very reason they often pullulated with unruly vigour and creativity, like the Southwark of Chaucer and Shakespeare (which the City sought from an early date to control) or the rough, riparian hamlets of boat people dotted downriver by Elizabethan times as far as the Isle of Dogs. So much was common to the cities of medieval Europe, generally well defined by walls and water: the suburb meant trouble, danger, vulgarity – and opportunity. Much later even, suburbs could cause major upsets of public order: in Paris, the riots that ended in the sacking of the Bastille in 1789 began outside the walls in the Faubourg Saint-Antoine. National and city governments therefore did what they could to check unplanned metropolitan expansion, issuing prohibitive edicts and sometimes pulling unlicensed suburban buildings down. In London, this long-sanctioned practice reached its climax in the early seventeenth century, during the reign of James I.

But it would be wrong to dismiss the pre-modern suburb as merely shambolic and sordid. Just as the city defined the parameters of regular civic life, so by the same token any activity too powerful, independent or hazardous had to find its place outside the tight confines of the walls. Palaces, monasteries, markets, hospitals and barracks all gravitated at an early stage to the outskirts, where space was not at a premium and institutions could impose their own rules.

Take just one example, that of Smithfield (fig. 3). Here, on the fringes of the medieval City, sprang up a market for livestock, a fair linked with the market, a place of execution, a priory and a hospital – vital activities all, but ones impossible to accommodate *intra muros*. Over the centuries, as London tightened its grip around the old suburb of Smithfield, the priory was suppressed, St Bartholomew's Hospital flourished and grew, while fairs and executions disappeared. Smithfield Market was rebuilt by the Victorians as a wholesale emporium for meat; but the live-cattle market was re-created, much enlarged, in a new and remoter suburb off the Caledonian Road. By this date other London institutions needing careful management and space such as cemeteries, docks, sewage works and certain types of factory and prison had copied the same pattern of suburbanization.

So tenacious has been the belief that the London suburbs are just a concatenation of old villages that we have almost forgotten how numerous, how powerful and often how *architectural* these extra-mural institutions were – and are. Great naval buildings give the keynote to Greenwich; barracks do the same at Woolwich; Chelsea, Kensington, Hampton, Kew, Richmond and of course Westminster have been profoundly shaped by their palaces and hospitals. Today it is often assumed that architectural scale and grandeur in cities are confined to the centre, whereas the suburbs are ordinary and domestic. Up to at least 1750 you could turn this around. The city core, with few exceptions (principally churches), was a repository of banal domestic buildings; the suburbs were the location for the great architectural projects. This applied to other dense cities as well – to Paris just as much as London.

When and why did the suburbs of these two great rivals start to differ so sharply? The answer has to do with the seventeenth-century tension and collision, political and geographical, between the City in the East and the Crown in the West. Westminster, where the epicentre of royal power lay, was never so much a suburb as a separate, Court-dependent community without walls, administratively and then also physically distinct from the City. By the time of the Civil War in the 1640s, the old city walls of London were an increasing irrelevance, whether for domicile or defence (the earthworks thrown up by Parliament to defend London took in a much larger area). Whereas other European cities kept on pushing out their administrative boundaries, built new rings of defences and kept the immediate areas beyond them clear of houses, London after the Restoration never had the military need or forged the political consensus between City and Crown to do so. The clear-cut enlargement and annexation of *faubourg* to city that several times took place in Paris, for instance, never occurred in London.

So the seventeenth-century squares built in the West End from Covent Garden onwards were created in a strange, administrative limbo. They were elegant yet periph-

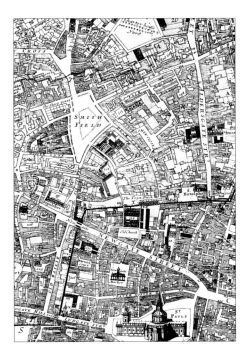

3

Morgan's map of London and Westminster, 1682

CITY OF LONDON

This detail shows St Paul's at the bottom, the line of the City walls, and beyond, the open space of Smithfield, top centre.

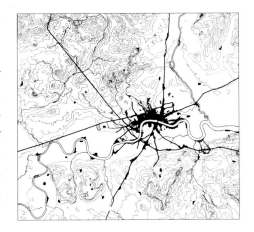

Seventeenth-century London

eral places that looked to Westminster and the Court more than to the City. Were they suburbs or not? That depends on your sense of the term. Covent Garden, the prototype of the 1630s, built in the tight, Franco-Italian classical idiom that came to define English urbanism, appears at first sight to be the very opposite to a suburb. Yet it occupied the edge of the built-up area, replacing (as its name recalls) the large garden of a former nunnery. In the same way, the whole succession of later London squares were laid out, for the most part, on orchard or market-garden ground. To deny them suburban status is to define the suburb in terms of style rather than topography. As yet there was no architectural style for the suburbs. Or rather, before the Great Fire, classicism of the type we now associate with urbanity was becoming the style of the ampler suburbs, while the vernacular tradition remained the idiom of the old and close-packed City.

Nor did the bad reputation of the suburbs vanish along with these handsome new constructions. The piazza of Covent Garden soon degenerated into a shabby market; the centre of St James's Square became, according to Macaulay, 'a receptacle for all the offal and cinders, for all the dead cats and dead dogs of Westminster'.[4] Proper management, not just architectural style, had to develop before the London suburb could achieve lasting respectability.

A devastating sequence of events was to be the making of the London suburb. These were the Great Plague of 1665 and Great Fire of 1666, twin catastrophes that underlined the drawbacks and dangers of urban life and the lure of the suburbs. For reasons of security and amenity alike, monarchs had long possessed Thames-side palaces within striking distance of the City: Greenwich in one direction, close to Henry VIII's naval port at Deptford; Richmond and Hampton Court in the other. Aristocrats and merchants who could afford them had likewise taken second homes up or down river (Osterley, built by Sir Thomas Gresham, is a well-known example). But the disasters of the 1660s – not the first, but the last and worst of their type – accelerated and propagated the movement. Though the City was fully rebuilt after the Fire and most of its citizens returned to reside there, many people had acquired a taste for life on the outskirts during the interim. In the new districts of Covent Garden, Soho and Bloomsbury they found streets, homes and gardens more spacious and pleasing than in the City itself. Neither Paris nor Amsterdam, London's main rivals in prosperity, enjoyed the topography and political circumstances that let them grow outwards in this smooth and permissive way.

Allied with this change was a social trend that gathered force in the eighteenth century: the ideal of bourgeois family life. To this, with its focus on personal security and tranquillity, Fishman largely attributes the rise of the London suburb. It is impossible to pinpoint a start to the process or judge the exact causes. One factor, certainly, was the secularization of morals during the Georgian era – the shift away from mere religious observance towards habits of communal and domestic respectability. Along with this went a growing intolerance of metropolitan vice, sickness and crime, signs of which can be found in the paintings of Hogarth, the social reformism of Henry and John Fielding and the many hospital foundations (mostly in the suburbs) of the period after 1720.

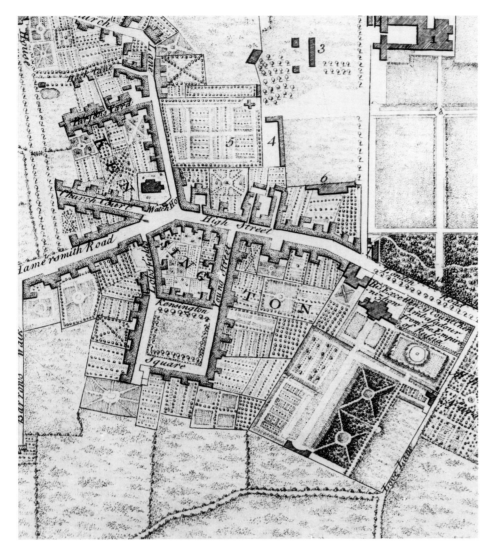

4
Rocque's map of London, *ca.* 1754
ROYAL BOROUGH OF KENSINGTON AND
CHELSEA
*A ribbon development in the outlying village of
Kensington. Kensington Palace appears in the
top right-hand corner, and Kensington Square
(begun in 1685) at the bottom. At this date
market and pleasure gardens continued to
occupy most of the space.*

In reality, London may have been no more dangerous, smoky, dirty, foggy or noisy than before. But among the better-off, a reaction against its moral and physical unruliness had set in. At the same time, London's unchecked commercial and industrial growth, its gallop to unprecedented urban extent, could make it a bewildering and belittling place to be. How much better to live, or at least send your wife and children to live, in some quiet, clean and finite newly built West End development (fig. 4), where the neighbours were civil, there was good shopping in Bond Street, you had a mews behind the house for your coach and pair, and Hyde Park was tolerably close by. How much better again to own a roomy villa in a quiet outlying village such as Hampstead or Hackney or Clapham or Camberwell and ride up to 'Change for the day or the week, as need be.

Patterns of that kind of life were common by the mid-eighteenth century but not as yet quite idealized. The suburban ideal of 'retreat' that we recognize today took time to mature; only when it had done so could it find its own architectural expression. It took

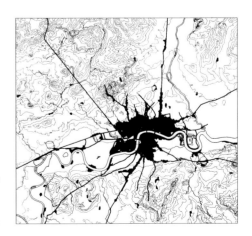

Eighteenth-century London

5

Clapham Common in 1800, from Smith's
*Actual survey of the roads from London to
Brighthelmstone.*

*Detached villas cluster around the common,
several of them belonging to the Thornton
family. South is at the top of the map.*

root with special strength in two districts with ties to the City and strong religious and intellectual communities. One was Hackney, where Georgian merchants' houses abounded and, at the time of the French Revolution, Church of England loyalists played cat and mouse with a controversial, unitarian-radical faction. The other was Clapham, where, during the destabilizing period of the French Wars of 1793–1815, William Wilberforce, Zachary Macaulay, the banking family of the Thorntons and the other so-called 'Clapham Saints' crystallized what was to become the standard of pious Victorian family life: prosperity, comfort and retirement coupled with prayer, intellectual effort and good works. Not that these habits had hitherto been lacking in English bourgeois

6

Park Village East, looking south, after a drawing by T.H. Shepherd

LONDON BOROUGH OF CAMDEN

This scene shows semi-detached villas built by Nash and Pennethorne after 1824 and the 'commercial cut' of the Regent's Canal leading down to the canal basin and Cumberland Market.

families. But around the common at Clapham (fig. 5) grew up, for the first time, a suburban community that offered something of a visible model for these virtues.

The Claphamites lived for the most part in ample, separate, Georgian villas, enlivened by bow windows or the occasional rustic touch. But as the speculative instinct for projecting 'urban' squares and terraces out into the fields weakens, the first shoots of a London suburban architecture, distinct from anything in Bath or Bristol or Edinburgh, emerge above ground. The immortal Paragon (1794–1807; see fig. 38) at Blackheath epitomizes the moment of transition. For here, the terrace, in up-to-date crescent form, couples with the Claphamite or Hackneyish villa (complete with bows at the back) to beget that lusty bastard, that misshapen key to the English suburb – the semi-detached house. Stranded out in a void, far from the intimacy and assurance of surrounding streets, the house-pairs of The Paragon hang on to one another, hold hands, as it were, for moral support, by means of linking colonnades. This equivocal blend of dependence and independence is the essence of suburban architecture – perhaps, indeed, of the whole modern manner of life.

The next step belongs indisputably to John Nash and his plan for Regent's Park. Here is displayed a panoply of suburban invention, in which villas and terraces of many articulations and sizes unite with road layout and landscape to ring the changes on all kinds of half-sketched or idealized relationships between city and countryside, civil community and august isolation. The upshot is a wealth of ideas, styles and motifs for the suburb of the future. The drollery and pretence involved, coupled with Nash's slapdash methods, his dubious business practices and the incompleteness of the development, make it easy to slight the whole enterprise as a mere essay in effects. But the 1820s was a decade not only of display but also of growing earnestness. If we are tempted to cynicism by the

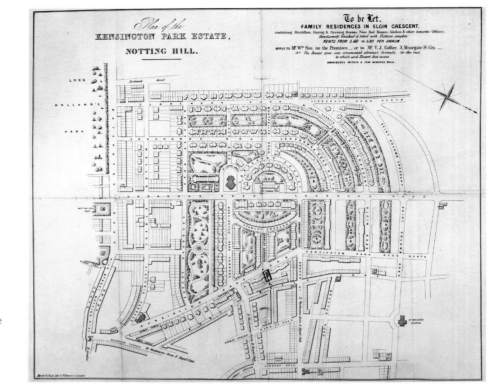

7

Plan of the Ladbroke Estate, North
Kensington, *ca.* 1855

ROYAL BOROUGH OF KENSINGTON AND
CHELSEA

*Terraces and semi-detached villas are set out
along straight and curving roads, with an estate
church left of centre and common gardens
behind the houses. The plan was substantially
modified in execution.*

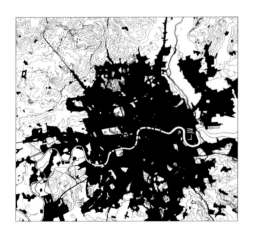

Nineteenth-century London

easy charm, slightness and intricacy of Park Village East (fig. 6) and Park Village West (see figs. 45–46), those miniatures of the forthcoming Victorian suburban villaed 'park', let us not forget that their precursor, Nash's circle of picturesque cottages at Blaise Hamlet (1811–12), outside Bristol, was built for a Quaker banker who wished to see his servants housed in respectable, rural interdependence.

Speculation and the suburb are indissoluble; the ideals of the reformer will always be watered down where profiteering is at stake. But it would be wrong to dismiss Regent's Park and its many successors – for instance, the inventive series of private 'garden squares' tucked away behind the stuccoed terraces of North Kensington (fig. 7) – as without serious aims. In the Victorian suburb, amenity, profit, comfort and the reinforcement of family life were all rolled up together in one ball. So much is shown not just by the middle-class housing that is the perpetual *leitmotiv* of the London suburb but also by the one building type which always accompanies it until about 1900 – the Anglican 'estate church' (or, in pre-Victorian times, the 'proprietary chapel'). Gothic though its tower may proclaim itself in contrast to the corrupt classicism of the houses all around, and starkly though its scale and ragstone facings may lour against domestic brickwork or smooth-coated cement, the distinctiveness of the estate church has a practical function that chimes in with everything around it. More than a symbol of spiritual values or community cohesion, it is a guarantee of respectability and order. It helps to ensure that the rental from the surrounding property stays high, and forms part of the overall calculation of the suburb.

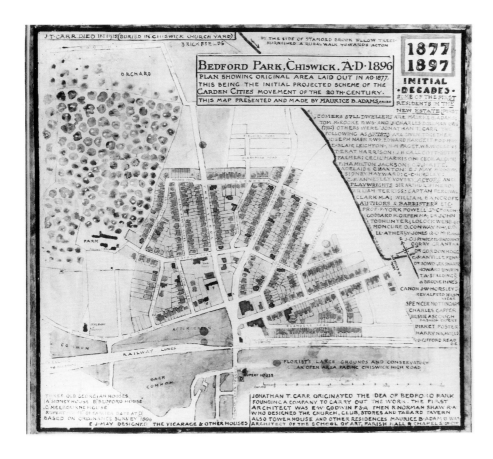

The map itself contains various handwritten annotations including:

BEDFORD PARK, CHISWICK. A·D·1896
PLAN SHOWING ORIGINAL AREA LAID OUT IN AD 1877.
THIS BEING THE INITIAL PROJECTED SCHEME OF THE
GARDEN CITIES MOVEMENT OF THE 20TH CENTURY.
THIS MAP PRESENTED AND MADE BY MAURICE B.ADAMS, FRIBA

1877
1897
INITIAL
·DECADES·

8

Map of Bedford Park, Turnham Green, Chiswick, of 1896

LONDON BOROUGHS OF EALING AND HOUNSLOW

This map of the earliest section of Bedford Park, laid out by 1877, shows the streets of houses, the site of the communal buildings and extensive planting. It was drawn by Maurice Adams, one of the architects of the estate and designer of the art school, parish hall and chapel. His plan is annotated with the names of some of the earliest residents, including Jonathan T. Carr, who, as the map states, 'originated the idea of Bedford Park', as well as numerous artists, architects, writers, thespians and lawyers.

Bedford Park (fig. 8; see also figs. 81–86), the most fetching of London's Victorian railway suburbs, begun in 1875, is a good instance of the mixed intentions and calculations involved in such places. Is it the 'first garden suburb', or a Bohemian community, or a doubtful speculation with botched detail? In some measure it is all three. Jonathan Carr, Bedford Park's promoter, was a risk-taker, haphazard about business and architectural detail. But he was also a social idealist who hoped and in part managed to create an egalitarian, secular, middle-class community with what we would now call 'leisure facilities' — club, pub, tennis courts and art school, as well as the inevitable church. Its street layout is nothing special and it peters out into banal development that dates from after Carr's financial collapse in the 1880s. That does not detract from its fresh and friendly tone, its respect for existing greenery and its rebellion against the dismal basements that until then had detracted from even the better suburban houses. Architectural perfection is not to be sought in Bedford Park. Like many suburbs, it is a vague sketch hinting at how busy people of moderate means may live, rarefied but also democratized in the process of being handed down from architect and freeholder to builder and tenant. Not by chance was visiting Bedford Park likened to 'walking through a water-colour'.[5]

By the time Bedford Park was created, the railway suburb was familiar. It had taken time to define itself. London's first railways, with a few exceptions such as the London Bridge to Greenwich route, were inter-city lines without many stations on the urban fringes or services calling at them. Early Victorian suburbs relied on omnibus routes (which multiplied after the repeal of restrictive legislation in 1832) or private stabling. Then the second railway boom of the 1860s, beginning with the Metropolitan and District Lines, ushered in a London suburban network that went on proliferating until the 1930s. A question then arose: how to confer the civilizing benefits of the suburb, now universally admitted, on London's poor and potentially discontented working classes?

The desire to reduce population densities in the centre had been expressed often enough since Elizabethan times; here at last was the means to do so. Uncoordinated metropolitan railway- and road-building during the 1860s had torn down so many homes (slum ones above all and deliberately) as to increase urban densities. This made housing reformers and parliamentarians keener to do something. The great obstacle was the cost of transport, which more than outweighed the cheapness of suburban land. The working man could afford to move his family to a healthy suburb only if rapid, subsidized trains ran very early and late in the day, taking him to and from his long hours of work in the centre.

Hence the Cheap Trains Acts, which took hold from the 1880s. They especially moulded the north-eastern outer suburbs accessible from Liverpool Street. Here and elsewhere (for instance, a swathe of southern suburbs stretching south from Peckham to Penge, Norwood and Anerley) the terrace tradition relentlessly perpetuates itself into the Edwardian years at a stunted two storeys, with bay windows thrown in as a sop to variety. Sometimes, as in Northern and Midland cities, the infinite procession of rows mutates into tiny, two-storey flats with pairs of adjacent entrances for each 'house'; Tooting and Walthamstow abound in this arrangement. Such tracts, with their pocket front gardens and their rear gardens half eaten up by back extensions, cannot vie with the advances in suburban theory and style portended at Bedford Park. The best estates, like those of the Artizans', Labourers' and General Dwellings Company at Shaftesbury Park, Battersea, and Queen's Park, Kilburn, boast broad streets, a certain overall discipline and some leavening touches of detail, yet at heart even they do not differ much from the 'by-law street' of Britain's industrial towns. In such places, the London railway suburb too often merits its glum reputation. They were never built for the poorest of the poor, needless to say, but for respectable artisans and the lower-middle classes (fig. 9) – the commuting clerks and 'lady typewriters' who were beginning to throng trains to and from the City.

Dominant though such models may have been, London was by now too big for consistency; by 1900 there were other types of suburban housing as well. Flats are instinctively looked on in Britain as inner-city dwelling types. But from the 1880s onwards, when, thanks to the hydraulic lift, middle-class flats began to spring up in substantial numbers, they were seized on by well-capitalized builders as a profitable alternative to the tired-out model of the terrace. Contrary to received opinion, flats in London were always popular, and occupied the outskirts as often as the core. Earl's Court and St John's Wood, for instance, offered Londoners outlying concentrations of the French,

9

'Let as fast as built'

Such was the original caption to this picture, which shows the construction of houses for the lower-middle classes on the outskirts of London; from George R. Sims, Living London, *London 1901.*

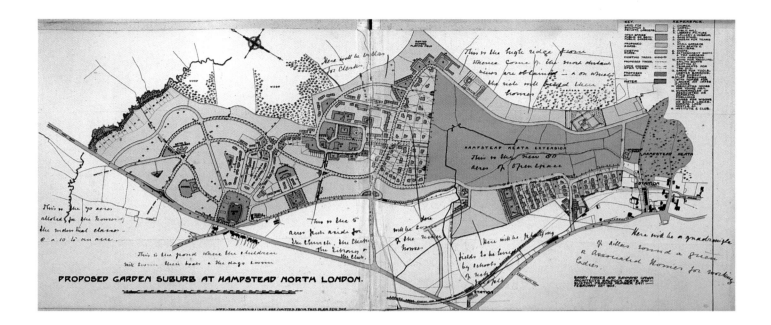

PROPOSED GARDEN SUBURB AT HAMPSTEAD NORTH LONDON.

horizontal style of living that grew in ease and acceptability as time enriched the styles and services of 'mansion flats'. The culmination of this trend was to be Highpoint, the pair of Modern Movement apartment blocks imposed upon the summit of Highgate by Lubetkin and Tecton in the late 1930s: not urban flats at all, but chic, Continental incidents breaking up the suburban grain, with picturesque garden landscapes attached by way of mollification. Earlier, the apology tended to take the guise of imitation or compromise. Maida Vale boasts street after unforgiving street of Edwardian 'mansion blocks' doing their implausible utmost to look like tall terrace houses. If suburbia is defined by commuting, Maida Vale's mansion flats are suburban, for their heads of household were largely sentenced to daily migration by tram, bus or, after 1915, the Bakerloo Line.

But with the Edwardian promulgation of the garden city and suburb, the separate dwelling as the definitive model for London's environs got new energy and heart. Narrowly speaking, the garden city did not affect London's fabric. Ebenezer Howard, the originator of the idea (or at least, the first person to set it out fully and rationally), hoped to ease the metropolis of its excess population by luring or deporting people of all classes to self-sufficient towns well beyond its limits. By this token, mindless suburbanization was to cease. But Howard's propagandizing did much to reinforce what was by now a general rush towards suburban dispersal. And the pattern of layout planned for the first garden city of Letchworth by its architects, Parker and Unwin, was to have an impact on all housing, not least on London's suburbs.

Hampstead Garden Suburb (fig. 10; see also figs. 89–93), laid out by Raymond Unwin from 1908 on the strength of his experience and travails at Letchworth, is the great exemplar – a model of almost inestimable importance. For here, thanks to the influence of his patrons, Henrietta Barnett and her committee, Unwin was able to smash

10

Henrietta Barnett's copy of Raymond Unwin's first proposed layout of Hampstead Garden Suburb of 1905

LONDON BOROUGH OF BARNET

Despite Dame Henrietta Barnett's wish to see the classes live side by side in the suburb she founded, in order to enrich each others' lives, she had definite ideas as to where it was appropriate for each class to live: the bigger houses with views over the heath were to be allotted to the wealthier classes, while the poorer classes were to be zoned off in the flatter land. The layout as built is more formal than Unwin had originally conceived it. This map has been annotated by Henrietta Barnett.

11, 12

Cité-Jardin Neuhof, Strasbourg, France

These images show a working-class garden suburb built in what was then part of Germany just before the World War I. Despite the local Alsatian style, the grouping of houses and the jardins potagers *show the influence of English garden city thinking.*

the codes and restrictions that had governed the extension of London ever since the Great Fire, by securing a private Act of Parliament to get round local by-laws. Narrow roads, wide verges, culs-de-sac, angled crossings, boundary hedges rather than walls, short terraces, set-back frontages, an end to the clumsy party wall rising above roof level and to the disfiguring back extension – these and other devices came down in scale at Hampstead Garden Suburb from outlying middle-class developments and were integrated into a fresh type of layout. The many architects who built there had to submit to rules that were different from the old ones that had obtained on London's great estates but every whit as stringent. On the maintenance of these rules down to the present day depend the continuing tone (and the property values) of 'The Suburb' – as it is justly often termed.

Seemingly in no time at all, Hampstead Garden Suburb was being visited and imitated: not just in the many garden suburbs and villages that sprang up all over Britain, only to be nipped in the bud by the First World War, but also all over Europe (in Germany most fully: Hellerau, outside Dresden, was the sincerest early copy) and the further-flung, English-speaking world. The Americans, with their boundless suburbs, were hot on it; even the French came up in double-quick time with their homespun version of the *cité-jardin*, more regimented and laid out with flats, not houses. This was the period of greatest international admiration for English architecture; the Unwinian suburb, with its deft layout and gamut of simplified vernacular styles, took centre stage in that story (figs. 11–12).

In two ways, Hampstead Garden Suburb never achieved all it set out to do. It was intended, revolutionarily, as a mixed-class development. But the less well-off (particularly

13

Stockton Gardens, White Hart Lane Estate, Tottenham

LONDON BOROUGH OF HARINGEY

White Hart Lane, begun in 1904, was one of the first LCC cottage estates to have been built in the suburbs. The layout and designs for the cottages by the Architect's Department moved closer to Raymond Unwin's ideal as set out in Cottage Plans and Common Sense *of 1902 (and subsequently realized at Hampstead Garden Suburb). Stockton Gardens is in the part of the estate north of Risley Avenue laid out and developed after World War I, where a more open, village-like plan was adopted.*

the East End working classes whom Henrietta Barnett had hoped to help) either never came or were ousted in time from their small 'cottages' by the middle classes. This was partly because of rents, partly because of distance from jobs and the cost of the journey from Golders Green by Tube, on which the Suburb relied. The other drawback was the void at its unfinished centre – its failure to create facilities other than the usual uplifting ones of churches, school and institute. If the London suburb was a moral as well as an architectural endeavour, the Suburb revealed its puritan roots at just the time when that philosophy was starting to look like a hindrance to city development. A paucity of shops was not so shocking in 1910; but the lack of pub, billiard hall, cinema or theatre betrayed a po-faced refusal of civic merry-making that was to scar suburban life in the secular new century.

So Hampstead Garden Suburb turned into a tranquil haven for middle incomes and, eventually, for the wealthy. Meanwhile, Raymond Unwin's design revolution trickled busily down. It first touched other co-operative or garden developments, such as the under-acknowledged Brentham in Ealing. It influenced the later stages of the four Edwardian working-class 'cottage estates' (Totterdown Fields, White Hart Lane (fig. 13), Norbury and Old Oak) built when the London County Council – for the next sixty-five years the critical force in metropolitan planning – switched from inner-city flats to suburban development, in a redirection of its housing policies after 1900. It pervaded the layout of London's two best estates built for munitions workers during the First World War, Roe Green in Brent and the bigger Well Hall at Eltham. And after 1918, through Unwin's influence as chief housing architect to the Ministry of Health, it was transformed

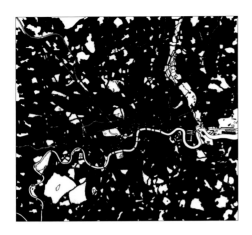

Twentieth-century London

into national policy and came completely to dominate the pattern of the inter-war English suburb.

Not only the big outlying LCC and other council estates of the 1920s, but also the vast swathes of private detached and semi-detached housing that enveloped London in the 1930s while the capital boomed and the rest of Britain slumped, owe their basic typology to Unwin. However healthy and popular their individual dwellings were, the inter-war council estates were built on too unremitting a scale. Austere and regimented to a fault, endowed with an over-extent of shaven open space and few social facilities, they culminate in the drab nullity of Becontree. This 'prairie' style of suburb was still sucking up land and Londoners after the Second World War. Or so Young and Willmott complained in their *Family and Kinship in East London* of 1958, which compared the LCC's moribund 'out-county' estate at Debden with the vibrant street life they found (or believed they had found) in inner-city Bethnal Green.

By then, among architects and sociologists at least, the virtues of city and suburb had been inverted. But between the wars, criticism was directed less towards social behaviour in the suburb than towards the tastelessness of private speculation, together with the rape of productive countryside which the philosophy of 'nothing gained by overcrowding' seemed to sanction. The spoliation was especially acute when the housing took the form of ribbon development – hated by Unwin and his fellow-planners, but difficult to control because planning law at that time was still rudimentary. Far from representing homage to the motor car, the linear march of semi-detached houses and occasional mock-Tudor pubs all along Eastern and Western Avenues, the North Circular Road and the Kingston bypass was construed by intellectuals as an insult to the dignity of the new traffic engineering and the culture of speed.

Meanwhile, the LCC's Green Belt policy of the 1930s, which started the business of capping London's growth by voluntary agreement with outlying authorities, came too late. Middlesex lost its heart by succumbing to 'Metroland'; the ancient county was to be abolished lock, stock and barrel in 1965, surviving thereafter only in the pathetic, illogical tribute of postal addresses. In truth, the enormity of London's suburban expansion in this period was too much to take in. Many people loathed it; John Betjeman and Osbert Lancaster celebrated its Englishness in a distant, teasing way, like travellers writing affectionately about the charm of colonies.

The real nature and worth of the 1930s suburb still elude us. What too often gets forgotten is how much of it depended on local employment, not commuting. While the rest of the country slumped, engineering firms were opening up all around the capital, notably the west and north, where the Americanizing factory fronts along the main roads – Aladdin, Firestone, Gillette and Hoover – were tokens of a new liberty and prosperity for London's skilled working class. As for the housing, pockets of it, where the gardens and street-planting are good, are graceful; much of it is as banal as the by-law street. Looking back on it from the vantage of post-war radical experiment in housing form and the reaction against it, we can say only that the model of private independent dwelling

14

It's a change you need – move to Osterley:
a London Underground poster of 1926
by Victor Hembrow

City smoke gives way to the fragrant calm
of Middlesex. London before the Clean Air
Act of 1956 was a grimy place. The suburb,
especially in the period of low traffic before
1960, was a quiet and clean environment.
A year's commuting would have cost the city
worker a mere £16.

evolved in the first half of the century has not been superseded. It may yet prove as durable as the 'classic' London terrace house.

Just a few people contemplated the ramification of London between the world wars as a whole. One was Frank Pick, the cerebral design-dictator, dispersalist and second-in-command at London Transport – the creation of which in 1933 did much to crystallize the concept of a 'Greater London'. Pick made sure that the outward extension of tubes and buses should coincide with a steady campaign of poster and leaflet propaganda commending the virtues of the metropolitan fringes (fig. 14). In that way, business opportunities could be linked to physical and spiritual reformation; Londoners could be prodded (outside peak periods) into taking country walks or exploring outlying attractions, even if they did not elect to inhabit the suburbs.

Another who saw the whole picture was the Danish architect-planner Steen Eiler Rasmussen, author of *London: The Unique City* (1937). For Rasmussen, the essence of London was the special style and civilization of its Georgian–Victorian ring of inner suburbs. He admired what London Transport was doing and agreed that low-density dispersal was a better policy than cramming the centre with Germanic blocks of flats. To Rasmussen especially is due the easy cliché that London is less of a unity, more of an agglomeration of urban villages. Certainly, the London planning régime and style of street layout in the centre has been looser and less inexorable than in other capital cities, because of the fragmentation of London's government.

In the suburbs, the point is moot. You can (as *The Companion Guide to Outer London*, London 1981, for instance, does) look benignly upon them in terms of their more agreeable environs and open spaces, of Blackheath, Dulwich, Greenwich, Highgate, Hampstead, Harrow, Richmond, Wimbledon or Hampton; or you can caricature them in terms of the 'spaces in between'. Not all the outlying centres are nice: think of Croydon or Watford or Ilford. What unites them is the way they have won battles against psychological (if not always administrative) incorporation into the grosser whole. The duration of these bastions of localism in the suburban landscape is due in part to the vociferous pride of their resident middle classes — many of them commuters and so at heart adherents of the suburban ideal. But in part it is due also to the flexible and modest nature of the Unwinian typology of housing around them.

A rare, full-scale celebration of those 'spaces in between' — really, of the outer London suburb at the climax of its popularity, but when it was fast losing ground among intellectuals — is offered by J.M. Richards in *The Castles on the Ground*. The book, Richards's second, appeared in 1946, at a moment of radical reflection on traditions of British architecture and planning. At the time it was written the author was still on war service in the Middle East, longing to come home. International modernism had not yet reasserted its grip on the future editor of the *Architectural Review*; and he found virtue and reassurance in the demotic Englishness of the suburb. This he identified with its ampler, sleepier, more Victorian, more settled manifestations — the leafy jungle of foliage, the whimsical architecture, the tradesman's van, golf clubs in the hall, girls going off for tennis, and so forth. *The Castles on the Ground* feels like an evocation of Chislehurst or Surbiton or Totteridge, not Penge or Edmonton or Becontree. Richards knew he was not supposed to like the suburb, but he did — at long distance. In the words of John Summerson, his book 'is not a plea for the tile-hung gable with the terracotta dragon, but a reminder that the life beneath and around such things possesses character and quality and that even if you despise the dragon you cannot be contemptuous of the human scene in which he plays his tiny part. There is, however, more to it; for Mr Richards will not allow that the suburbia which he depicts would be the same without the dragon —

KEY PLAN FOR RE-DEVELOPMENT

FINAL STAGE OF RECONSTRUCTION

KEY.
TWO STOREY HOUSES
THREE STOREY FLATS
FOUR STOREY FLATS
TEN STOREY FLATS
SCHOOLS & HOSPITALS
PUBLIC BUILDINGS
SHOPS
COMMERCE
INDUSTRY
PUBLIC OPEN SPACE
PRIVATE GARDENS
RAILWAYS
CANALS
EXISTING BUILDINGS

SCALE. 0 500 1000 1500 2000 FEET

T. L. Marshall.

15

Plan for a proposed reconstruction area in Shoreditch, from Abercrombie's *County of London Plan*, 1943

LONDON BOROUGH OF HACKNEY

The key shows how rebuilding was intended to follow Abercrombie's 'mixed development' principle, with a mixture of houses and walk-up flats and a few tall blocks of ten-storey flats (centre, darker) arranged in lines and surrounded by plenty of open space. Commercial and industrial areas are zoned well away from the housing.

still less, that it would be better. May a man not keep a dragon?'[6]

The answer of the post-war generation of urbanists, once it got into its stride, was resounding: he could not. Suburbs were now once more out of ideological favour; and if Londoners insisted on hanging on to individual houses with gardens, as they did whenever they could, why, they could put themselves on lists and emigrate to new towns, to Harlow and Basildon, Stevenage and Hatfield, Welwyn Garden City and Hemel Hempstead, Crawley and Bracknell. There they put up plenty of that sort of thing – updated versions of the suburban house but in a planned context, with secure industrial employment only a bike-ride away and a nice new school just around the corner for the children.

Alas, it did not work out so quickly or neatly. All through the 1950s London was fast losing population through voluntary and assisted dispersal. Meanwhile, commuter trains were more packed than ever, and doctors' surgeries filled up with housewives diagnosed as suffering from 'new town blues'. Some of this had to do with adjustment. The strategic central planning on garden-city lines adumbrated by Abercrombie in his two great plans for London (of 1943 for the LCC area (fig. 15), of 1944 for the periphery) was

16

The opening of the *Homes for London* exhibition, 1949, by the Minister for Health and Housing, Aneurin Bevan

Homes for London was the most popular of a series of exhibitions held in the entrance foyer of Charing Cross Underground station and was seen by over 120,000 commuters. It explained to Londoners the ideas behind modern town planning and housing design, and showed them that new homes for rent really were on their way – if mostly in the LCC's 'out county' estates. As an advertisement for the LCC's Valuer's Department, however, it was a disaster. The exhibition caused an outrage in the architectural press and within a year housing was back with the Architect's Department.

breathtakingly ambitious. It took time to build new towns, lure employers and retailers to them and conjure up social facilities and networks. There was another dimension to the problem. By containing London and drawing the excess population well away, the new-town and green-belt policy was meant to spell the end of sprawl (fig. 16). But neither towns nor jobs came on stream fast enough to appease the colossal post-war demand for housing. To make up the shortfall, the LCC went on well into the 1950s building its undifferentiated 'out-county' estates of suburban council housing: Aveley, Borehamwood, Debden, Hainault, Harold Hill, Oxhey and St Paul's Cray were the biggest of them. It was here rather than in the nascent new towns that 'blues' proved the more measurable reality.

The tardiness in the delivery of new towns and the dullness of the early results were a godsend to advocates of the high-density, compact city, as they started to stir during the 1950s. Mainly they debated how to tackle the war-damaged centre of London, where it was agreed that extra height in the form of offices and flats would generate prosperity and community and add pep to a dull skyline. But what about the suburbs, so dreamily described by Richards? They needed pep too. Abercrombie's vision of the new London had been one of 'mixed development'. This meant a medley of tall, middling and low buildings in rings of diminishing densities, packed fairly tight in the centre but fewer per acre at the edges. He had assumed that the London suburbs would consist mostly of houses. But he had never said there should not be high buildings there, just that they would have to be balanced by even more open space, which seemed to mean a saving of land. Lubetkin had given an inkling of the alternative vision – handsome towers in beautiful gardens – in his Highpoint flats. The Swedes and Danes had begun to experiment with 'point blocks' on outlying housing estates during the 1940s, to be followed smartly by Le Corbusier's imposition of his slab-block type, the ominous Unité d'Habitation (1948–52), on the edge of Marseilles. Monumentalism in the suburbs was back with a vengeance.

Such was the thinking which generated the first high-rise estates of the LCC, at Woodberry Down in Stoke Newington, and at Ackroydon and Roehampton on opposite sides of Wimbledon Common (fig. 1; see also figs. 128–31). Each of these estates was built on the sites and grounds of former villas (in Roehampton's case, very grand ones overlooking Richmond Park). They were suburban by virtue of their historic location, but urban in that they recolonized previously inhabited sites at much-increased densities, and because the types of housing built there had ceased to be specific to the suburb. It all seemed like a clean break, and a disavowal of the suburban past. Yet Roehampton, the largest and most famous of the LCC's housing developments, visited by architects from all over the world, was hailed by Nikolaus Pevsner as a rolling, picturesque landscape smack in the English tradition, an updating of Regent's Park with slabs and towers for the common man assertively replacing the gentry's temples and follies. Try as the urbanists might, when building in the suburbs they could not escape the suburban tag and tradition. By contrast, when the identical mixture of flats and houses was deployed by the LCC on inner-city sites, nobody took much notice. The landscape was the key.

A more conciliatory and pragmatic accommodation with the suburb came from Eric Lyons and his partners in the deft, private developments built piecemeal by the Span development consortium from 1953 onwards, most remarkably at Blackheath (see fig. 138). Again the backdrop, more often than not, was a well-treed enclave of Victorian villas, fragmented by bombing and the vanishing of the servant class. Span operated on a far smaller scale than the LCC and worked interstitially, rebuilding a pair of deep plots here, plugging a hole there, coaxing and enhancing the landscaping, making more of what already existed. Without the location, without the planting, Lyons's ground-hugging flats and neat houses with their cleanly tang of Scandinavia would amount to little. Yet here the particularity of the Richards vision dies the definitive death. Here a fresh type of middle-class suburban Londoner, as caricaturable as ever, has come into her own. Miss Joan Hunter Dunn has got a professional qualification, bought a Moulton bicycle and taken to shopping at Habitat.

Shameful though it is to say so, the work of Span amounts to almost the latest distinctive contribution to the architecture of the London suburb. Thamesmead, the Greater London Council's township on the marshy foreshore between Woolwich and Erith, was the most ambitious project of the 1960s and 1970s, but can hardly be classed as more than a noble failure that got enmeshed in the complexities of planning a new peripheral community at high density on very difficult terrain. The collapse since then of

17

Robin Crescent, Beckton, *ca.* 1985

LONDON BOROUGH OF NEWHAM

Brick paving and neo-Victorian housing in
Docklands: estate agents prefer to call places
such as this 'urban villages' rather than suburbs.

an architectural commitment to housing, private or public, has much to do with this loss of nerve about the suburbs. The 'volume builder' has reigned there supreme, with even less guidance or authority than in the days of ribbon development – save in matters of traffic management, turning circles and access for firemen or dustmen. A partial exception is Park Hill, Croydon, where the builders Wates in the late 1960s promoted an estate akin to the Span developments on old villa sites. But it is indicative that the most sophisticated sector of Park Hill, a development by the Swiss architects Atelier 5, was whittled down to 21 houses instead of the original 147.

Since the 1980s there has been a surge of meritorious housing schemes in Docklands (fig. 17) and other sectors of London's inner ring. The last thing the creators of these 'urban villages' wish them to be tarred with is the suburban brush, even when they feel as if they were light years away from Charing Cross, and a dearth of public transport makes their residents slaves to the motor car. Among the design professions, the ideal of the London terraced house is often invoked; never the London suburb. Why is this? The answer lies in a campaign of sociological warfare waged against the suburb since the 1950s by architects and others who wanted to fortify threatened inner-city communities against the dispersalists. As a corollary, they felt obliged to lump together and denigrate almost any of the many possible modes of suburban lifestyle. Ever since, the high priests of architecture have been calling for dense inner-city communities, high-rise or medium-rise, in a Canute-like effort to stem the voluntary flight from the cities.

That flight from, to be precise, city centres continues to go on all around the world. Counter to this runs an equally unstoppable and far greater influx *into* city regions from rural areas. No genius is needed to guess where these two masses are ending up: in alternative types of suburb. The suburb is the future, no matter what its character: dense or open; zoned or unzoned; accessible by train, bus or car; focussed upon church, school or supermarket; a concentration of apartment blocks bristling out of a shabby tide of tarmac; shanty-ish, with tenants at the margins of the economy improvising walls and roofs bit by bit on and around basic 'sites and services' laid down by the authorities; a tissue of finite streets and medium-height terraces; or a somnolent drip, drip, drip of low, leaf-shaded dwellings and their garages.

Now a fresh charge has been levelled against the suburb: that it fails the test not only of ethics but also of greenness. Verdant it can be, sustainable (we are told) it is not. The suburb stands accused of being an accessory to waste, pollution and even apartheid. Instead of travelling weary distances each day, segregating ourselves in ghettoes where we meet few people different from ourselves and live unchallenged lives, we are invited to renew and reinhabit the serviceable inner city; discover stimulus, strangeness and civic value; take part in events and excitements; chatter in street cafés like erstwhile Parisians; bike, walk or ride.

In fact, London is innocent of the worst charges of one-way suburbanization. The term and the practice of 'gentrification' were coined in London, which, from the 1960s, saw a broadly based return of the middle classes to central districts – accurately, from outer suburbs to inner ones. The health of the inner area of London is crucial, for it sets the framework within which the whole south-east region operates. But the belief that we must all be crammed into dense communities and deprived of our cars is as apocalyptic and improbable as its opposite counterpart, the supposition that we are going into a spin of incremental decentralization and alienation, and shall all soon be isolated from one another and communicate only through our modems.

Moreover, the relentless puffing of metropolitan life and culture is unbalanced – lazy, even. It devalues the sub-centres of which London has so many prized and varied examples, whence people so often derive their sense of belonging, from the elegance of Hampstead or Blackheath to the ordinariness of Bromley or Ealing. It does nothing for the poorer inner suburbs, for that deprived swathe of southern and eastern territory between the poles of Clapham and Hackney (first of the bourgeois suburbs), the transformation of which should be an early challenge facing a future London-wide government. And it ignores the vitality of the outer suburbs today, where mobility, changes in employment patterns, and the modern mix-up of building types and scales mean that it is becoming less and less meaningful to generalize about the suburb in either sentimental or pejorative terms.

The London suburb today is no dormitory but an integral and equal part of the greater metropolis. Heathrow, to take the prime example, has become a major focus for the whole London region, encircled by a network of businesses, many in cheapjack and depressing offices but others housed in glamorous architecture, notably at Stockley Park. To insist on the Heathrow periphery's subservience to the historic and cultural centre is a dangerous mistake. It hinders us from seeing it as an environment with a strength and magnetism of its own as well as planning problems that sorely need addressing.

The attractions that the centre of London now offers are profound for those who are young, rich, single or obsessive. They, perhaps it will be argued, are the vanguard of the metropolitan culture. That does not give architects and planners licence to ignore the rest. Most people want to live quite ordinary lives. For a civilized kind of ordinariness, nothing the city centre offers has yet been invented to beat the suburb; and for a humane model of suburb there is nothing to beat the best of London's suburbs. By loving, respecting, studying and renewing them better, we shall be on the way to inventing the successful new communities that the world's population demands and must have.

NOTES

1. John Summerson, foreword to H.J. Dyos, *Victorian Suburb*, Leicester 1973, p. 8.
2. Quoted in Julian Treuherz, *Victorian Painting*, London 1993, pp. 88–89.
3. Geoffrey Chaucer, 'The Canon's Yeoman's Prologue', *The Canterbury Tales*.
4. Robert Fishman, *Bourgeois Utopias*, New York 1987, Chapter 1.
5. Edwin Abbey, quoted in Moncure D. Conway, *Autobiography*, 1904, pp. 339–41.
6. From Summerson's review of *The Castles on the Ground* in *Architectural Review*, May 1947, p. 187.

Chapter One
From Aristocratic Ideal to Middle-Class Idyll: 1690–1840

CHRIS MIELE

'Tis true that the suburbs of London are much larger than the body of the City, which make some compare her to a Jesuit's hat, whose brims are far larger than the block; which made Count Gondamar the Spanish Ambassador himself to say, as the Queen of Spain was discussing with him, upon his return from England, of the City of London, 'Madam, I believe there will be no City left shortly, for it will all have run out the gates to the suburbs!'

James Howell, *Londinopolis* (1657)

Londoners have been seeking refuge in the suburbs for as long as records have been kept.[1] In the thirteenth century the numbers of out-dwellers were small, and very few of them would have travelled between city and country every day. We can surmise that their reasons for moving outside the city walls were not so different from those of the City merchants who flocked to Islington or Clapham in the 1790s. Plague – which occurred with terrifying regularity between the mid-fourteenth and the seventeenth century – provided the motivation for some,[2] but perhaps more were impelled by a number of intangible cultural factors.

Some medieval merchants purchased what could be called 'suburban seats' as investments, but others were making a bid to raise their social standing. Land helped them to infiltrate the aristocracy; it enabled them to marry their daughters into the great county families, enter county government, serve on public commissions, acquire hunting rights, and renovate their newly purchased properties.[3] Nostalgia for rural life had something to do with it as well. A significant number of London's merchants and apprentices-made-good had roots in the Home Counties and so were inclined to send their children to one of the many village nurseries in the orbit of the City; Croydon and Stratford were favoured spots. Those who chose to retire from business naturally gravitated to these places and eventually these suburban adopted homes came to rank higher in their affections than the City itself, a trend reflected in the large number of monuments and tombs to London grandees still to be found in the ancient parish churches of places that have now been swallowed up by the capital. How many followed this trajectory will never be known for sure but the number was significant: on leaving for Agincourt, Henry V was so concerned at the number of aldermen residing outside the City that he ordered them to return to strengthen its defences.[4]

Undoubtedly the most popular place of resort was Hackney, almost directly north of Bishopsgate. The parish was free from plague and said to have healthy air. Rich citizens,

18

Camberwell Grove, Camberwell

LONDON BOROUGH OF SOUTHWARK

Running north from Camberwell Green, an old village centre, is Camberwell Grove, an excellent collection of late eighteenth-century suburban terraces and semis, many of the latter linked by lower entrance porches. The street was developed along a private avenue that had previously belonged to a mansion house, the grounds of which were split up in a sale of 1776. Grove Lane to the west has a similar history but is less coherent architecturally.

19, 20

Sutton House, Homerton High Street, Homerton

LONDON BOROUGH OF HACKNEY

The pen drawing (right) shows Sutton House as it probably looked when first built in the 1530s for Ralph Sadeler, a favourite of Henry VIII. Hackney was then one of London's most prosperous suburbs, home to many merchants with regular business in the City. The house's picturesque silhouette later gave way to a Georgian parapet (above), and sash windows replaced the originals, but many of the earlier interiors are intact.

aldermen and goldsmiths (the predecessors of modern bankers) began acquiring land here in the thirteenth century. Hamlets at Clapton, Dalston, Homerton, Kingsland and Shacklewell absorbed the overspill in the fourteenth and fifteenth centuries. Speculators exploited the rising fortunes of these places and built short runs of houses that suited metropolitan taste. By 1602 Hackney had four residents who were titled and one hundred who were described as 'Citizens of London'; indeed, so elevated was the general run of Hackney-dweller that from 1617 a special system of elected local government, a select vestry, prevailed. Certainly by this date there is strong evidence to demonstrate a pattern of full-time commuting rather than occasional residence. Daniel Defoe noted, with a touch of Puritan disdain, that the place had more than one hundred coaches. Many of the great late medieval houses built by these carriage folk were still to be seen when John Stow made his tour in the early seventeenth century.[5] One of the grandest, Brooke House, was demolished after World War II. One that has survived is Sutton House (figs. 19–20), built in 1535 by Ralph Sadeler, a royal courtier who also had apartments in Whitehall Palace and possibly at Greenwich. Initially a place of occasional retirement, by the 1550s Sutton House was lived in by John Machell, a cloth merchant

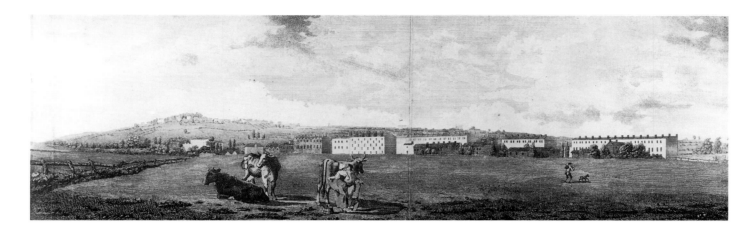

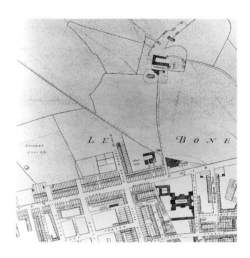

21, 22

Horwood's map of London, 1794–97

CITY OF WESTMINSTER

The hard edge between city and country is evident in the panoramic view (top), published as the frontispiece to Horwood's map of London. It captures Marylebone from Willans Farm to the north, with Baker Street, then under construction, on the right. The extract from Horwood's map itself (above) shows another farm, Alsops, about to be engulfed. The diagonal field boundary to the north would wind up as the south side of modern Allsop Place, the backdrop to Nash's Cumberland Terrace. Willans Farm was Crown property; it stood on land now incorporated into Nash's Regent's Park.

who also owned a house in Milk Street in the City – in other words, the sort of person who would have more regular business in the City.[6]

Tottenham was also home to Londoners as early as the twelfth century and, like Hackney, had a number of large merchant houses by the sixteenth century.[7] There were similar settlements in St John's Wood and Battersea, and also in West Ham, where the Cobhams Estate is an interesting example of a suburban property that was handed on from one City man to another, starting in 1329.[8] In the fifteenth century the number of villages drawn into the orbit of the capital increased, but not dramatically or uniformly. Edmonton, Islington and Woodford saw an influx of Londoners, but Stoke Newington, which was no further from the City than Hackney, did not. Acton, however, did, largely because Londoners had purchased land there centuries before as investments. So did Chiswick, the riverside location of which made it an ideal place from which to travel to the Court at Kew. The most developed of the ancient suburbs was Southwark, a lone outpost that grew up to the south of London Bridge. The lack of other bridges meant that there was very little in the way of suburban development south of the Thames until the late eighteenth century.[9] The reasons for suburban growth, both then and now, depended greatly on particular circumstances: proximity to the capital, transport, amenities and the structure of land tenure were only the most obvious variables.

The great burst of trade associated with the reign of Elizabeth I was responsible for a suburban building boom. Hoxton, a small hamlet in the parish of Shoreditch, was one of the first places to feel the impact of new money and was particularly favoured by foreign merchants and ambassadors. St Katharine's by the Tower, Whitechapel, Mile End New Town, Moorgate, Clerkenwell, Holborn, Wapping, Radcliffe, Bromley-by-Bow, Bermondsey; according to John Stow's *Survey of London …* (1603), all these places had 'increased mightily' over the previous fifty years. For Stow, the suburbs of London were less an ideal than a physical reality, which was, in places, very unpleasant. Many of the new dwellings were filthy, but the worst thing about the suburbs was the loss of countryside that their construction entailed (figs. 21–22). Spitalfields had become, in his words, one 'continuous building … of Gardens, houses, and small cottages', with the fields taken

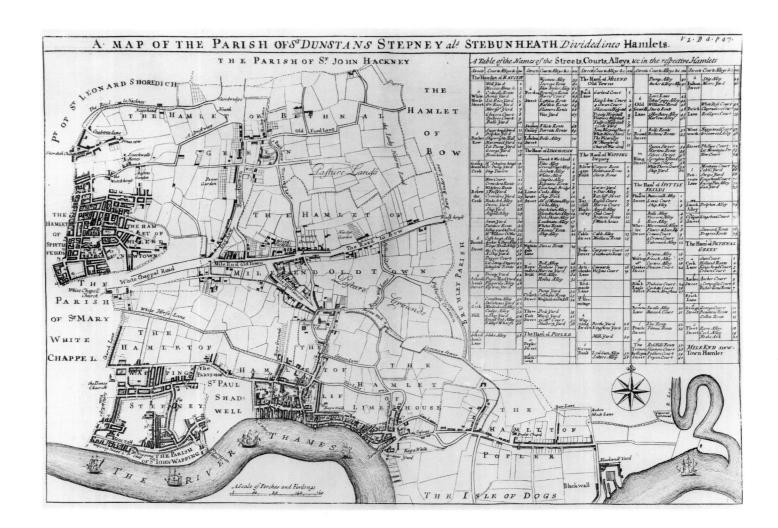

23

A map of the parish of St Dunstan's, Stepney,
from John Strype's *Survey of the Cities of*
London and Westminster, 1720

LONDON BOROUGH OF TOWER HAMLETS

This map shows one of the most intensively
suburbanized parishes adjacent to London.
Stepney, Shadwell and Limehouse were,
according to Strype, 'as a city', continuing the
intensive development of London itself, but at
the periphery: particularly in Mile End, city and
country mingled in a way that he found
especially pleasing.

up entirely by market gardens and bowling alleys. Within living memory it had offered up a small slice of Arcadia, 'fayre hedgerowes of Elme trees, with Bridges and easie stiles to passe over into pleasant fields' fit for shooting or walking.[10] Shadwell experienced the same transformation another fifty years later, when it was overrun with speculative housing of modest to middle-class proportions, making it one of London's first industrial suburbs.[11] John Strype's fascinating *Survey of the Cities of London and Westminster* (1720; fig. 23) captures the texture of these early inner suburbs a century later. Stepney, Strype observed, had the character of a city by the river, but on the north 'this Parish has the face of the country'. In Mile End New Town, less densely settled, houses built in the previous century for the 'Country Retirement [of] Citizens ... other wealthy Men ... and Persons of the Greatest Quality' had been taken over by 'Sea Captains and Commanders of Ships ... and Persons of Good Quality'.[12] Thus there existed a suburban life cycle that is recognizable today, in which once aristocratic or upper-class suburbs are settled by middle- and then working-class people, forcing the aristocrats further afield (fig. 24).

In addition to Stow's *Survey*, this first great wave of suburbanization has left us with some of the earliest firm evidence of the meaning Londoners attached to their suburbs. Shakespeare's contemporaries were deeply suspicious of the outlying neighbourhoods, where the City generally had less control. In short, the Elizabethan suburbs were a free-trade zone and as such constituted a threat to the City's legal and financial hegemony. Minor industries were thriving outside the City walls by the second half of the sixteenth century, undercutting the established trade monopolies. Guildsmen petitioned for relief. A Royal Proclamation of 1580 prohibited all new building within three miles of the City gates. Several Acts of Parliament attempted to curb development, culminating in one of 1657 that extended the radius of the *cordon sanitaire* to ten miles. None had the desired effect.[13] Inns, theatres, pleasure gardens, archery grounds and other less salubrious 'entertainments' sprang up, marking the suburbs as a site for pleasure as crudely under-stood and prompting a steady stream of invective, some of it very entertaining in itself:

Oh there [in Clerkenwell and Shoreditch] are they which think that fornication

Is but youthful, sportful recreation ...

Their venery will soon consume their stocks,

And hang them to repentance with a pox.[14]

Even the élite aristocratic suburb, just outside what was, in effect, a high-growth inner suburban ring, was affected by the trade boom. The affluence of London's villages com-pared with rural villages is measured in the late seventeenth-century hearth-tax returns. In 1664 nearly half of the 230 houses assessed in Chiswick had two or more hearths.[15] In Brentford the same percentage had three or more.[16] In West Ham 30% of the houses had five or more hearths. In Walthamstow the figure was slightly higher. To put these figures in perspective it helps to know that, on average, only 17% of houses in rural Essex had five or more hearths.[17] The returns for Barnes, Hampstead, and Putney tell a similar story of wealth.[18]

Under the influence of metropolitan money a new landscape emerged at such places as Chelsea, Highgate, Kensington, Richmond, Roehampton, Twickenham and Walthamstow, a hybrid topography that would show itself wherever London struck out into the surrounding countryside. Market gardens and nurseries mingled loosely with farms, paddocks, and houses of every description, from mansions to hovels, with perhaps an almshouse or two.[19] Arable farming gave way to livestock and hay production to satisfy the capital's insatiable appetite, in some places as early as the sixteenth century.

Whether there evolved a specifically suburban architecture in the linear develop-ments leading out of the City and Westminster is difficult to say. The concept of 'subur-bia' is not obviously inscribed on a great house such as Balmes (fig. 25) in Hoxton, grandly rebuilt in about 1635 by Sir George Whitmore (Lord Mayor 1631–32, who had trading interests in the New World). This, or something very like it, could well have been found in deepest countryside.[20] Alternatively, the short, mid-seventeenth-century terrace

24

Monument to Sir Richard Newdigate (1602–1678) and his wife Mary (died 1692), Harefield parish church

LONDON BOROUGH OF HILLINGDON

This monument was carved by Grinling Gibbons and positioned to the left of the altar. Like many monuments in the old parish churches on the edge of the the cities of London and Westminster, it commemorates one who made his fortune and reputation in the capital before retiring to one of its quiet suburban parishes. Born in Warwickshire, Sir Richard entered Gray's Inn in 1620 and was subsequently called to the Bar and went on to become a chief justice. Harefield was in fact the ancient seat of his family, which had been alienated from it in the sixteenth century.

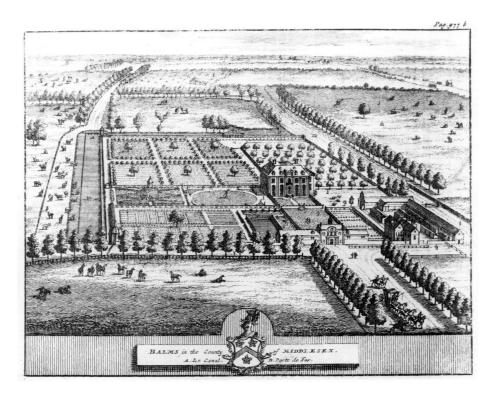

BALMS in the County of MIDDLESEX.
A. *Le Canal.* B. *Porte de Fer.*

25

Balmes House, gardens and home farm, as they appeared in 1727

LONDON BOROUGH OF HACKNEY

This grand suburban seat was built at the north end of Hoxton Street in 1653 by Sir George Whitmore, sometime Lord Mayor of London and Master of the Haberdashers' Company. Kingsland Road can be glimpsed in the upper right-hand corner. Sir George gave his name to the present Whitmore Estate, built as social housing by the LCC in 1925. The north portion of the gardens was laid out with middle-class villas in the first half of the nineteenth century as part of De Beauvoir Town (see fig. 47).

now known as nos. 52–55 Newington Green (fig. 27) in Islington resembles, at least superficially, terraces constructed in Great Queen Street and Lincoln's Inn Fields in the preceding decades, even though Newington Green was then most definitely suburb, not town.[21] Perhaps this consonance of building type should be taken as evidence that people regarded the suburb as a small town of independent character, rather than as a dependent satellite of the capital. Indeed, Georgian commentators often used the word 'village' where we would 'suburb'. For them, the difference between London's satellite villages and independent ones was shown by the greater prosperity of the former as expressed in the wealth of the residents and the quality of the shops.

There may well have been an intermediate way of building – intermediate because it is neither rural nor urban – with symmetrical façades and plan forms that were redolent

26

Reconstruction of Kingswood Lodge as it would have looked when built in 1708

LONDON BOROUGH OF CROYDON

The unknown builder of Kingswood Lodge was working in the same four-square, brick idiom as could be found nearer town, but in a place such as Croydon, where the pressure of development was less than in the city, single, detached houses rather than terraces were still the rule.

FROM ARISTOCRATIC IDEAL TO MIDDLE-CLASS IDYLL

of urban classicism but distinguished from their town cousins by having generally broader proportions and fewer storeys. A view of Kingswood Lodge (fig. 26) in Croydon as it probably appeared when newly built in 1708 gives some idea of the form and scale of a typical middle-class suburban house.[22] A more modest expression of the same tradition can be found in 327 Hoxton Street, a now rare example of a type that was once common along the high streets of those London villages that spanned the gap between city and country. Originally one room deep and five bays wide, it has the relatively wide plot frontage and low profile that mark it out as a suburban house. In the words of one historian, these characteristics reflect its position outside 'the fashionable core ... [where] land values were lower and plots often developed individually or in small groups'.[23] There was a variety of plan form even at this modest level, which is probably explained by the fact that many such buildings were erected piecemeal on encroachments from manorial estates and not as part of a large estate development.[24]

27

Nos. 52–55 Newington Green, Islington

LONDON BOROUGH OF ISLINGTON

Securely dated by a plaque to 1658, these houses constitute London's oldest surviving terrace. When it was built the metropolis was still far off, and the locality a rural hamlet with only a smattering of Londoners. Nevertheless, the developer decided on a form that would be entirely at home in Covent Garden or St James's Square.

Engraved for Harrison's History of London, &c.

A View of HAMMERSMITH from Chiswick.

28

Hammersmith as it appeared from Chiswick Mall in the second half of the eighteenth century

LONDON BOROUGH OF HAMMERSMITH AND FULHAM

The position of Hammersmith on the north bank of the Thames and just south of an ancient road leading west from London (now King Street) virtually guaranteed the district's development as a suburb. In 1725 Daniel Defoe was unsettled by the intrusion of suburban terraces: 'In this village we see now not only a Wood of great Houses and Palaces, but a noble Square built as it were in the middle of several handsome streets, as if the Village seemed enclined to grow up into a city.' He was probably referring to the development of the Broadway, not, as we see here, the Upper Mall, but this image suits his words very well.

Suburban townscapes were famously incoherent and patchy, and stayed so, a fact lamented by Defoe, who saw London and its dependants as an ungainly, formless spread. He longed for geometric purity, for all of the capital to fit neatly into a regular figure – ideally a circle – as Rome did, and for it to be separated from the suburbs by a clear green zone.[25] As it was, such places as Islington and Hammersmith (fig. 28) seemed no more than extensions of the towns. Similar complaints were made by John Gwynn in his visionary *London and Westminster Improved* of 1766, in which he argued for the suppression of building on the main roads leaving the City and Westminster and for clear boundaries to be drawn around each of the suburban villages. Within the suburbs themselves, Gwynn imagined buildings of uniform appearance, which would give a foretaste of the grandeur he hoped to see imposed on the rebuilt capital itself.[26]

Gwynn demanded an architecture of the suburbs that would be distinctly suburban, that would signal the intermediate state between rural nature and metropolitan culture, but his Enlightenment ideal was not reflected in what actually happened in suburban developments. From the perspective of the late twentieth century, the fact that there was no self-consciously architectural response to the suburb until the end of the eighteenth century seems perverse, or at least eccentric. Perhaps the most striking instance of this is to be found in Kensington, where in 1685 Thomas Young laid out Kensington Square on the green verge of the Court suburb, making no apparent concession to the rural character of the place.[27] The same disregard for the interface of town and country was found at Richmond, where the proximity of another royal palace had attracted genteel and merchant folk since at least Tudor times. Richmond's allure was increased by the discovery of mineral wells in 1696, and in the last years of the seventeenth century the aristocratic village clustering about Richmond Green was in the throes of a suburban

FROM ARISTOCRATIC IDEAL TO MIDDLE-CLASS IDYLL

boom. Speculators, following the example of West End builders, erected terraces and single houses (and even one very early pair of semi-detached houses, The Rosary and The Hollies in Ormond Road), their ventures underwritten by the Londoners who had established second residences there.[28]

The social demography of London's suburbs, medieval to Georgian, is still not well understood. Certainly the evidence encoded in the buildings themselves is difficult to interpret. Take the case of Church Row (fig. 29) in Hampstead, built probably in the 1720s. None of these houses had stables or mews attached, which suggests that the residents were not commuters – but horses and carriages could be hired near by, and by 1740 there were two daily coaches into town. So, these substantial houses could have been used as summertime retreats, as full-time suburban houses for commuters, or as the full-time homes of people who rarely strayed outside the borough. The latter would almost certainly have been professionals who had retired from business in the City or Westminster, as the local economy could not have supported the wealth reflected in the many fine Georgian houses known to have been built here and in the surrounding streets.[29]

Inevitably, transport was a key factor in defining the suburban zone. Daily commuting by river was well established surprisingly early. In 1636 the Privy Council tried to restrict the number of journeys between Hampton and London on account of plague, observing that 'divers Londoners' had obtained houses upstream, 'and these they inhabit going daily to and from London'.[30] Relatively long distances overland did not deter those in search of an elegant retreat, particularly in the summer season. Epsom is a good case in point. By 1650 its mineral springs had transformed this retiring Surrey town into a key stage in the genteel entertainment circuit. It bristled with City men, many of whom were

29

Church Row, Hampstead

LONDON BOROUGH OF CAMDEN

Most of the early eighteenth-century terraces to survive in Greater London now consist of only half a dozen houses or so. Church Row in Hampstead, built largely, it appears, between 1710 and 1728, is unusually complete. The church tower of St John's (the rebuilt parish church was dedicated in 1747) closes off the view splendidly. Many residents would have had houses in town as well, resorting to Hampstead in the summers only, while others seem to have resided there permanently. How the commuters got to town is not clear, as the houses were built without stables (although they could be hired near by). In 1740 there were only two daily coaches from Hampstead, one to High Holborn and the other to Covent Garden.

30

Nos. 810–812 Tottenham High Road

LONDON BOROUGH OF HARINGEY

This mid-eighteenth-century semi-detached house is part of an impressive, albeit much neglected, group lining what was once one of the country's most important land routes, the Great North Road. According to Daniel Defoe, Tottenham was an unbroken linear development from the Green northwards and lived in by a very particular type: 'There is not anything more fine in their degree, than most of the Buildings this way; only with this observation, that they are generally belonging to the Middle sort of Mankind, grown Wealthy by Trade, and who still taste of London; some of them live both in the City and the Country at the same time: yet many are immensely rich.' This photograph illustrates how the relatively deep front gardens, which are a distinguishing characteristic of Georgian and later suburban terraces, have been encroached upon. The parlous state of many of these Georgian houses in Tottenham is a testament to the social demography of modern London; transported to Spitalfields or Highgate, and each and every one of these buildings would by now have been gentrified. This illustrates as well as any example one of the difficulties facing conservation officers in the outer boroughs.

said to have braved the long journey every day. In 1710 one traveller made the return journey in just under six hours.[31] A little later, Defoe observed that it was common for successful merchants 'to place their families here, and take their Horses every morning to London'.[32] Another eighteenth-century commentator observed that *en promenade* in season at Epsom it was easy to believe oneself 'on the Exchange or at St James's, or in an East India factory'.[33] Those who could not face the daily grind could at least conduct business by daily post, established in season here by 1684.[34] Epsom seems to have defined the radius of feasible commuting into London in the Georgian period, a perimeter which is nowadays more clearly marked by the M25 motorway.

Less is known about the commuting habits of the Georgian professional and merchant classes, but a few fragments unearthed by diligent archival research suggest daily trips in and out of town were not beyond the means of the middling sort.[35] In 1709 one Edmond Skinner was exempted from parochial office in Enfield (his place of residence) because he had to travel daily to the City, where he was a haberdasher of petty wares. Defoe, our best guide to the early Georgian suburb, sheds some light on the quality of life in this part of Middlesex, observing that 'most of the Buildings' lining the Great North Road from Tottenham (fig. 30) to Edmonton belonged to 'the Middle sort of Mankind, grown Wealthy by Trade, and who still taste of London; some live both in the City, and the Country at the same time ...'.[36] Middlesex was able 'to partake of the influence of London', as Defoe put it, because of the relatively high quality of its roads; between 1700 and 1720 all the principal ones were turnpiked. Essex also was easily accessible, but Kent and particularly Surrey were cut off from the capital by the sheer brute fact of the

FROM ARISTOCRATIC IDEAL TO MIDDLE-CLASS IDYLL

Drawn by Schnebbelie & Engraved by Sparrow.
Entrance to London by the OBELISK in the Surry Road.
For Dr Hughsons Description of London
Published by J. Stratford 112 Holborn Hill June 9th 1810.

31

Obelisk at St George's Circus, Southwark, in 1810

LONDON BOROUGH OF SOUTHWARK

The grand new avenues that led south from Blackfriars and Westminster Bridges crossed at St George's Circus, where this obelisk was erected in 1771. It has since been removed to Geraldine Mary Harmsworth Park. In the 1790s Sir George Dance the younger developed a plan for the area around this junction, which sadly was never realized. This print is interesting for showing commercial carriages that were typical of the day, and in the middle distance, a pair of toll houses, a reminder that all the arterial road improvements carried out in Georgian London were financed privately by turnpike trusts.

Thames, which was spanned in the heart of the capital only by London Bridge until the middle of the eighteenth century.[37] Land in Lambeth and the part of Southwark then known as St George's Fields was worth a fraction of the value of land on the opposite bank of the river. The suburban potential of London south of the Thames was first unlocked by the construction of Westminster Bridge, finished in 1750, and then by Blackfriars, finished in 1769 (see fig. 32). As soon as these opened, new suburbs sprouted along their southern approaches but in spasmodic bursts. Sustained, intensive, speculative development (fig. 31) had to wait for that magnificent trio of post-Waterloo bridges designed by the great Scottish engineer John Rennie: Southwark (1814–19), Vauxhall (1811; demolished 1898) and Waterloo itself (1811–17).[38]

Commuting on horseback was only for the robust. Less physically demanding were stage or mail coaches or (for those who could afford them) private carriages. Even in a private carriage the journey was likely to be a long series of sickening lurches. In the late eighteenth century new suspension systems led to increased comfort and in the 1790s came lighter, snappier Phaetons; four-wheeled and owner-driven, they were the sports cars of their day. 1804 saw the introduction of elliptical metal springs which permitted lighter designs. Single-horse cabriolets came soon after, enabling more people to become 'carriage folk'.

Commuting by coach was possible in theory, though in practice the vagaries of land transport made it unreliable.[39] One of the earliest regular suburban coach routes was to Clapham Common, where a daily return service was established in 1690. By the 1770s, when, according to directories and handbooks, a total of eighty coaches left the City and Westminster each evening bound for suburban destinations, commuting was becoming

32

Nos. 122–128 Kennington Park Road

LONDON BOROUGH OF LAMBETH

Kennington Park Road was built in 1788, when the area around Newington Butts was first opening for development. The catalyst was Blackfriars Bridge (opened in 1769), which brought hundreds of acres of open land within the reach of Westminster, thereby making it highly desirable. Many of the earliest groups of houses were semi-detached with generous spatial allowances, but swiftly rising land values tempted builders to maximize profits by building terraces (which had a lower unit cost). Nevertheless, what John Summerson called the 'snob appeal' of the semi induced some builders to create the illusion of detachment by recessing the ranges at party walls.

33, 34

Highbury Place viewed across Highbury Fields, 1790s (*right*); **Bakers' map of Islington, 1790s** (*far right*)

LONDON BOROUGH OF ISLINGTON

Islington's proximity to London made it attractive to wealthy citizens fleeing the plague, while in the late seventeenth century the discovery of mineral springs at Saddler's Wells brought a fashionable crowd. Despite this, however, the area did not really become a suburb until the late eighteenth century, when development, previously confined to Upper Street and the southern end of Essex Road (then Lower Street), began to reach into the surrounding fields. The fine terraces and raised pavement on the south side of Cross Street (1760s) and the contemporary houses in Colebroke Row are interesting survivals from this first burst of growth, as are the very grand houses in Highbury Place at the north end of the former parish. This was speculatively developed by John Dawes, a stockbroker who lived in nearby Canonbury. Completed in the late 1770s by the Southwark builder James Spiller, this development had as its front garden all of what is today Highbury Fields. This lithograph (right) of the 1790s shows Highbury Place still enjoying its exclusive isolation amid Islington's farms. The map of the same period (far right), by Edward and Benjamin Baker, shows development concentrated at the Angel and the Green, with Barnsbury still largely in agricultural use.

commonplace. By 1805 the number had increased fourfold, and out of the increased total, two-thirds of the journeys were to the City and one-third to Westminster. There were more than six hundred daily journeys by 1821, and the proportion going to the City had increased. Evidently workers in the Square Mile were more likely to be commuters than their West End counterparts.[40] Some areas on the western edge of London — Edgware and Finchley, for example — remained relatively untouched by this expansion of public transport.[41]

The real revolution in overland, suburban transport occurred in 1829, when George Shillibeer opened a London–Greenwich service featuring his own invention, the omnibus. Although early models bounced along uncomfortably, Shillibeer's omnibuses were affordable if you were a clerk or shopkeeper. Very soon they were ubiquitous, herds of them lumbering out of town each day bound for Putney, Kew, Lewisham, Peckham, Brixton, Norwood, Dulwich, Streatham and, proverbially, Clapham.[42]

Towards the end of the eighteenth century, then, the suburb was beginning to be more than merely a fact of London life but rather a cultural force with a recognizably modern form. The messy vitality that had hitherto been characteristic of the suburbs slowly gave way to a greater visual coherence, at least in parts, a coherence that was itself the product of larger historical forces, of swiftly increasing population and increased wealth. The agent of this physical transformation was the large-scale speculative builder. Whereas previously his work had been confined to the West End and a few select suburban locations (Richmond, for example, or Kensington), now it was to be seen overrunning formerly 'greenfield' sites, the value of which, as agricultural land, gradually slipped as demand for housing increased.

The methods of exploitation were more or less those that had been used by the great London estates since the seventeenth century: landlords granted building leases to speculators and builders, who, having put up a certain number of houses according to some agreed plan, then passed on their leases to a building owner, who in turn let it to a tenant.[43] In plan and elevation the resulting houses, particularly along the main suburban arteries, followed the precedents established in West End developments, but subtle differences reflected a less citified setting. Perhaps the most conspicuous was the provision of a front garden, in some cases so slight as to seem vestigial but in others grand and dramatic. In the new developments on Lambeth Marshes, immediately south of Westminster and Blackfriars Bridges, these setbacks were vast, 50 feet (15.25 m) or more. In the City Road in Islington the proportions were less generous, though the visual effect is nonetheless striking. In contrast to the brick canyons of central London, these newly built suburban ways must have created the impression of broad avenues and generous spacings. At Highbury Place (fig. 33), also in Islington, the freeholder of the property extended the concept of the front garden to all of what would become Highbury Fields by guaranteeing his lessees that the land opposite their houses would remain open to Holloway.[44] Behind the main arterial roads, with their mix of new-generation terraces and the patchwork of earlier suburban building, entirely new quarters sprang up. The lower density of construction in these areas directly reflected the relative cheapness of land beyond the arterial roads in fast-growing suburban villages (figs. 34–36).[45]

35

Islington Green, 1850

LONDON BOROUGH OF ISLINGTON

Islington is less a Georgian suburb than a Regency and early Victorian one. The area around the Green and west into Barnsbury boasts more terraces and semis of the 1820s, 1830s and 1840s than almost any other place in the country, and much of this new housing was meant for City clerks and successful artisans, who relied on the omnibus to ferry them to points south and west. This engraving shows a view of the Green from the south, with an omnibus in the right foreground.

36

Islington in 1780, woodcut by Walter
Thornbury, 1883

LONDON BOROUGH OF ISLINGTON

*Built in the 1750s to improve communications
between the City and the West End, the New
Road (now Marylebone, Euston and Pentonville
Roads) encouraged suburban development to
the area south of Islington Green so that, by
1780, the village atmosphere was swiftly being
transformed. Although to our eyes the scene
seems rustic, the presence of carriages and the
number of houses were signs of this place's fast-
changing fortunes. What is more intriguing is the
fact that this sort of view should have been
published in 1883, when Islington had slipped
far down the ladder of gentility and the Green
had lost its air of suburban respectability.*

A more significant formal trait of this new generation of suburban, speculatively built housing was detachment and its various permutations. Many suburban seats of earlier days had been isolated from their immediate surroundings by walled pleasure grounds, parks or even farmland. Late Georgian 'detachment' was something else entirely, for it was detachment relative to an overall development: detachment, in other words, as signifier of status. The 'villa' denoted the highest status; the 'semi' or 'quasi-semi' expressed subtle gradations lower down the social scale.

It is common to see the semi-detached house as an invention of the late eighteenth century but in fact the form can be traced back to the late seventeenth century. The Grove in Highgate, of about 1688, is a remarkable survival of a short run of suburban semis, built as an investment and designed to appeal to purchasers who wanted something with more cachet than a run-of-the-mill terrace. Summerson identified a similar development in Horseferry Road, built by the Dean and Chapter of Westminster for exactly the same reasons in 1719–20.[46] Writing in the 1950s, Summerson regarded these two examples as isolated instances but recent research suggests that there were others. Early semis can be hard to spot because many, such as Southside House (1748; fig. 37) in Wimbledon, have since been turned into single houses.[47] This gentle revision of the picture sketched by Summerson does not contradict his principal point, which was that semi-detachment and quasi-semi-detachment played a significant part in the late Georgian unfolding of the capital's suburbs, particularly in the previously underdeveloped areas south of the Thames.

The key event was the opening of Blackfriars Bridge in 1769, which led to a series of speculative developments in and around the area known as Newington Butts. Nos. 123–133 (odd) Kennington Road (1773–75) are excellent early examples of speculatively built semis, but within a decade the provision of relatively ample space around each building was discouraged by rising land values. The result was quasi-semi-detachment (fig. 32), essentially a single terraced development where entrance ranges paired at the party walls have been set back into a recess. Thus the speculator achieved the economies of terraced construction while preserving the appearance of individuality.

37

Reconstruction of Southside House, nos. 2–3 Woodhayes Road, Wimbledon, as it probably appeared when first built in 1748

LONDON BOROUGH OF MERTON

Southside is an early and very grand example of a suburban semi-detached house. Alterations made in this century to convert it into a single dwelling hid its origins as a semi. It is hard to know just how unusual Southside House was in its own day, but we can be sure that this is a rare survival. The wing projecting from the right rear is part of a pre-existing house that was incorporated into the serving arrangements of the right-hand house.

The Paragon, Blackheath

LONDON BOROUGH OF GREENWICH

The Paragon, the most superb group of Georgian semis in London, was developed as a grand entrance-piece to what was meant to be a small villa quarter. John Cator, a rich timber merchant, bought the Wricklemarsh Estate in 1783, sensing that Blackheath was ripe for development, but he didn't get around to commissioning this first element from Michael Searles (a surveyor to the nearby Rolls Estate and with long-standing south London connections) until 1793/94. A few houses went up quickly (Searles himself was the first resident) but then building had to be suspended owing to credit restrictions during the Napoleonic conflict. The group was finally completed ten years later but the houses were not bought immediately. The architecture of The Paragon speaks for itself: as a piece of monumental building, the crescent rivals anything put up earlier in Bath by the Woods or later in Regent's Park by Nash. The key to Searles's composition is the use of the linked colonnades, which gave a sense of scale as the houses curve off into the distance. The distance between each block is also nicely calculated, allowing a view in depth that lends the whole group a sculptural solidity. Alterations and war damage compromised the purity of design until the whole group was carefully restored in the 1950s. At this time most of the houses were made over into flats.

Perhaps no better illustration can be found of this tightrope-walk between profit motive and consumer demand than the houses in Kennington Park Road now numbered 122–128 (built in 1788; fig. 32), where detachment has been whittled away to the absolute minimum. Summerson concluded, and he must be right, that this paring away at the idea of separateness, from semi to quasi-semi, should been seen as a sign of the 'snob appeal' of detachment.[48]

Further away from the centre, runs of semi-detached houses continued to be built along generous lines long after they had ceased to be profitable in the nearer suburbs. Some of them, such as The Paragon (1794–1807; fig. 38) at Blackheath, were on an almost palatial scale. Shorter and less ostentatious runs of semis can be found near by in Eliot Place (1792–1805) and in Bruce Grove (*ca.* 1798), Tottenham, north of the river. The form has never really fallen from favour.

In order to enhance the illusion of social distinction still further, builders routinely provided pairs of semis with a single pediment and treated the fronts as a single eleva-tion, discreetly removing the entrances to the returns of the houses or tucking them into understated side bays. In this way a pair of fashionable houses took on the appear-ance of a single great one (see fig. 18). In the Regency period speculators went to extreme lengths to deploy this mark of social distinction on houses that were otherwise

39

Lloyd Square, Finsbury

LONDON BOROUGH OF ISLINGTON

Thomas John Lloyd Baker developed his father's farmland south of Pentonville Road from 1818. The project was begun by John Booth, a surveyor, and completed by his son William Joseph, who must be credited with the distinctive appearance of the estate. What is remarkable about the elevations is the scale of the pediment gables, which span each pair of houses, and the illusion of detachment achieved by recessing the first floor above the shared entry porches. Seen obliquely, the houses in Lloyd Square and Lloyd Baker Street have something of that geometric grandeur that Searles built into The Paragon, Blackheath; the residents of the Lloyd Baker Estate were, however, a modest lot – gentlemen tradesmen, small-time merchants, skilled craftsmen and solicitors.

of fairly middling proportions. In the case of the quasi-semis on the Lloyd Baker Estate (fig. 39) in Islington, the results are dramatic, but the deep, slightly overscaled pediments are just a little bit meretricious. Greater cachet was often achieved by laying out a run of semis on a crescent plan, a device that became increasingly common after 1800. With the front and two sides of each pair exposed to public view, the semi assumed the form of a free-standing villa, resolutely distancing itself from the more pedestrian terrace.

The villa had, after all, something of the elegance associated with a foreign import. Brought from Italy to England in the seventeenth century, it was vigorously developed by architects and patrons in the circle of Lord Burlington during the 1720s and 1730s. At the heart of the Palladian villa was an approach to planning, a compact arrangement of interior spaces around a circuit (as opposed to the linear plans commonly found in seventeenth-century great houses), which was reflected, on the outside, in a dense form with a strong sense of cubic geometries. This directness conjured up notions of rustic simplicity, a trace association surviving from the Italian farmhouses designed by the sixteenth-century architect Andrea Palladio. Something of that simplicity was, it must be said, lacking in the great English Palladian show houses built for the Whig ascendancy from 1720 to 1740 and represented in the suburbs of London by Wanstead House (Colen Campbell, 1714–20; demolished 1824), Moor Park (remodelled in the 1720s, probably by Leoni), and Wricklemarsh (John James, 1724–27; demolished by 1800). However, less ostentatious dwellings built on the Palladian model contain a germ of the suburban style of the Regency period. Marble Hill House (Roger Morris, 1724) in Twickenham and the White Lodge (Morris, 1727) in Richmond would gradually exert a strong influence on the middle-class suburban ideal.

FROM ARISTOCRATIC IDEAL TO MIDDLE-CLASS IDYLL

That influence bore fruit at a favourable moment in the economic cycle. As the slow growth of the 1740s yielded to the boom of the 1750s and especially the 1760s, the renewed interest in the medium-sized Palladian villa among London's suburban élite led to a surge of suburban villa building.[49] All the principal designers of the period tried their hand at the form: Sir William Chambers, more usually associated with great houses, built Manresa House (1760–68), Roehampton, while Robert Taylor and James Paine specialized in villas. There were complete 'villa quarters' in Richmond, Twickenham and Roehampton. Fashionable day-trippers came upstream to marvel at buildings that were said to mark the progress of the arts in Britain. Observers reported villa quarters in Islington, South Kensington, Hampstead, Highgate, Muswell Hill, Clapham, Walthamstow, Wanstead, Woodford, Ealing and even in such remote spots as Southgate, Monken Hadley and South Mimms.

The villas designed by Robert Taylor are particularly interesting since most were built with new money earned by men involved in commerce, banking and government contracting. Danson House (1762–70) embodies the late Georgian villa ideal as well as any surviving example; a portrait of the house painted in about 1766 (fig. 40), just as the interior decoration was commencing, captures some of the social significance of the villa style with its fascinating play between seeing and being seen. Standing on an eminence, Danson, like many villas, was meant to excite the eye of the beholder; its situation also made it the perfect place from which to survey the surrounding parkland and agricultural estate, some six hundred acres of gently rolling Kentish country. The prismatic form of the villa itself (fig. 41) answers this dual purpose: by presenting a series of facets, it excites the eye; yet those same bays that break up the blocky form provide the viewer within the house with splendid panoramas. This is the architecture of spectacle: as an object, Danson is calculated to excite, but is also a kind of viewing platform, a belvedere from which successive views of the outside world would be presented like so many choice dishes. This sweeping domain was the personal reserve of the builder of the house, a merchant called John Boyd, and his family, who occupy an important position in the right foreground of

40, 41

Danson House, Danson Park, Bexleyheath
LONDON BOROUGH OF BEXLEY

Designed and built in the 1760s for John, later Sir John, Boyd, the geometric purity of this stone-faced villa was the height of fashion in its own day. Sitting in splendid isolation, both an object in the landscape to be surveyed and a promontory, houses such as Danson provided the model for less exalted suburban dwellings, where the aim was to create an individual space. Physical detachment became the icon of independent family life, in which the individual and his family are constructed as independent units, self-created and outside the traditional bounds of social obligations, a frame of mind well expressed in the accomplished oil painting of Boyd and his family, executed probably in 1765 by the artist George Barrett the Elder. This oil shows the principal front of the house, with wings containing stables and offices, demolished in the first years of the nineteenth century, not long after Boyd's death. The photograph shows the other – south – side of the house, as it appears today. English Heritage began restoring the house in 1996.

Pl. 4.

Three small Houses intended to be built in Vauxhall Road,
whose exterior appearance are intended to convey the idea of one entire Villa.

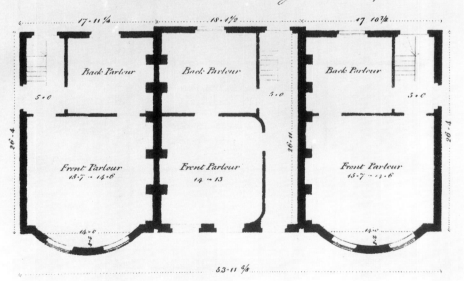

Vide the Explanation given in the Letter Press.

W. Pickett sculp.

the painting. Their territory is self-sufficient, enclosed, almost Edenic. Here is the anti-social side of the suburban ideal writ large, in which the private experience of family life is placed outside, or rather, above society in general. No doubt Boyd's medieval precursors had something of this same sense of difference, but nothing they have left us expresses it in quite so compelling and direct a fashion as this house-and-family portrait.

From this acme of elegance the villa ideal percolated down the social scale. Charles Middleton's *Picturesque and Architectural Views for Cottages, Farm Houses, and Country Villas* of 1793 describes the villa in terms that suggest its pleasures could be enjoyed by people of lesser means than Boyd. In his *Essay on Rural Architecture* (1803), Richard Elsam published a design for 'three villas' at Vauxhall (fig. 42), in which the splendid isolation of Danson House is made to fit – rather uncomfortably, it must be said – on to what was, in essence, a short terrace. Known locally as 'Villa House' or 'Villa Building' (note the singular nouns), Elsam's design was circulated well into the Victorian period, being published in three separate editions of the *New Practical Builder*.[50]

Boyd's Danson House and Elsam's triple villa were single structures. When did single villas, or semi-detached houses pretending to be villas, come to be arranged as self-contained suburban estates, thus making that final evolutionary jump to a built form that fully reflects our own understanding of the suburb as the intermediary environment between country and city? The change came in the last decade or so of the eighteenth century and it was worked not by builders but by architects. One of the innovators was George Dance the younger, the eminent City architect and surveyor, who replicated the revolutionary city planning forms devised by the Woods of Bath for the great Circus and Royal Crescent (1754–75) in London estate plans. His proposal for the Bedford Estate of 1766 shows the clear influence of the Woods' set pieces of city planning; several more sub-Bathian schemes for City lands were made in the 1770s and 1780s, but then, in 1790 or so, came a plan for the Earl of Camden's estate at Camden Town, in which the Woods' grandiose terraces have been translated in part into semis and villas. In 1794 there followed a most remarkable plan for the development of the Eyre Estate in St John's Wood, where the transformation of urban into suburban form was complete. It shows only semis, none of them with colonnades. The start of the Napoleonic Wars slowed developments but in the first decade of the new century the story was taken up where it had been left and once again the focus was the north-western fringe of London, that is, in the corridor that runs north-west from Regent's Park. At the Royal Academy in 1803–04, the architect John Shaw exhibited a plan for a 'British Circus' on the same estate. Descriptions of this lost work suggest it was similar to the earlier, anonymous Eyre plan. Then came Dance again, in 1807, with a scheme showing crescents and rows of semis built behind and in between the principal roads in St George's Fields, Southwark. Dance was at this very moment actually building nine pairs of semi-detached cottages (he called them 'double cottages') in the village of East Stratton. Five remain.[51]

With the exception of this one commission in East Stratton, all the rest was paper architecture. Nevertheless, during these years several suburban villa estates were con-

42

Elevation and plan for three houses known as Villa House, Vauxhall, from Richard Elsam's *Essay on Rural Architecture* of 1803
LONDON BOROUGH OF LAMBETH
Paired villas treated as a single house, spanned by one gable, were common at the turn of the century, lending middle-class houses a touch of grandeur. Elsam's design pushes the illusion one step further, treating a trio of houses as a single three-part composition, the informal elegance of which would have been more suitable for the occasional residence of a duke in, for example, Brighton or Tunbridge Wells than a group of what were, in fact, quite ordinary and small suburban houses. No other building illustrated as vividly the social aspirations of villa architecture. Sadly, it was demolished later in the nineteenth century.

43

Villas of *ca.* 1840 in Clifton Hill, St John's Wood

CITY OF WESTMINSTER

St John's Wood retains the sense of special separateness that it had in the early nineteenth century, a fairy-tale effect underscored by the mingling of architectural styles in one street: Gothic and Italianate, and the more modern Classicism that is the hallmark of Regency style.

structed, which show the influence of the ideals of the Picturesque (fig. 43), an easy configuration seen as the opposite of the contrived geometries of the West End speculative builder, although most of these early essays in the Romantic suburban mode lacked the coherence and sweep of the earlier plans discussed above. Typical of the more informal approach were houses built after 1800 in Alpha Road, St John's Wood, which were described by Summerson as 'low slung' with 'wide eaves' and laid out in no particular order.[52] A few years later the Eyre Estate offered the architect John Nash, who was about to commence his Regent Street and Regent's Park development for the Crown – which did much to stimulate the suburbanization of south Hampstead – the chance to design semi-detached pairs to the north. He passed the job on to his assistant James Burton, and in 1813 the construction of North and South Bank, not far from Alpha Road, commenced. The residents of these new developments were, for the most part, prosperous tradesmen (not necessarily carriage owners), some City commuters, a sprinkling of artists and a few titled names.[53] What is now Keats Grove was developed at the same time, where villas and semis in several styles respectfully mingle before an elegant proprietary chapel. Grander plans for the nearby Maryon Wilson Estate were made as early as 1821 but continually frustrated by the legal restrictions imposed by the terms of the bequest. Nevertheless, the development of other parts of south Hampstead with suburban villas and semis commenced, athough the financial collapse of 1825 meant that schemes were laid aside or progressed slowly. In the 1830s, however, things picked up again, leaving handsome suburban villas in abundance on the Eton College Estate. A more exotic stylistic mix came in the 1840s and 1850s in the streets around Adelaide Road (fig. 44).[54] Villa quarters on the scale of Alpha Road sprouted in

several parts of London after 1804 or so. One of the first was the Twickenham Park Estate (from 1805), built on the edges of the former park; ambitious plans for the Kennington Oval, produced in 1804, were begun but promptly scaled back.

What most of these developments sorely lacked was an overriding architectural coherence, in which the design of individual buildings complemented each other and at the same time interacted with the layout of the streets. For this the genius of John Nash was required. We have seen how the development of Regent Street and Regent's Park stimulated the suburbanization of London north and west of the Park. The forms of Nash's terraces, even the highly picturesque ones that faced the Park, exercised very little influence on the villa boom. Much more influential were two small developments on the north-east corner of the Park. Plans for the picturesquely arranged streets of Park Village East and Park Village West, on either side of the Regent's Canal, are dated to 1823. The Crown granted the leases to Nash himself in the following year, and until his

44

Provost Road, Primrose Hill

LONDON BOROUGH OF CAMDEN

The Chalcot Estate comprised 230 acres owned by Eton College. Its development began in earnest in the early 1840s, when Samuel Cumming proposed erecting houses in what would become Adelaide Road, Bridge Approach, Eton College Road, Provost Road (shown here) and Eton Villas. Cumming, fortunately, was minded to do good work, and if the planning of these streets is nothing special, the houses nevertheless have a robust charm.

45, 46

Park Village West

CITY OF WESTMINSTER

Park Villages East and West, laid out by Nash in 1823 on either side of the Regent's Canal, constituted the most calculatedly picturesque villa quarter in London before 1850. The subtle play of sinuous street line and asymmetrical architecture can now be appreciated only in Park Village West, which is an influential masterpiece of suburban planning. Half of Park Village East was demolished ca. 1900 for the London and North Western Railway cutting.

retirement in 1834 he filled the plots with essays in the Picturesque manner, some Italianate, some vaguely vernacular, some Gothic. The informality of the Alpha Road villas is reined in, given a stronger, clearer and more dramatic effect, although loss through railway widening and in World War II has meant that only the smaller of the two, Park Village West (figs. 45–46), survives. The great planned suburbs of the Regency period – De Beauvoir Town (fig. 47) in Hackney, Clapham Park, Blackheath Park and Ladbroke Grove – all bear the influence of the villa tradition as it developed from Alpha Road to Nash's Park Villages. This influence, a product of English Romanticism and the Picturesque, survived the advent of Victorian respectability to develop into a comfortable tradition.

NOTES

1. D. Keene, 'London in the Early Middle Ages, 600–1300', *The London Journal*, XX, no. 2, 1995, pp. 9–21, esp. pp. 14–15. The most important recent studies are M. Carlin, *Medieval Southwark*, 1985; K. McDonnell, *Medieval London Suburbs*, Chichester 1978; and A.G. Rosser, *Medieval Westminster, 1200–1540*, Oxford 1989.
2. John Warde, a City merchant reared in the countryside, proposed continuing to live in his native Hertfordshire even after his election as Mayor in 1485; the reasons given were plague and political strife.

47

De Beauvoir Square, north side

LONDON BOROUGH OF HACKNEY

The 130 acres of the De Beauvoir Estate once boasted the fine suburban seat known as Balmes House (see fig. 25). The estate was developed by its owners, the de Beauvoir family, from 1834, when a spacious plan was adopted, designed by W.C. Lockner, architect of the estate church, St Peter's, and built by one Thomas Smith. The square itself, which has lost its east side, is unusual for being entirely in a medieval style. The only other of London's squares to wear this same style is R.C. Carpenter's Lonsdale Square, De Beauvoir's exact contemporary.

Some merchants who had purchased suburban seats as investments reserved one part for their own use, especially in times of plague. See S. Thrupp, *The Merchant Class of Medieval London*, Ann Arbor MI, rev. edn 1962, pp. 144–45, 226–31.

3. McDonnell, pp. 126–29; Thrupp, pp. 127–29, 229–30, 245, 280–81.

4. Thrupp, pp. 226–31.

5. *The Victoria County History* [hereafter *VCH*], *Middlesex*, X, ed. C.R.J. Currie, 1995, pp. 11–13.

6. Ex info. V. Belcher in advance of forthcoming publication on Sutton House to be published by English Heritage and The National Trust.

7. *VCH, Middlesex*, V, ed. R.B. Pugh, 1976, pp. 309–15. Bruce Castle in Tottenham is as rare and noteworthy a survival as Sutton House in Hackney.

8. *VCH, Essex*, VI, ed. W.R. Powell, 1973, p. 71.

9. H.J. Dyos, 'The Growth of a Pre-Victorian Suburb: South London, 1580–1836', *Town Planning Review*, XXV, 1954, pp. 59–78 and *passim*.

10. *A Survey of London by John Stow, Reprinted from the Text of 1603*, ed. C.L. Kingsford, Oxford 1908, I, p. 127.

11. M. Power, 'Shadwell: The Development of a London Suburb in the Seventeenth Century', *The London Journal*, IV, no. 1, 1978, pp. 29–48.

12. John Strype, *History of the Cities of London and Westminster ...*, I, London 1720, p. 47.

13. Dyos, 1954, pp. 61–62.

14. George Wither, 'The Scourge of Villainy', 1613, quoted in Manley, p. 171.

15. *VCH, Middlesex*, VII, ed. C.R. Elrington, Oxford and London 1982, p. 56.

16. *VCH, Middlesex*, VII, pp. 113–14.

17. *VCH, Essex*, VI, pp. 52–53, 245.

18. P. Brandon and B. Short, *The South East from AD 1000: The Regional History of England*, London 1990, p. 261.

19. Brandon and Short, pp. 182–83, 211–12.

20. P. Metcalfe and K. Sugden, 'Balmes House', *Hackney History*, II, 1996, pp. 3–8.

21. Richard Lea, draft report on nos. 52–55 Newington Green, Islington (Historical Analysis and Research Team, English Heritage, 1995), ISL 40.

22. Richard Lea, unpublished report on Kingswood Lodge, Kingswood Lane, Croydon (London Region Survey Section Report, English Heritage, October 1993).

23. E. McKellar, 'The City and the Country: The Urban Vernacular in Late Seventeenth- and Early Eighteenth-Century London', in *Georgian Vernacular*, ed. N. Burton, London 1995, pp. 10–18.

24. This was particularly true in Hampstead. See F.M.L. Thompson, *Hampstead: Building a Borough, 1650–1964*, London 1974, pp. 13–14 and *passim*.

25. Daniel Defoe, *A Tour thro' London about the Year 1725*, extracts therefrom, edd. M.M. Beeton and E.B. Chancellor, London 1929, pp. 1–5, 81, 89 and *passim*.

26. Suburban planning is discussed on pp. x–xi and 14–15 of the first edition (London, privately printed).

27. *The Survey of London, South Kensington: Kensington Square to Earl's Court*, 52, London 1986, pp. 1, 4ff.

28. J. Cloake, 'The Growth of Richmond', *Richmond Local Historical Society Paper*, 8, 1993, pp. 24–36; and *idem, Richmond Past*, London 1991. See also C. Hussey, 'Richmond Green, Surrey', *Country Life*, XCV, 12 May 1944, pp. 816–20.

29. F.M.L. Thompson, *Hampstead: Building a Borough, 1650–1964*, London 1974, p. 25.

30. M. Robbins, 'Transport and Suburban Development in Middlesex down to 1914', *Transactions of the London and Middlesex Archaeological Society*, XXIX, 1978, pp. 129–36.

31. In July 1710 von Uffenbach traversed the fourteen miles from Westminster in just under three hours. See *London in 1710, from the Travels of Zacharias Conrad von Uffenbach*, trans. and edd. W.H. Quarrell and M. Mare, London 1934, p. 105.

32. As quoted in Dyos, p. 65.

33. Brandon and Short, pp. 160–61.

34. Dyos, p. 63.

35. Robbins, p. 130.

36. Defoe, p. 82.

37. Robbins, p. 130. For a survey of road building in the period, see H.J. Dyos and D.H. Aldcroft, *British Transport: An Economic Survey from the Seventeenth Century to the Present*, Leicester 1971, pp. 20–39 and *passim*.

38. Dyos, pp. 65–66, 68. Rennie was replaced at the last by James Walker. For a compact survey of Thames crossings, see M. Tucker's chapter in B. Cherry and N. Pevsner, *The Buildings of England: London 2: South*, Harmondsworth 1994, pp. 707–16.

48

Blomfield Road, Little Venice

CITY OF WESTMINSTER

Overlooking the Regent's Canal, the villas in Blomfield Road were built in the first half of the 1840s, and although nothing special in architectural terms, the waterside setting, enhanced by mature trees, makes this one of the best groups of early Victorian houses in London.

39. P. Sumner, *Carriages to the End of the Nineteenth Century*, London 1970; and J. Copeland, *Roads and Their Traffic, 1750–1850*, Newton Abbot, n.d., pp. 134–37.

40. Dyos, pp. 69–70.

41. *VCH, Middlesex*, IV, edd. J.S. Cockburn and T.F.T. Baker, Oxford and London 1971, p. 152; VI, p. 43.

42. Dyos, p. 70.

43. The system is described in John Summerson, *Georgian London*, London 1942, rev. 1962.

44. M. Cosh, *The Squares of Islington*, I, London (Islington Archaeological and Historical Society) 1900, pp. 102–03.

45. See, for example, the development of the Phillimore Estate, as described in *The Survey of London, North Kensington*, XXIII, London 1973, pp. 42, 58, 68–71 and *passim*.

46. J. Summerson, 'The Beginnings of the Early Victorian Suburb', *London Topographical Record*, XXVII, ed. A. Saunders, 1995, pp. 1–48.

47. I am grateful to my colleague Richard Lea, whose splendid analysis of this building deserves to be more widely known. See his drawings and report in the Historical Analysis and Research Team files, English Heritage, LD 3616 and MERTON 48 (1995 draft).

48. J. Summerson, 'Beginnings', pp. 3–6.

49. The standard source on the villa ideal remains Summerson's 'The Classical Country House in Eighteenth-Century England', reprinted in *The Unromantic Castle and Other Essays*, London 1990, pp. 71–120, esp. pp. 83–101. For a recent review of this area see G. Worsley, *Classical Architecture in Britain: The Heroic Age*, New Haven and London 1995, *passim*.

50. The 1823, 1836 and 1842 editions. See Summerson, 'Beginnings', pp. 11–14.

51. Summerson, 'Beginnings', pp. 15–19, and D. Stroud, *George Dance, Architect*, London 1971, pp. 125–27, 144–47, 203.

52. Summerson, 'Beginnings', pp. 18–19. Little remains of this important initiative; the present-day Alpha Close is the vestigial remnant of Alpha Road.

53. M. Brown, 'St. John's Wood. The Eyre Estate before 1830', *London Topographical Record*, XXVII, ed. A. Saunders, 1995, pp. 47–68, esp. pp. 51–60.

54. Summerson, 'Beginnings', pp. 28, 31–41; Thompson, pp. 124–28, 218–50.

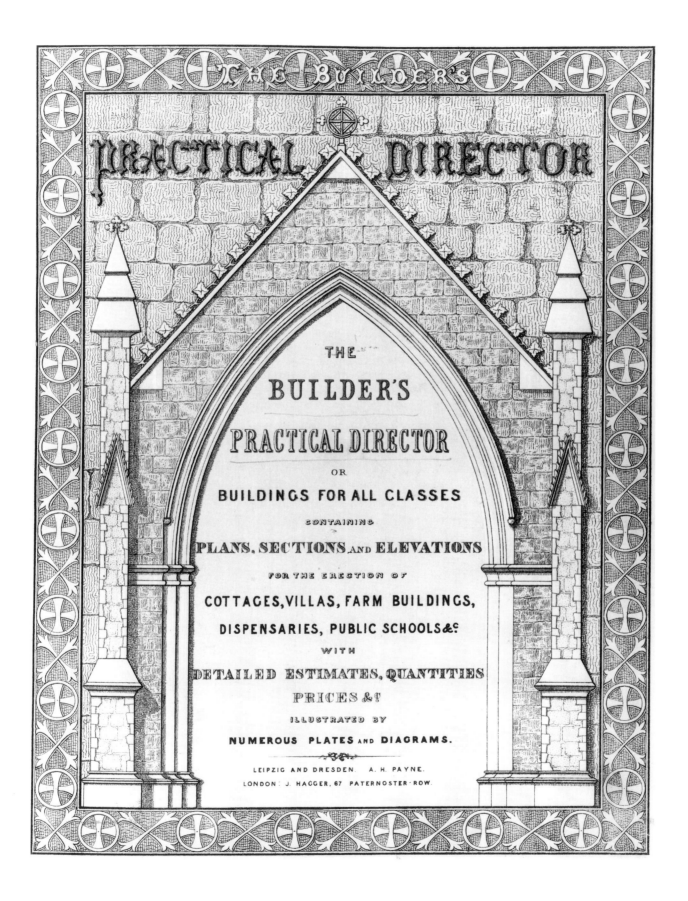

THE BUILDER'S

PRACTICAL DIRECTOR

THE

BUILDER'S

PRACTICAL DIRECTOR

OR

BUILDINGS FOR ALL CLASSES

CONTAINING

PLANS, SECTIONS AND ELEVATIONS

FOR THE ERECTION OF

COTTAGES, VILLAS, FARM BUILDINGS,

DISPENSARIES, PUBLIC SCHOOLS &c.

WITH

DETAILED ESTIMATES, QUANTITIES

PRICES &c.

ILLUSTRATED BY

NUMEROUS PLATES AND DIAGRAMS.

LEIPZIG AND DRESDEN.   A. H. PAYNE.

LONDON: J. HAGGER, 67 PATERNOSTER-ROW.

Chapter Two
Infinite Variety in Brick and Stucco: 1840–1914

SUSIE BARSON

Goodness me, but isn't London big? It seems to start about twenty minutes after you leave Dover and just goes on and on, mile after mile of endless grey suburbs with their wandering ranks of terraced houses and stuccoed semis that always look more or less identical from the train, as if they have been squeezed out of a very large version of one of those machines they use to make sausages. How, I always wonder, do all the millions of occupants find their way back to the right boxes each night in such a complex and anonymous sprawl?

Bill Bryson, *Notes From A Small Island* (1995)

A certain jaundiced and patronizing view of the seemingly endless suburbs encircling 'proper' London has been voiced many times by many different writers since the development of the land around the tightly packed capital first began to get under way in earnest one hundred and fifty years ago. In 1873 Ruskin complained, 'What a pestilence of [houses] and unseemly plague of builders' work – as if the bricks of Egypt had multiplied like its lice, and alighted like its locusts – has fallen on the suburbs of loathsome London?'[1] Meanwhile, William Morris yearned with a passion for the pre-industrial city:

> Forget six counties overhung with smoke,
> Forget the snorting steam and piston stoke,
> Forget the spreading of the hideous town;
> Think rather of the pack horse on the down,
> And dream of London, small, and white, and clean,
> The clear Thames bordered by its garden green.[2]

If Ruskin and Morris were among those who most forcefully articulated the idea that the growth of the Victorian city was a threatening prospect, there were plenty of others willing to back them up. Most authors who comment on the suburbs, especially those writing before World War II, imbue their writing with scorn, cynicism or passionate hatred, perhaps mostly cogently expressed by H.G. Wells in *The New Machiavelli*. Wells bewailed London's 'vast endlessness', foreseeing the Londoner of the year 2000 as having 'the whole of England and Wales south of Nottingham and east of Exeter as his suburb'. His revulsion had its roots in childhood memories:

> I was in the full tide of building and growth from the first; the second railway with its station at Bromstead North and the drainage followed when I was ten or eleven, and all my childish memories are of digging and wheeling, of woods

49

The Builder's Practical Director, a pattern book of 1855 by E.L. Tarbuck

This was typical of the pattern books produced in the mid-nineteenth century. It gave thorough and practical advice to the speculative builder and was truly Vitruvian in its range. It covered such topics as the choice of site, methods of construction and the vexed matter of style. For the last he offered a choice of Italianate and Gothic (with no hint of any 'battle' between them) to suit a range of sizes and classes of property.

50

Eaton Square (north side), Belgravia

CITY OF WESTMINSTER

*Massive in extent, Eaton Square was developed
over the course of thirty years, beginning in
1826. The north side, arguably the finest, was
the work of Thomas Cubitt, who began at the
west end, working steadily east through the
1840s. Each of the surviving three sides has a
'palace' front.*

51

Topsfield Hall, Crouch End, in 1894

LONDON BOROUGH OF HARINGEY

The photograph captures the final days of this late eighteenth-century house. Suburban development was going on all around the house and estate owned by the Elder family: Weston Park and Cecile Park to the north was being developed by John Farrer, architect to the Elders. The house was sold in 1894 to Edmondsons, the builders and developers of Muswell Hill. In its place they put up a parade of shops, curved at the corner, called Topsfield Parade, now in the heart of Crouch End.

invaded by building, of roads gashed open and littered with iron pipes amidst a fearful smell of gas, of men peeped at and seen toiling away deep down in excavations, of hedges broken down and replaced by planks, of wheelbarrows and builders' sheds, of rivulets overtaken and swallowed up by drainpipes. Big trees, and especially elms, cleared of undergrowth and left standing amid such things, acquired a peculiar tattered dinginess rather in the quality of needy widow women who have seen happier days.[3]

The 'tide of building and growth' was an intense period of house construction between 1840 and 1914, when the isolated villages around London and the eighteenth-century developments outside the city boundaries described in the previous chapter were engulfed by new building, with some of the older, sturdier and more useful buildings incorporated and others swept away by infilling and redevelopment (figs. 51–52). There were many reasons for this massive increase in development, but by far the most important was the huge increase in population during the period.

The total population in London in 1801 was 959,000; by 1921 it was 4,483,000. Most of these people lived in the central area in 1801: 787,000, as opposed to 64,000 in the 'inner ring' (Battersea–Chelsea–Islington–Lambeth–Paddington), and 108,000 in the 'outer ring' (Hampstead–Poplar–Wandsworth–Hammersmith). By 1921 the numbers of people living in the central area and inner ring were about the same (1,364,000 and 1,186,000 respectively), with a higher figure of 1,933,000 in the outer ring. The biggest leap in the population figures of the outer ring occurred between 1861 (542,000) and 1881 (1,093,000). The figures show that almost 500,000 people were housed in the outer suburbs within twenty years: an extraordinary achievement.

INFINITE VARIETY IN BRICK AND STUCCO

The other major factors driving the development of the suburbs were the need – or the desire – to escape the squalor and overcrowding of inner-city slums occupied by the working classes and the unemployed, and a demand for new houses for an expanding middle class with social aspirations. The inner boroughs were becoming less attractive: the Georgian residential quarters were fragmented by the cutting-through of new roads and railway lines, and neighbourhoods around station termini lost respectability as they gained accessibility. Thomas Cubitt, having laid out Belgravia (fig. 50) and Pimlico from the 1820s onwards, was opposed for this very reason to the construction of Victoria Station in the 1850s, seeing it as a threat to his ordered stucco domain. Factory owners, small businessmen, civil servants, doctors, teachers, shopkeepers, and bankers and their clerks all wished to live in salubrious areas and in new houses, designed for single-family occupancy, that reflected their respectable social positions. The early Victorian suburbs in Clapham, Camberwell, Hackney, Newington and Islington were primarily middle-class residential suburbs from where the wage-earning male could travel daily into the City or West End. The home to which he returned was expected to provide respite from his daily cares, a place of well-ordered routine and stability, a private and primarily feminine domain run by a wife with the help of mostly female staff: cook, maid and nanny.

The suburban building boom that began in earnest in the 1840s was entirely the result of private enterprise. In the early years of Queen Victoria's reign most of the population lived in rural communities and gained their living on or from the land. Increasing industrialization brought people to the cities in search of work, overcrowding the centres and creating pressure for some kind of expansion outwards. The next one hundred years saw such development of the cities that by 1940 most people were living in a suburban rather than an urban environment.

An important reason for this phenomenon in London was change in land use. The land on which the houses were built usually came from large country estates. The landowner would first secure an Act of Parliament to abolish manorial rights on the land. Building leases on small parcels of land (a few fields at a time) were then offered to builders, who erected houses for rent. The actual process of development was not usually carried out by the landowners themselves, but by small-scale speculators – either the builders who put up the house or minor capitalists who employed builders but made profits from the development of a whole area.

Most speculative developments were built by small firms building houses in small numbers. The builder needed to raise the initial capital to acquire the lease on a parcel of land for two or three houses and to pay for building materials and labour to erect the houses. He then needed to sell on the leases as quickly as possible for as much as possible to cover his costs and allow a small margin of profit towards the cost of the lease for the next parcel of land. The capital was raised by mortgages from building societies and solicitors, typically at the rate of 5% interest over fourteen years. By 1880 a completed house cost around £90 to build and could be let at an annual average rent of £26.[4] Many small builders were unable to sustain this system and went bankrupt, while large building

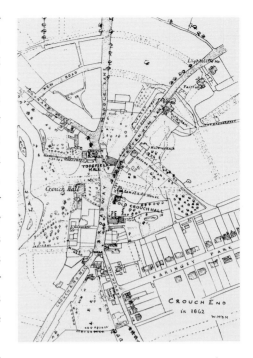

52

Map of Crouch End of 1862

LONDON BOROUGH OF HARINGEY

This map shows several large Georgian houses and villas – Crouch Hall, Old Crouch Hall and Topsfield Hall – which were a feature of the rural villages on the outskirts of London. The railway arrived in the 1860s and signalled the beginning of a building boom. Development of the area began in earnest in the 1880s and 1890s, transforming Crouch End from village into suburb, physically discrete from but economically dependent on the city centre.

53

Shaftesbury Road, Hornsey

LONDON BOROUGH OF ISLINGTON

Terraced housing of the 1880s by different
builders using a variety of styles and materials.

contractors with more reliable cash flow, such as Cubitt, could undertake whole estates. Cubitt, acting as both builder and developer, gave advances to his builders but no more money until the builder had satisfactorily completed his part of the work.

Around the middle of the nineteenth century there was a shift away from the 'measuring and valuing' system of payment as the work went up, to a new procedure whereby the builder estimated the cost of the work beforehand and entered into a contract to do the job at a fixed price, within a time limit and according to plans and estimates. For builders of speculative houses there was no 'client', but building agreements, covenants and conditions of borrowing money amounted to much the same thing as a contract. In nineteenth-century speculative house building, the eighteenth-century custom of putting up the shell or carcass of the house and moving on, leaving the buyer to organize the rest of the trades to finish the work, was replaced by the practice of one firm undertaking all essential parts of the construction. Most speculative builders were individuals or small firms, with bigger firms taking a larger proportion of the housing market by the end of the nineteenth century.[5]

Much of the Victorian and Edwardian suburb was developed piecemeal, sometimes giving a fragmented appearance with later infilling that could end up lowering the tone of a neighbourhood and sending the middle classes elsewhere. The results of small operations of the 1850s and 1860s can be seen in streets where small contractors developed short sections before moving on, leaving the street to be continued by others in a different style or size. One of the pleasures of perambulating the London suburbs is to detect, in the scale or appearance of the houses and the layout of the streets, the extent of one development and the beginning of the next; Shaftesbury Road (fig. 53) in Hornsey illustrates this neatly.

INFINITE VARIETY IN BRICK AND STUCCO

Some estates would employ an architect or a surveyor to ensure the quality of building, the aesthetic appearance of individual houses and the architectural coherence of the estate. In 1859 an article in *The Builder* describing the development of part of Kentish Town attributed the superior quality of the estate to the involvement of a professional architect.[6] The article offers some illuminating comments, beginning with an expression of surprise that the land had not hitherto been built upon, 'particularly when we take into consideration the fact that within the last few years nearly all the fields lying between Kentish Town and Haverstock Hill have been covered with a small but respectable class of houses'. The author admires the way in which the land, formerly belonging to the Dean and Chapter of Oxford, has been laid out by forming wide roads and large plots with gardens for the houses instead of the 'long streets of seven-roomed dwellings peculiar to the neighbourhood'. The sewers, drains, gas and water supplies were put in at an early stage, before the 'handsome ten-roomed houses conveniently appointed, having each a 20-foot forecourt and faced in malm brick and stucco' were built. Smaller runs of terraced cottages, a parade of shops and a large tavern with handsome elevations were included in the estate. The whole was laid out by Philip Hardwick, architect and surveyor to Christ Church, Oxford, and the resulting buildings (fig. 54) were far better than the 'inferior

54

Gaisford Street, Kentish Town

LONDON BOROUGH OF CAMDEN

Part of an estate laid out from the 1850s on land belonging to Christ Church, Oxford, by the architect Philip Hardwick and consisting of a mixture of semi-detached villas and terraced houses. The contemporary building press admired the wide streets and generous plot sizes as well as the handsome elevations of the estate.

55

'St Valery', Beulah Hill, Norwood,
by Sextus Dyball

LONDON BOROUGH OF CROYDON

Sextus Dyball, architect–builder working in Beulah Hill, Norwood, in the 1880s, gave a French château-style roof to the tower of this house, 'St Valery', to produce a rich, eclectic composition that works well on a generous scale.

suburban buildings which we have noticed'. This is a reference to what the defenders of standards in the building profession perceived as a high failure rate of new houses. In 1862 *The Builder* reported on an inquiry into the causes of an accident in which three workmen lost their lives while working on a terraced house in Hackney. The inquiry exposed the dangers of under-regulated building sites where speculative builders boosted their profits by using inferior materials and providing insufficient support to houses under construction.[7] There was little centralized control over house building until about the 1870s, and few local restrictions or guidelines. Most building was carried out by builders with only their pattern books to guide them. Conditions were improved by the Public Health Act of 1875, which gave local authorities the power to lay down regulations concerning the sanitation, specifications for construction, the widths of streets, building lines and so on. The effectiveness of control varied from area to area, but the majority of houses were more

INFINITE VARIETY IN BRICK AND STUCCO

56

No. 23 Carleton Road, Tufnell Park

LONDON BOROUGH OF ISLINGTON

George Truefitt's houses of the 1860s on the Tufnell Park Estate in Camden were original in the treatment of the elevation, often preferring to eschew the Venetian Gothic detail made popular by the writer John Ruskin in favour of the more abstract effect of broad, plain, assymetrical façades. This house in Carleton Road has a Flemish-inspired crowstepped gable.

soundly built as a result. Although some houses undoubtedly failed through 'jerry building' and many have been demolished, making it impossible to say how long they could have continued in use, speculatively built houses have survived in sufficient quantity to suggest that, overall, building standards were reasonably high.

Articles in *The Builder* also highlight the enduring rivalry between the professional architect and the speculative builder, a battle in which the architect aimed to distinguish himself either by increasing specialization in a building type other than housing (E.R. Robson with schools, A.W. Cross with public baths, Saxon Snell with hospitals and asylums, Frank Matcham with theatres) or by stamping his own individual character on his domestic work. Sir John Summerson has shown how architects of single houses and groups of houses in north London (Charles Gray, Charles Hambridge, George Truefitt, Batterbury and Huxley) – and, it should be added, elsewhere – distinguished their buildings by the use of quirky,

57

Victorian 'vernacular': Tufnell Park Estate

LONDON BOROUGH OF ISLINGTON

The double bay window shown here has different details: the upper has a foliage design in the composition stone window lintel picked up by the round capitals on the colonettes; the lower bay has broader, square pilasters with freer, intertwining foliage on the capitals.

58

Victorian 'vernacular': Park Road, Hornsey

LONDON BOROUGH OF HARINGEY

The capitals on these small Victorian houses show the finesse of naturalistic detail in flora, fauna, and faces that could be achieved in the composition stone capitals cast from moulds. The monkey, among fully rounded grapes, has a tail that entwines with the stem of the vine.

inventive features (figs. 55–56).[8] In some cases the speculative builder could also attempt originality through eclecticism, employing a Victorian (and later, Edwardian) 'vernacular' that had little to do with the work of the great architects of the day (figs. 57–61).

Examples can readily be seen in the composition stone decoration of the 1870s and 1880s, in window surrounds and capitals on porch pillars or bay pilasters: Ruskinian assemblages of fruit, flowers, swags, entwining vines, monkeys, birds and squirrels; neo-Norman, Gothic and Classical elements often crowded together hugger mugger on the simple brick façade.

INFINITE VARIETY IN BRICK AND STUCCO

59

Edwardian 'vernacular': Duke's Avenue, Muswell Hill (*top left*)

LONDON BOROUGH OF HARINGEY

These Edwardian houses have many features typical of the period around 1900: ornate scrollwork in plaster relief in the pediments, with an incised scroll pattern in the window lintels below; a moulded brick egg-and-dart cornice under the eaves and around the top of the bay; and turned wooden balusters in the porch and sash windows with small panes over plain-glazed frames.

60

Victorian 'vernacular': Mount View Road, Hornsey (*top right*)

LONDON BOROUGH OF HARINGEY

A French château-style roof with overlapping 'fish-scale' slate tiles surmounted by cast-iron decorative cresting distinguishes this house of the 1880s.

61

Victorian 'vernacular': Tufnell Park Estate

LONDON BOROUGH OF ISLINGTON

Houses on the Tufnell Park Estate (for example in Anson Road and St George's Avenue) were built in a variety of styles: castellated with Tudor-style flattened window arches, Italianate or Gothic.

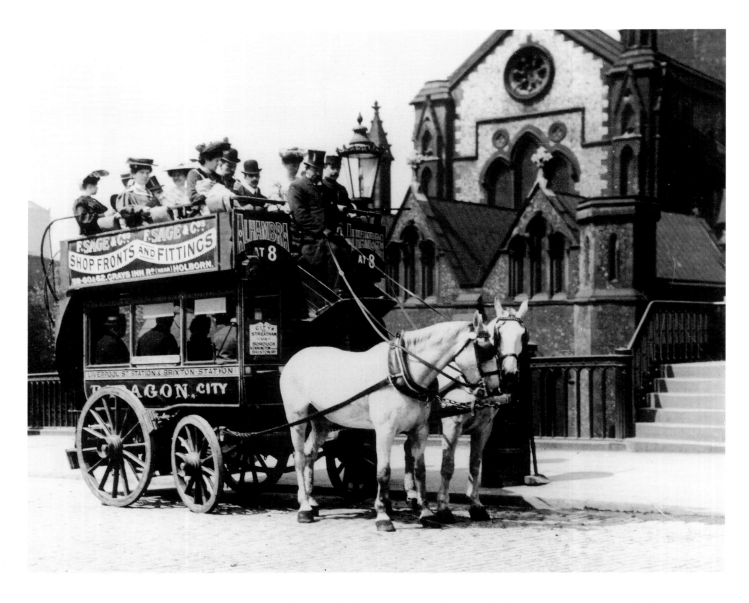

62

Horse-drawn omnibus

A horse-drawn omnibus outside Southwark Cathedral en route from the suburb of Brixton to the City. This type of carriage had served London from the 1870s. This photograph was taken in 1906; a motor bus had been brought out two years earlier, and an electric tram service was begun in 1903 by the LCC. Both marked the demise of the horse-drawn bus.

Another significant factor to affect London's suburban development in the nineteenth and early twentieth centuries was transport. The relationship between the spread of new suburbs and the growth of the transport network around London is a complicated one. The first omnibus service began in 1829 (fig. 62) and the first tram service in 1861; the Metropolitan Railway opened in 1863 and the first Tube service ran in 1890; cable trams were introduced in 1884 (fig. 63) and motor buses followed in 1897. In 1901 the first electric tramway (faster than the horse-drawn tram and cheaper than the bus) ran from Shepherd's Bush to Acton; the service was later extended to Hounslow and Uxbridge. By 1914 tram services went out as far as Edgware, Edmonton, Barnet, Enfield, Walthamstow, Bexley and Croydon (fig. 64). Commuter routes were extended on the existing railways, bringing in middle-class passengers from up to twenty miles from the centre. Electrification transformed the Underground network. The Metropolitan Line

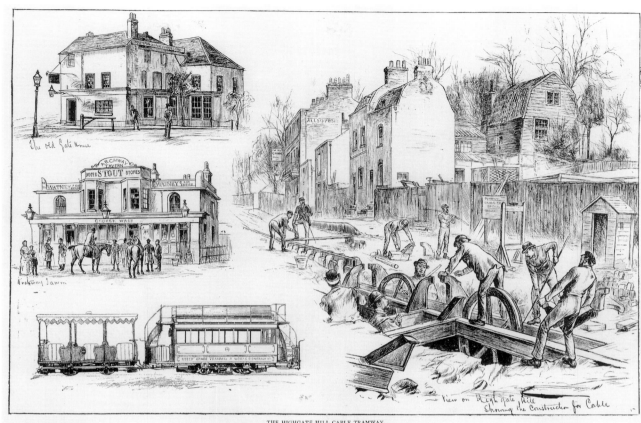

THE HIGHGATE HILL CABLE TRAMWAY.

63

Cable tram

Constructed in 1884, the Highgate Hill Cable Tramway was a pioneering form of public transport. Developed in hilly San Francisco in the 1870s, the cable traction system moved cabs using a steel cable in the middle of the track. The first cable tramway in Europe ran up and down the steep hill between the old coaching inns and taverns at Highgate and Archway, as its horse-drawn predecessors had done. Both pubs, illustrated in the vignettes, were to be rebuilt shortly afterwards.

64

Tram

The LCC tram shown here was photographed in 1913.

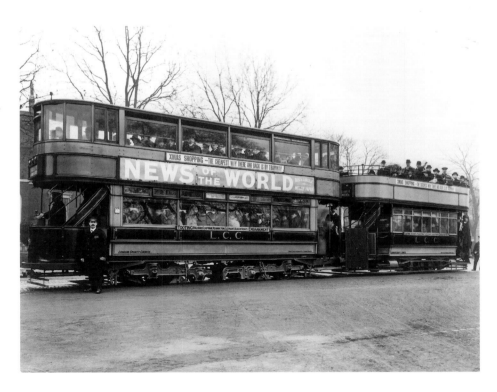

65

Railway cottages in Sulgrave Road, Shepherd's Bush

LONDON BOROUGH OF HAMMERSMITH
AND FULHAM

Houses such as these symmetrical, brown stock-brick cottages, with some tile hanging in the gable and red-brick 'aprons' under the sills, were built in south and west London in the 1850s and 1860s as a direct result of the expanding railway network.

(begun in 1863) was gradually extended in the 1870s, and the Circle Line was completed by 1905. The potential of the first electrified Tube, which ran from the City to Stockwell from 1890, was realized in the early years of the twentieth century by an American, Charles Tyson Yerkes. Yerkes's investment in the enterprise enabled three new lines to be built: the Bakerloo, Piccadilly and Hampstead lines, which not only laid the foundations of the modern Underground system, but also opened up north London for development. Concurrent with these services was the growth of the number of people who chose to live further out from London's centre. What has interested recent historians of suburban development in London and elsewhere is the relationship between these two phenomena: was the coming of railways the cause or the result of the development of the outlying areas?

The conclusion from numerous studies of particular areas is that no simple cause-and-effect can be proved: suburbs existed for many years with a poor transport service and the building of a station did not always attract development (although it was usually only a matter of time). Even when development came it might be of only the poorest

INFINITE VARIETY IN BRICK AND STUCCO

kind. F.M.L. Thompson has made the important point that the development of suburbs preceded the provision of railway services by periods of at least a decade or two, for each of the larger cities.[9] Thompson argues that early improvements in transport originally carried off the wealthy minority to the outlying areas; better transport made the creation of a suburb possible, but not inevitable. In certain areas, such as Bromley in the 1850s and west London in the 1860s, there was a response to the arrival of the railway (fig. 65), but the existence of the railway was not a precondition for suburban growth. In many cases a suburb would be expanding and an omnibus service into town would follow the expansion, not the other way around.

From the 1840s railway stations sprang up in rings around central London: to the south at Battersea, Wandsworth, Brixton, Balham, Peckham, Dulwich, New Cross, Brockley, Forest Hill and Lewisham, and to the north at Kentish Town, Kilburn, Crouch End (fig. 66), Hornsey and Wood Green. Their arrival encouraged the construction of middle-class villas, semi-detached houses and respectable terraces.

66

Crouch End Station

This typical suburban railway station of the 1860s, where commuters could change for the City on to the Great Northern Railway line, served the branch railway between Finchley and Finsbury Park. It is a brick-built, single-storey, unpretentious building, which has since been converted into a café.

The railways, long used by the middle classes as a means of getting to work, were only gradually taken advantage of by the working classes when the fares were reduced: in outer London, commuting to a job in the centre was impossible until affordable, and the introduction of cheap tickets transformed many suburbs from middle-class enclaves to a social patchwork much closer to their class make-up today. Working-class suburbs developed rapidly around Edmonton and Walthamstow from the mid-1860s, when the Great Eastern Railway provided cheap 'workers' trains' into London, but in general workers' cottages and lower-class terraced housing tended to go up on sites that builders did not feel were sufficiently attractive for middle-class housing: next to factories, docks or railways.

Despite the powerful presence of the railways, other factors had to be in place before development occurred. These have been identified by Thompson as an attractive location (high up, or near water) with suitable building ground; an established nucleus; landowners willing to develop at a good moment in the building cycle; and access to decent and frequent transport.[10]

Suburban development took place earlier on the north side of the river than on the south, partly owing to the pattern of land ownership and partly because of the lack of good-quality building land to the south. Along the south bank of the river and the roads leading back from the main bridges, some building of mixed type and quality had taken place by the middle of the nineteenth century, but the potential to develop salubrious suburbs here was blighted by poor drainage, industrialization and, later, the multiplication of railway lines to Clapham Junction. In contrast, the availability of large tracts of good-quality building land to the north encouraged the expansion of Georgian suburban nuclei at Hampstead, Highgate, Tottenham, Clapton and Hackney into well-to-do suburbs. Providing enough drainage for an ever-increasing population was a problem, and the Metropolitan Board of Works and later the London County Council had to spend £316 million between 1856 and 1930 on mains drainage and sewage disposal works, a gargantuan undertaking initiated by the celebrated Sir Joseph Bazalgette.

The general pattern of provision of working-class housing in the nineteenth century was in tall tenements erected from the 1850s in inner-city areas. As we have seen, the coming of railways enabled workers to move out and live in their areas of work, and the effect of this is the subject of many published local historical accounts of the development of particular boroughs. In 1848 the parish of Battersea, for example, was lightly populated and characterized by open common and farmland. Its population was clustered on the riverbank at Battersea village and on higher ground around Clapham Common. By the 1880s the area was covered with railway lines and houses. Nine Elms, with its railway yards and gasworks, was where the labouring classes were concentrated and many rows of small, terraced houses were erected to accommodate them.[11]

The Shaftesbury Park Estate off Latchmere Road in Battersea was built in 1872–77 by the Artizans', Labourers' and General Dwellings Company, a philanthropic company formed in 1867. It was the earliest estate of cottages built by this or any other group (the

Peabody Trust was the first to build housing specifically for the working classes, but provided high-density blocks in inner-city areas). The company architect, Robert Austin, planned over one thousand cottages with gardens laid out in tree-lined streets, for better-paid workers who could afford the rent of between seven and thirteen shillings a week. The cottages varied in type, size and design, but most were built of the same materials: stock brick, with a little decorative red and black banding and some Gothic ornament (fig. 67). The inhabitants were governed by strict rules, especially with regard to subletting, and neither churches nor pubs were allowed within the estate boundaries.

68, 69

Fifth Avenue, Queen's Park Estate

CITY OF WESTMINSTER

The Queen's Park Estate, begun in 1875 by the architect Rowland Plumbe, benefited from jollier designs than had previously been employed. Plumbe used the Victorian Gothic Revival

The entrances at the four corners of the plot were announced by turrets: built for and occupied by skilled labour, Shaftesbury Park was a social fortress of the respectable working class. Another, similar development by the Artizans', Labourers' and General Dwellings Company is Queen's Park (figs. 68–69).

The Housing of the Working Classes Act of 1890 was an attempt to address the housing problem, which in London had become acute. Local authorities were empowered to buy as much land as might be necessary for the long-term planning of improve-

ment schemes, to rehouse people displaced through slum clearance, and to build houses themselves. It took time for local authorities to embark on programmes of new building; of all new houses built between 1890 and 1914, fewer than 5% were provided by local authorities. This was largely because the expense of rebuilding had to be borne from the rates: refurbishing existing housing was the cheaper and therefore the more popular course of action. Liverpool was the first city to build its own council housing, and Manchester and Sheffield built some small suburban cottage estates after the Act, but it

vocabulary to ornament the façades of the small houses: colonettes, drip hood moulds around the windows and polychromatic brickwork. Some of the corner houses are emphasized by square turrets with pyramidal roofs. The estate contained more than 2000 artisans' houses, a meeting hall and a Methodist church.

INFINITE VARIETY IN BRICK AND STUCCO

70, 71

Old Oak Estate, Hammersmith

LONDON BOROUGH OF HAMMERSMITH
AND FULHAM

The progressive LCC architects adopted several garden city principles in the planning of this estate, begun in 1911: a serpentine road offering a picturesque view of vernacular-inspired houses, and the use of a splayed 'butterfly' plan for houses at the corners, reminiscent of Unwin's handling of junctions at Hampstead Garden Suburb. Subtle variations of style were introduced to add interest to the terraces of houses.

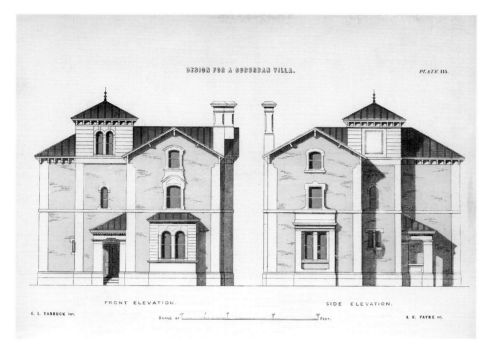

DESIGN FOR A SUBURBAN VILLA.

PLATE 115.

FRONT ELEVATION.

SIDE ELEVATION.

E. L. TARBUCK inv.

SCALE OF FEET.

A. H. PAYNE sc.

72, 73

Elevations and plans for a suburban villa, from *The Builder's Practical Director*, a pattern book of 1855 by E.L. Tarbuck

Tarbuck's text that accompanied this design in The Builder's Practical Director *stated: 'This house is planned with studied irregularity, with the view of obtaining the greatest amount of picturesque effect.' The tower contained the staircase, and at the top was a smoking-room. The coal-cellar and WC could be entered without going into the kitchen, and space was provided for china and wine. A side entrance was provided for tradesmen and a veranda was built at the back of the dining room; altogether a 'convenient family residence in brick and cement for the sum of £1500'.*

was the London County Council that finally got to grips with the problem in the early twentieth century.

By 1914 the LCC had housed 25,000 people in a variety of estates. The LCC Architect's Department included gifted young architects under Thomas Blashill and, from 1899, W.E. Riley. They took their inspiration from Philip Webb and W.R. Lethaby, and produced some of the most progressive housing and public buildings in the country. They sought to bring to the working-class cottage the dignity, individuality and quality of design and materials that a wealthy private patron would expect in his country house. The best of their cottage estates built in the outer ring of London were Totterdown Fields (1903–11) in Tooting, White Hart Lane (1906), Old Oak (1911; figs. 70–71) in Hammersmith, East Acton (1913) and Roehampton (1924), all consisting of humane, Arts and Crafts-influenced, two-storey cottages of the type built at Letchworth and Hampstead Garden Suburb.

In middle-class suburbs, the general pattern of development during the 1840s and 1850s consisted of either large villas set in their expansive grounds or overlooking a park (figs. 72–73), or, for the less well-off, runs of Italianate terraces forming squares and crescents. A new form of dwelling, the semi-detached house, which broke loose from the confines of Regent's Park (the Park Villages and Gloucester Gate) and St John's Wood (the Eyre Estate), appears in large numbers from the 1850s in Maida Vale, Holloway, Hackney, Highbury, Willesden, Blackheath, Greenwich, Camberwell and Dulwich. By the end of the nineteenth century these generously proportioned houses with gardens at both front and back had become the quintessential suburban house form (figs. 74–75). For the lower-middle class during the 1860s and 1870s it was

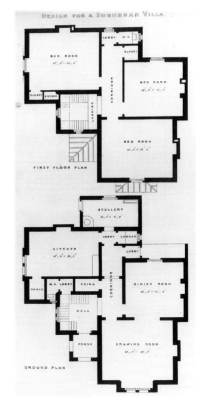

DESIGN FOR A SUBURBAN VILLA

BED ROOM

LOBBY W.C.

CLOSET

BED ROOM

CLOSET

CISTERN

LANDING

CORRIDOR

BED ROOM

FIRST FLOOR PLAN

SCULLERY

KITCHEN

LOBBY LARDER

LOBBY

COAL

W.C. LOBBY CHINA

CORRIDOR

DINING ROOM

HALL

PORCH

DRAWING ROOM

GROUND PLAN

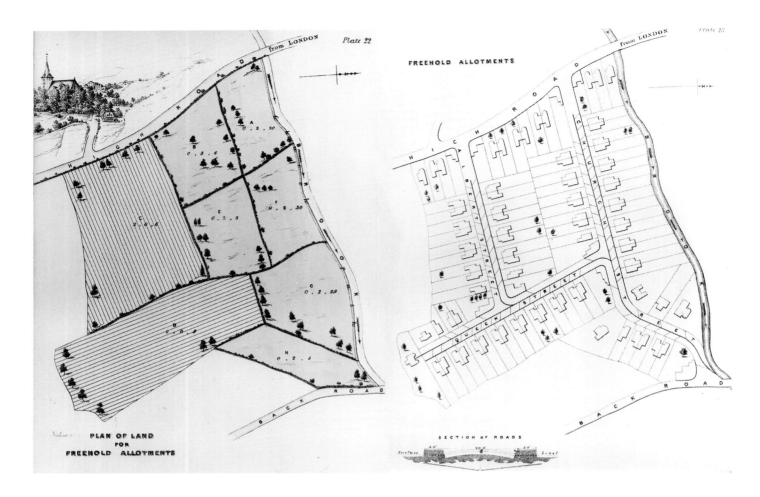

74, 75

Plan of land for freehold allotments (*above left*) and plan of the proposed development (*above right*), from *The Builder's Practical Director* of 1855

The initial plan shows a 'typical' tract of land likely to be bought by a speculative builder. In the layout of the proposed development of semi- detached houses the streets follow the boundaries of the hedges; the larger plots front the High Road. Note the quintessential Victorian suburban names, in particular Albert Road and Church Road.

the small terraced house, two-storey with slate roof, terracotta chimney-pots and back extensions for scullery and wash-house, which dominated the suburban landscape, in row upon row (figs. 76–77).

Houses varied in rental cost from about £20 per year for a six-room house (two rooms each at basement, ground-floor and first-floor level) to about £55 for a ten-room family house or as much as £100 for a sixteen-room house with dining and drawing rooms, two servants' rooms in the roof, kitchens in the basement and lavatories on the ground floor.[12] The materials and method of construction were the same for all classes of house: load-bearing brick faced with stucco (usually moulded in imitation of stonework) under pitched roofs of tiles or slate. Sash windows were ubiquitous, but the size and shape of the openings and the profiles of the glazing bars varied enormously.

Builders responded to the incomes and tastes of the likely tenants with a variety of housing types – terraced, semi-detached and detached. The speculatively built house was usually a simplified, scaled-down version of what architects were using for custom-built houses. Designs and architects' plans were published in technical trade guides specially produced for speculative builders, such as *The Illustrated Carpenter and Builder* and *The Builder's Practical Director* (figs. 72–73 and 78–79; see also fig. 49), and experienced

INFINITE VARIETY IN BRICK AND STUCCO

76, 77

Albany Road, Ealing

LONDON BOROUGH OF EALING

The exterior photograph of ca. 1890 shows a range of variously sized terraced houses, which still survive. An interior view of one of them, 'Redcliffe', shows the heavily patterned wallpaper and ornate gasolier typical of a Victorian suburban parlour.

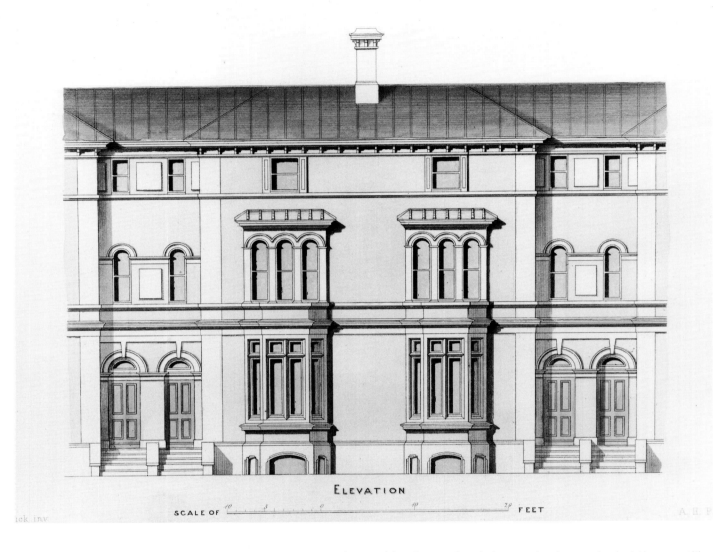

ELEVATION

SCALE OF   FEET

78, 79

Victorian pattern-book designs

In his introduction to The Builder's Practical
Director *of 1855, its author, the architect
E.L. Tarbuck, defined the book's content and
purpose: 'Plans, specifications and estimates in
detail clearly to be understood by the Million
will be exhibited. In a word it is intended to lay
before our readers a Handbook of Building, a
reference to which will be of use to the initiated
as well as to those about to purchase plots of
ground and to build houses.' Other architects*

builders were quite capable of executing their own drawings and calculating quantities
without professional assistance (fig. 80). The customer had little influence over the
design. The result at the lower end of the market was little innovation in house plan,
construction or materials and a monotonous appearance in the repetition of façades. At
first glance it might appear that little had changed since the Georgian period, although a
closer look revealed subtle variations in window design or changing taste in ornament.
The decorative style of these houses was predominantly Ruskinian Gothic, with builders
using moulds to cast composite stone for the capitals *in situ*. The capitals that adorned
the pillars of the porch or bay window depicted a variety of fruit, animals and foliage. At
close range, these details often turned out to be admirably intricate and naturalistic.

One feature that distinguished the front elevation of the house from that of its
eighteenth-century predecessor was the bay window, which not only enlarged the room

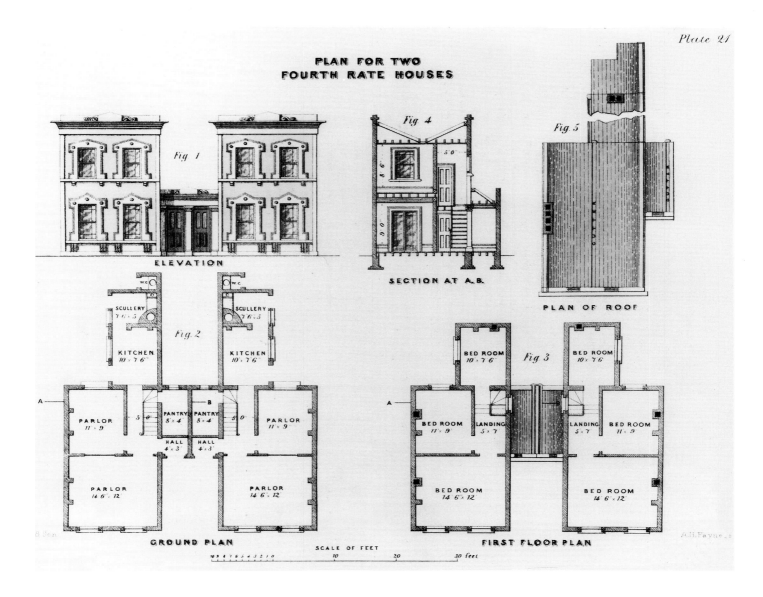

Plate 21

**PLAN FOR TWO
FOURTH RATE HOUSES**

Fig 1

ELEVATION

Fig 2

w.c.   w.c.

SCULLERY
7·6·5   SCULLERY
7·6·5

KITCHEN
10·7·6   KITCHEN
10·7·6

A

PARLOR
11·9   PANTRY
8·4   PANTRY
8·4   PARLOR
11·9

HALL
4·3   HALL
4·3

PARLOR
14·6·12   PARLOR
14·6·12

GROUND PLAN

Fig 4

SECTION AT A.B.

Fig 5

PLAN OF ROOF

Fig 3

BED ROOM
10·7·6   BED ROOM
10·7·6

A

BED ROOM
11·9   LANDING
5·7   LANDING
5·7   BED ROOM
11·9

BED ROOM
14·6·12   BED ROOM
14·6·12

FIRST FLOOR PLAN

SCALE OF FEET
10   20   30 feet

a few feet and let in more light, but also broke up a row of terrace fronts and gave it depth, pattern and an air of distinction. The bay window also served a social function. As one late Victorian suburbanite reminisced:

> The main attraction for us all was the window. Our house stood at the corner of the two roads, and gave us a good view down most of the length of one of them, affording us plenty of information of the doings of our neighbours and passers-by. Up and down they went, the hawkers of various goods, each with the appropriate cry: 'Flowers all a-blowing and a-growing', 'ornaments for your fire-stove', 'a pair of fine soles', 'bird cages, ironholders, brooms, brushes and baskets'.[13]

While such houses made up the majority of speculative developments in London, a private development occurred that was to change the style of subsequent speculative domestic building. Bedford Park in Turnham Green, west London, was laid out by the

also produced pattern-book designs to suit a wide range of requirements and budgets.

80

Belsize Park

LONDON BOROUGH OF CAMDEN

The semi-detached pair of houses shown here closely follow Tarbuck's suggested formula as set out in his pattern book, The Builder's Practical Director, *of 1855, but any unnecessarily time-consuming or expensive ornament has been omitted.*

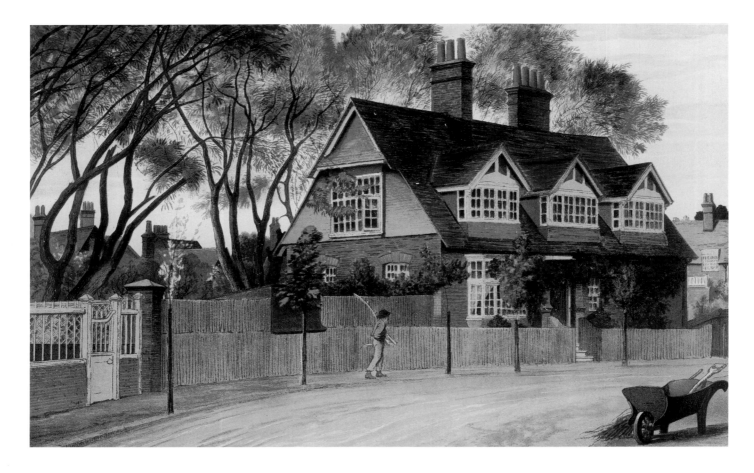

81

Queen Anne's Gardens, looking north by H.M.
Paget

LONDON BOROUGH OF EALING

*The aim to achieve good taste on a budget was
the challenge facing the architects designing
houses for Bedford Park. This lithograph shows
one such attempt, at no. 7 Queen Anne's
Gardens, designed in 1878 by W. Wilson for the
painter T.M. Rooke.*

entrepreneur Jonathan T. Carr in 1875 and subsequently built up with 'artistic' houses by
Richard Norman Shaw (employed by Carr as the architect for the estate between 1877
and 1886), E.J. May and Maurice Adams in the 'Queen Anne' style. In order to attract the
highest rents, Carr promoted the estate as an exclusive enclave for discerning aesthetes
and artists. The architecture was an important aspect of his marketing campaign; Shaw's
Bedford Park houses are characterized by red-brick or tile-hung walls with decorative
panels of carved brick or moulded terracotta, deeply coved cornices and sweeping
rooflines with tall chimney-stacks. The fenestration in these houses is particularly inventive: Venetian windows or 'Ipswich oriels' are glazed with small panes in white-painted
wood frames or with leaded quarries. The houses are irregularly and picturesquely
grouped, particularly on corner sites, and have distinctive garden walls and fences. There
are no basements or large rear extensions, and the houses, although modest in scale, are
provided with generous front doors and entrance halls (figs. 81–86; see also fig. 8).

Bedford Park was novel because the houses were specially commissioned for the site
and because of the large number of trees and green spaces, both communal and private,
that were incorporated into the estate; it is the first example of the village or market
town idiom being adopted for a speculatively built suburb. As such, it was well received
by the architectural schools and the building press. It was praised by the German techni-

INFINITE VARIETY IN BRICK AND STUCCO

No. 6 Bedford Road, Bedford Park,
Turnham Green, Chiswick

LONDON BOROUGH OF EALING

*R. Norman Shaw's 'Type D3', for which
designs are shown in fig. 83, becomes no. 6
Bedford Road, a detached house with tall
chimneys, steeply pitched tiled roof, gabled
dormer, wooden bay window, no basement
and wooden fences rather than iron railings.*

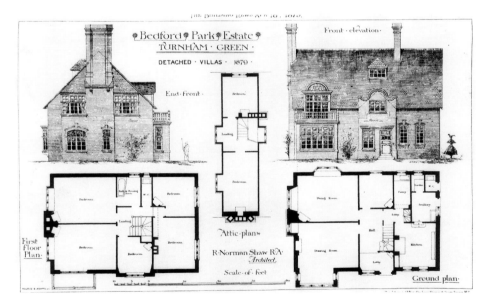

83

Designs of 1879 by R. Norman Shaw for
detached villas for the Bedford Park Estate,
Turnham Green, Chiswick

LONDON BOROUGHS OF EALING AND
HOUNSLOW

*These plans, of 'type D3', were published in
The Building News in 1879. The text that
accompanied the design approved of the
'quaint and homely effect', the low cost of
building (£1400), the use of quality materials
(red bricks and red roof tiles) and the economic
planning within the house.*

cal attaché Hermann Muthesius in his seminal survey of English domestic building, *Das englische Haus*.[14] Despite the lampooning of its inhabitants by metropolitan wits such as Gilbert and Sullivan and G.K. Chesterton, Bedford Park was considered a great architectural success by the time it was completed in 1883. Its stylistic influence is to be seen in such later developments as the nearby Grove Park Estate belonging to the Duke of Devonshire (particularly nos. 80–94 Grove Park Terrace of 1888, with Shaw-inspired

84

Tower House and Queen Anne's Grove
by S.M. Trowtschold, 1882

LONDON BOROUGH OF EALING

*A contemporary account of Bedford Park noted:
'The first thought of the proprietor of these
hundred acres was how to spare the greatest
number of trees and build artistic houses among
them that might look as though surrounded by
the growth of centuries' (Lady's Pictorial, 3,
1882, p. 34). This lithograph, by one of the
many artist-residents of Bedford Park, shows
Jonathan Carr's own house, the Tower House,
in the background; in the large gardens in the
foreground the trees are rendered in a
fashionable Japanese style.*

Bath Road, Bedford Park, Turnham Green, Chiswick, in 1881

LONDON BOROUGH OF HOUNSLOW

On the left is the church of St Michael and All Angels; on the right, the Tabard Inn and shops that were purpose-built for the community of Bedford Park. The ensemble was designed by Richard Norman Shaw and recently completed when this photograph was taken.

detail), where it brings a touch of fashionable 'Queen Anne' to an otherwise conventional late Victorian suburb of Italianate villas.

The influence of Shaw and his school can be seen in many suburban terraces and semi-detached houses from the 1880s and into the early years of the twentieth century: the Bush Hill Park Estate (from 1878), near Enfield, Heathfield Park (1883) in Willesden, and Duke's Avenue (1906) in Muswell Hill all contain good examples. The smaller, more economically planned housing of Shaw, Voysey and Ernest Newton provided the prototypes for much housing in south London, too, in particular the Wimbledon Common area, and Bickley and Chislehurst in Bromley. The houses in Camden Park

86

The Avenue, Bedford Park, Turnham Green, Chiswick

LONDON BOROUGH OF EALING

R. Norman Shaw's style for the Bedford Park Estate, a reinterpretation of seventeenth-century rural vernacular with Renaissance, Dutch and Flemish details, is shown here in these semi-detached houses of 1880.

(1893–1916; fig. 87) in Chislehurst clearly show the influence of Shaw: with their broad gables, tile-hanging and prominent chimneys, these are evidently the offspring of Bedford Park parents.

What the suburban house succeeded in doing by the turn of the century, which urban housing could not, was confer a sense of status on the house-owner. It expressed his attachment to family life, to a smoothly run household, to privacy, convention and moral rectitude. The gardens in which the suburban house was set made clear the distinction between the public and the private spheres: the front garden was – and often still is (fig. 88) – for public display, the rear garden for vegetables or family relaxation.

The image of suburbia that emerged by the end of the nineteenth century was resolutely middle class. An essay entitled 'From London Tenement to London Mansion' by P.F. William-Ryan and published in 1903 describes the East End tenements with a sombre, dispassionate tone, then shifts gear when discussing the suburban house and lifestyle:

> Step into a train and let us away to the suburb with its villas detached and semi-detached, its roads with their avenues of saplings and bay windowed houses. Every suburb is in fact a town in itself, with villas standing in their own grounds proclaiming the presence of an aristocracy, while democracy is represented by terraces of four-roomed and six-roomed houses. Somebody has said that the London suburbs are sad. They are only peaceful.[15]

The author goes on to describe the interior and the life of the inhabitants 'neither rich nor poor'. The houses are immaculately kept, 'the wall hung with a few popular prints, flowers on the hall table'. The mistress of the house, he imagines, will dust the piano,

88

Meadvale Road, Brentham Garden Suburb

LONDON BOROUGH OF EALING

The public display of the front garden has long
been a feature of the suburban house, as here,
in one of the earliest garden suburbs. Pre-dating
Letchworth Garden City and Hampstead
Garden Suburb, it was built in 1901–15 by a
co-operative society, Ealing Tenants. The layout
of the estate and the Vernacular Revival
architecture were supplied by Parker and
Unwin, who were involved from 1907.

89, 90, 91, 92

Hampstead Garden Suburb

LONDON BOROUGH OF BARNET

*Barry Parker and Raymond Unwin published
The Art of Building a Home in 1901 and
Cottage Plans and Common Sense in 1902;
both books emphasized their belief that Arts
and Crafts principles were 'equally applicable to
the £200 cottage or the £10,000 country
house'. Their skill in the design of the exterior
and internal layout of a range of residences on a
planned estate, demonstrated at New Earswick
and Letchworth, was the reason that Henrietta
Barnett chose them, in 1904, to design a
garden suburb for all classes, her 'green golden
scheme'. Shown here is the variety of sizes and
styles of houses and cottages built at
Hampstead Garden Suburb in the early years of
the twentieth century, with features in common
such as front gardens, hedges and trees.*

sideboard and sofa before supervising the preparation of a cosy little dinner, to be eaten at 6.30 with her husband when he returns from the City. He concludes that 'homeliness is the keynote of suburban life'.

Hampstead Garden Suburb was an attempt to convey that pride in homeliness to all classes in a mixed development. It was founded in 1906 through the inspiration of Dame Henrietta Barnett, whose motives were twofold: to prevent the building-over of rural land on Hampstead Heath by speculative builders following the opening of Golders Green station in 1900; and to provide a model community of rich and poor living together, enriching each other's lives and residing in beautiful houses surrounded by vegetation both wild and cultivated. The principal architect and planner of the estate was Raymond Unwin, who was known to Barnett through his planning work at New Earswick and Letchworth Garden City, which was based on the principles evolved by Ebenezer Howard for the self-sufficient satellite town.

Unwin's primary concerns at Hampstead Garden Suburb were to avoid monotony and uniformity by rethinking street layout; to make use of the existing contours and natural features of the site; and to make the houses and groups of cottages varied but architecturally harmonious. The style of his houses is based on sixteenth- and seventeenth-century English vernacular architecture, but made highly individual and tailored to the anticipated occupants and to modern living (figs. 89–93). There is no doubt that Unwin succeeded in his aims. 'The Suburb', as it has become known to its residents, was – and remains – an internationally famous landmark in the development of the planned estate.

Unwin's innovative work at Letchworth and at Hampstead Garden Suburb formed a decisive step in the evolution of a new approach to town and country planning, which attempted to provide some control and conditions on the development of the suburbs. As stated earlier, there had been little professional supervision or control over the design and building of new developments before the Public Health Act of 1875. The by-

INFINITE VARIETY IN BRICK AND STUCCO

laws spawned by this Act concerning the layout, width and lines of new streets were strengthened and expanded by the Building Act of 1894, which contained restrictions on height, proximity to neighbours and internal planning. By the end of the nineteenth century the old by-laws introduced in the 1875 Act were no longer adequate; more-over, as Unwin noted, they had led to visual monotony and environmental sterility:

> ... much good work has been done. In the ample supply of pure water, in the drainage and removal of waste matter, in the paving, lighting and cleansing of streets ... probably our towns are as well served as those elsewhere. Moreover by means of our much abused by-laws the worst excesses of overcrowding have been restrained; a certain minimum standard of air, space, light and ventilation has been secured; while in the more modern parts of town a fairly high degree of san-itation, of immunity from fire, and general stability of construction have been maintained, the importance of which can hardly be exaggerated. We have laid a good foundation and have secured many of the necessary elements for a healthy condition of life; and yet the remarkable fact remains that there are growing up around our big towns vast districts, under these very by-laws, which, for dreariness and sheer ugliness it is difficult to match anywhere and, compared with which, many of the old unhealthy slums are, from the point of view of picturesqueness and beauty, infinitely more attractive.[16]

Gradually the movement for the extension of sanitary policy into town planning united the interests of public health and architecture. The result was the first legislation bearing the term 'town planning': the Housing, Town Planning etc Act of 1909. The Rt. Hon. John Burns MP, President of the Local Government Board, introduced the Bill with these words:

> The object of the Bill is to provide a domestic condition for the people in which their physical health, their morals, their character and their whole social condition can be improved by what we hope to secure in this Bill. The Bill aims in broad

93

Denman Drive South, Hampstead Garden Suburb

LONDON BOROUGH OF BARNET

Denman Drive South was laid out and developed in 1912 with houses designed by George Lister Sutcliffe. These gabled and rendered buildings are ornamented by red-brick, diamond-patterned quoins. The canted bay windows on the ground floor were either roofed with red tiles or flat-roofed, to soften the symmetry.

outline at, and hopes to secure, the home healthy, the house beautiful, the town

pleasant, the city dignified and the suburb salubrious.[17]

The Town Planning Act of 1909 was an extension of the existing legislation in order to respond to the rapid growth of suburbs. In London, over half a million acres of land had been converted from agricultural or rural use to housing, factories, industrial complexes and railways between 1892 and 1908, and the new Act aimed to raise standards of new building. But it did not deal with the problems of existing towns or badly built areas in large cities. Cumbersome procedures contained within the Act discouraged new building. As far as town planning was concerned, little real progress was made until the Town and Country Planning Act of 1932, but improvements in the design of housing were enshrined in the Housing and Town Planning Act of 1919, which implemented many of the recommendations made in the Tudor Walters Report of 1918 (although named after the MP who chaired the committee that produced it, this report was written largely by Raymond Unwin): to provide three-bedroom houses with baths and gardens for the working classes, at a density of not more than twelve houses to an acre. The Act of 1919 also recognized the principle of state subsidies and heralded an era of massive council estate building.

The spread of the suburbs of London throughout the nineteenth century, although appalling to William Morris watching it happen, represented, it might now be argued, the meeting of town and country that Morris envisaged in his Utopian novel *News From Nowhere*, with mutually beneficial effects on the inhabitants of both. It is clear that the developments of the period, the 'classic' suburbs, housed thousands of people, but how much do we value the results today? The historian of London Sir Walter Besant deplored the life of the suburb for being as 'dull as mankind ever tolerated'. Many critics, particularly J.M. Richards in *The Castles on the Ground*, have attempted to appreciate suburban style – the picturesqueness of the streets, the anarchic 'builder's vernacular' of the exteriors, the marrying of house and garden; other writers, such as Bill Bryson, continue to find them incomprehensible and unappealing.

Urban historians such as Professor H.J. Dyos, F.M.L. Thompson and D. Cannadine have come to the subject another way. By studying individual districts such as Camberwell or Bromley, they have dissected and analysed the process of building estates to illustrate the rationale behind seemingly anarchic and disparate areas. Such studies, argues Thompson, 'are a triumphant demonstration that the suburbs, far from being featureless wastelands, possess individuality of character in the distinctive layouts and buildings .... The process of creating suburbs was only translated into shapes on the ground through perfectly rational and orderly decisions by people.' He concludes: 'Suburbia represents what a great number of people wanted to live in: it is not necessary to admire it in order to wish to understand how it has happened.'[18]

Victorian and Edwardian suburbs remain a key physical part of the everyday experience of most Londoners. Only by getting to grips with the history of these suburbs can we appreciate what is special about them and then make sensible efforts to preserve it.

A close inspection of apparently uniform suburban architecture reveals the variety of decoration afforded by eclectic mixtures of historical styles and features. The decorative details – ridge tiles, polychromatic brickwork, iron cresting, Chinese fretwork, terracotta panels, stained or painted glass – often dismissed as merely pretentious, can be fun, intriguing and, at times, highly accomplished. Abundance was relished before tastes changed and stripped-down neo-Georgian or the clean lines of Modernism changed the face of the London suburb.

We must not only identify and appreciate these details, but we must also understand their place in the larger scheme of the suburb: the relationship of the individual house to the treatment of the terrace as a whole, the relationship of the terraces to the topography of the site, the planting of beech, cherry, chestnut and rowan in the streets, the contrast between the modest scale of the houses with the grandeur of the local civc buildings. When viewed from a descending aeroplane, the low-lying sprawl of red-brick houses and brown-tiled pitched roofs, laid out in straight lines, does indeed appear vast and intrusive on the green belt straining to keep the buildings in check. But equally striking is the amount of greenery within the built-up areas: tree-lined avenues, squares, parks, commons and grass-covered reservoirs, where Nature has been cherished amid man's civilizing infrastructure. This is, perhaps, the crowning achievement of the London suburbs: the attainment of a certain kind of rural environment, picturesque, clean and contained, on one's own scrubbed doorstep.

NOTES

1. John Ruskin, Letter 29, 'La Douce Amie', *Fors Clavigera* (Library Edition of the Works of John Ruskin, XXVII), London 1907, pp. 528–30.
2. William Morris, *The Earthly Paradise* [1868–70], London 1896: the opening of the 'Prologue: The Wanderers'.
3. H.G. Wells, *The New Machiavelli* [1911], London 1994, p. 30.
4. Ian Marshall and Ian Willox, *The Victorian House*, London 1986, p. 35.
5. For a full account of the ways in which speculative developments were organized and financed, see Stefan Muthesius, *The English Terraced House*, New Haven and London 1982, p. 28.
6. 'Works in the Suburbs of London', *The Building News*, 8 April 1859.
7. *The Builder*, 22 February 1862, p. 138.
8. John Summerson, 'The London Suburban Villa, 1850–1880', *Architectural Review*, CIV, 1948, pp. 63–72; reprinted in Summerson, *The Unromantic Castle and Other Essays*, London 1990.
9. F.M.L. Thompson (ed.), *The Rise of Suburbia*, Leicester 1982, p. 19.
10. *Ibid.*, p. 19.
11. Janet Roebuck, *Urban Development in 19th-Century London*, London 1979, esp. 'Lambeth, Battersea and Wandsworth, 1838–1888', pp. 128–29.
12. John Burnett, *A Social History of Housing, 1815–1985*, 2nd edn, London 1986, p. 200 (footnote).
13. Molly Hughes, *A London Family, 1870–1900*, Oxford 1981, p. 5.
14. Hermann Muthesius, *Das englische Haus*, Berlin 1904; trans. as *The English House*, Oxford 1979, pp. 146–48. Under the subheading 'The Small Suburban House', Muthesius sets out the 'pros and cons' of houses in the 'dreary English suburbs'. His views still influence the public perception of the suburbs.
15. Quoted in George Sims, *Living London*, III, London 1903, p. 314.
16. Raymond Unwin, *Town Planning in Practice: An Introduction to the Art of Designing Cities and Suburbs*, London 1909, pp. 3–4.
17. *Parliamentary Debates*, CLXXXVIII, col. 949, 12 May 1908.
18. F.M.L. Thompson, *op. cit.*, p. 23.

Chapter Three
Between the Wars: 1914–1940

ROGER BOWDLER

Gaily into Ruislip Gardens

Runs the red electric train,

With a thousand Ta's and Pardon's

Daintily alights Elaine;

Hurries down the concrete station

With a frown of concentration,

Out into the outskirt's edges

Where a few surviving hedges

Keep alive our lost Elysium – rural Middlesex again.

John Betjeman, 'Middlesex' (1954)

London and its outskirts became Greater London during the inter-war period. Great swathes of Middlesex were built over and large parts of Essex, Kent and Surrey disappeared beneath the expanding capital. This was the age of 'Stockbroker Tudor', arterial roads and new Underground stations; playing fields, metal-framed windows and aerodromes. Immortalized as 'Metroland' by Betjeman, London's inter-war suburbs form a huge yet coherent part of the city's housing stock and represent, for many, the epitome of the edge-of-town development. By the time of the outbreak of war in 1939 most of the area of Greater London as we know it today was built up.

During World War I central government, in the form of the Ministry of Munitions, had become involved in suburban building for the first time, providing housing for the influx of workers to the munitions and aeroplane factories that multiplied in south-east and north-west London (fig. 95). Continuing the impressive tradition of publicly funded housing established by the London County Council, developments such as Aeroville, built to house workers at the Grahame-White aircraft factory at Hendon, or Roe Green, built at Stag Lane in 1917–19, were designed by HM Office of Works, headed by Frank Baines. As rare examples of government-funded residential schemes, these estates form interesting and unusual episodes in the development of outer London.

The privations and sacrifices endured in World War I led to great things being anticipated on the cessation of hostilities. For the first time in its history, London had endured aerial bombardment. Thousands of its civilians had been engaged on war work while thousands more had enlisted in the armed forces. Tens of thousands never returned, and many who did were maimed and broken; some estates, such as the Douglas Haig Homes (fig. 96) in Morden, were specifically designed for these living casualties and included novel provision for their disabilities. Increased levels of state

94

The builders **by Harry Bush,** *ca.* **1933**

This watercolour, probably set near the artist's home in Merton Park (London Borough of Merton), shows the construction of a standard pair of semis. Behind are houses from an earlier period of suburban expansion.

95

Well Hall Road, Well Hall Estate, Eltham

LONDON BOROUGH OF GREENWICH

The LCC's tradition of public housing built in a vernacular style and set amid generous open spaces was followed by the Ministry of Works when it built this estate during World War I for munitions workers based at the Woolwich Arsenal. A tram connected the workers with their work place.

intervention during the War prompted the question of whether the state should not mobilize its considerable resources in meeting the challenges of peace, just as it had done to meet the threat of an armed aggressor. The state recognized the debt owed to the people for their sacrifice, and the suburbs were to be markedly affected by the intense, if short-lived, attempt to improve the domestic lot of London's working-class population, and create – in Lloyd George's ringing phrase – 'Homes fit for Heroes'[1] (fig. 97).

London between the wars was subject to dramatic expansion. The rate of growth had slowed down slightly from its peak in the late nineteenth century, but the sheer quantity of new arrivals was startling. It was calculated that in 1935 Greater London's population stood at some 8.5 million, and that the population had been growing by about three-quarters of a million people each year. In other words, the area within a 25-mile radius of the centre had been absorbing the equivalent of a large provincial city's whole population *each year*, and some 24,000 new families annually sought accommodation in the metropolis. About a fifth of the nation lived within an area constituting less than 0.8% of Britain's land area.[2] The growth of Greater London was also uneven. Between 1921 and 1937 the national population rose by 7.5%; during those years, the population of inner London (as represented by the LCC area) actually declined by almost half a million persons while the Greater London conurbation grew by a million and a quarter.[3]

These statistics vividly suggest the challenges facing the local authorities, many of them new and inexperienced, that had to cope with this influx of humanity. They also suggest the opportunities that existed for the builders, estate agents and building societies that sought to meet the demand for housing. Public and private sectors each strove

96

Douglas Haig Memorial Homes, Morden

LONDON BOROUGH OF MERTON

An estate of 'friendly' neo-Georgian houses, designed by Grey Wornum in 1929 to house disabled ex-servicemen of World War I. Field Marshal Haig's portrait appears in the terracotta roundel, a constant reminder of the Western Front.

to provide housing within – or within reach of – the capital. Initially, public bodies took the lead in providing housing, but from the mid-1920s onwards the commercial sector dominated the scene. Houses were cheaper and more plentiful by the mid-1930s than they had ever been before.

Improved housing for London's working classes was regarded as a high priority. It was an important means of reducing popular discontent, and of demonstrating the state's post-war commitment to public welfare. In 1919 the Housing or Addison Act was passed, which offered substantial government subsidies to local authorities for council house building. It laid down densities per acre and minimum room sizes, and made the provision of internal bathrooms mandatory. About 170,000 such houses were built across the country before the Act was superseded by the Chamberlain Act of 1923, which shifted subsidies away from the public sector and into the private. During this short period some 60% of all new houses in the London area were built by local authorities, a tenfold increase on the pre-1914 ratio.[4]

The Homes fit for Heroes movement was of great interest in terms of the effect that it had on the suburbs. The Addison Act encouraged the building of suburban housing, and thereby enshrined – for the first time in official housing policy – the desirability of the suburb, an important development in the evolution of the city. In the debates leading up

97

'Homes fit for Heroes': Sundew Avenue,
Wormholt Estate, Shepherd's Bush
LONDON BOROUGH OF HAMMERSMITH
AND FULHAM

*Part of the large estate planned immediately
after the end of World War I by Hammersmith
Borough Council. Such estates sought to rehouse town dwellers in well-designed and solidly
built houses set within spaciously laid-out
estates. The restrained, vernacular look of such
developments owed much to the LCC tradition.*

98

Aerial view of the Bellingham Estate

LONDON BOROUGH OF LEWISHAM

The formal planning of the Bellingham Estate, built by the LCC in 1921, is immediately apparent in this aerial view. The triangular site, wedged between two railway lines, was planned around a hexagonal green and flanked by two sports grounds. Almost 2700 houses were built here. Few other suburbs were to attain such geometrical neatness.

to the Act of 1919 the Conservative Member for Chelmsford, Ernest Pretyman, neatly summed up the appeal of this type of living. He was very content that

> houses shall be provided in semi-rural conditions with good garden plots and with good transport access to work in which the man is engaged, so that he can do his work in the factory while his family can live in fresh air and in a properly constructed house and where, when he gets home at night, he will find not only a healthy family, but healthy occupation outside where they can go and work together in the garden.

Fresh air, space, gardens, ease of communications: the age-old appeals of the London suburb remained as desirable as ever.

The London County Council was responsible for some of the largest housing estates in Europe. By purchasing land well beyond the capital's fringes (and on the less commercially attractive south and east edges), the LCC kept costs down but maintained their celebrated building standards. Houses could be laid out at a lower density than that demanded by inner-city estates, and thus the democratization of the garden suburb became possible (much the same thing was happening at Welwyn Garden City, founded in Hertfordshire in 1920). South of Lewisham are the Bellingham (fig. 98) and Downham Estates, commenced in 1921 and 1924; the latter, much the larger, was not completed until 1937. Between them they contained some 10,000 houses, enough to constitute a medium-sized town. Also commenced in 1921 was the largest council estate of all: the Becontree Estate (figs. 99–100) at Dagenham, which eventually housed some 120,000 people. Applicants for these new 'out-county' estates were vetted for suitability and obliged to demonstrate a record of regular rent payment before being allocated a place. The LCC Architect's Department was headed by G. Topham Forrest from 1919 to 1935. Its predominantly neo-Georgian work at its best possesses a dignity and wholesomeness

A prize-winning garden at no. 50 Kingsmill Road, Becontree Estate, in 1931

LONDON BOROUGH OF BARKING AND DAGENHAM

Householders personalized their homes on the sprawling and repetitive Becontree Estate by putting their horticultural prowess to work: gardens were one of the few areas for expression within a municipal estate.

that remains unsurpassed in Europe. The charge of monotony, however, is a difficult one to shake off: the sheer scale of the Becontree or Downham Estate is daunting, and economies of scale, together with the desire for a rationalized equality, conspire to produce a slightly impersonal settlement.

The War had revealed what poor physical shape much of the young male working-class population was in. Health considerations loomed large in inter-war attitudes to town planning and encouraged the creation of generously laid-out developments with adequate amenity grounds. Critics were to attack the suburb's tendency to spread: 'sprawl' became one of the most frequently voiced and pejorative objections against inter-war building on the edge of the capital. Deplorable though the loss of countryside was, between the wars London's population was still growing at a dramatic rate, and this growth required more land than ever before. The countryside at the fringes of London was largely sacrificed in the interests of a healthier populace.

The issue of space raises the question of transport. Commuting had long been a crucial determinant of London's growth, and this was never more true than in the inter-war period. How far could the Londoner be expected to travel to work? How much should the daily journey cost? And how long would it take? Electric trains and motor vehicles arrived in London to supplement the steam trains, trams, horses and feet that had carried the Georgian, Victorian and Edwardian Londoner to and fro. The extension of the London Underground to the outer suburbs during the 1920s and 1930s was one of the most important developments in the capital's growth (fig. 101). In 1920 the Central Line was extended westwards from Shepherd's Bush

100

Wood Lane, Becontree Estate, in 1927

LONDON BOROUGH OF BARKING AND DAGENHAM

The LCC's largest housing estate was begun in 1921 and was to consist of no fewer than 26,000 dwellings. This row of restrained brick houses set the pattern for thousands of others across the country. The houses are already occupied but the road has yet to be made. The row of mature trees is all that remains of this formerly rural part of Essex.

to Ealing Broadway; in the later 1930s it pushed eastwards into southern Essex, and in a north-westerly direction to Ruislip. The Northern Line was eventually to link north and south London with the 17-mile tunnel that connected East Finchley with Morden (the longest continuous tunnel in the world at the time of its construction). The Edgware branch (fig. 102) worked its way to the northern fringe of Middlesex, reaching its destination in 1924, and the High Barnet branch was built between 1935 and 1940.

In many ways the Piccadilly Line is the quintessential inter-war Underground branch. Originally serving stations between Finsbury Park and Hammersmith, it was extended westwards to Uxbridge and eastwards to Cockfosters in the early 1930s. What distinguished the Piccadilly Line from the others was the quality of its stations. Never before had the modern preoccupation with speed found so happy an architectural expression as in Charles Holden's station buildings. Their bold geometry, sleek interiors (dramatically lit by night) and unabashed modernity embodied the swiftness and efficiency of Greater London's expanded transport network. South and north-east London, then as now, were under-served by the Underground but some solace was to be found in the modernization and expansion of the surface railways: the Southern Railway in particular was extremely active in creating a system that served Kent, Surrey and beyond, and kept the Underground out of its domain. The LCC tram network continued to offer the cheapest rides in London, and a growing network of bus routes connected suburbs with each other (across the routes leading into the centre) as well as with the principal shopping centres. By the mid-1930s two and a half million people were travelling every day within Greater London, and an astonishing quarter of a million people were

101

Why not live at Sudbury Hill?: London Transport poster of 1930 by Christine Jackson

As the poster makes clear, the great advantage of the modern suburb was that it made it possible for the city worker to live in spacious, leafy surroundings. This drawing shows what the suburban dream was all about.

102

Hendon Central Station, Hendon Way

LONDON BOROUGH OF BARNET

The station was designed by S.A. Heap and opened in 1923 as part of the Northern Line extension. It was soon surrounded by an elegant shopping parade: such complexes became the nuclei of London's swelling outer suburbs.

103

Hoover Factory, Western Avenue, Perivale
LONDON BOROUGH OF EALING
*Inter-war factories got no jazzier than this.
Designed by Wallis, Gilbert and Partners in
1931 for the American vacuum-cleaner giant,
this is the best example of the flamboyant,
attention-grabbing commercial premises that
sprung up alongside London's arterial roads. The
concrete frame was enriched with red and blue
glazed tiles, set against green and gilt windows:
even at speed, the factory is unmissable.*

employed in the transport sector.[5] In 1933 the LCC tramways, the Underground lines and the London General Omnibus Company united to form the London Passenger Transport Board: it was a measure of the scale of the challenge facing London's transport chiefs that this amalgamation was agreed to. The London worker might have had further than ever to travel, but he or she could take comfort in possessing a transport network unrivalled elsewhere. Should the network ever run into problems, solace could always be sought between the covers of a paperback or library book: higher literacy rates than ever, combined with more comfortable methods of transport, made the reality of the journey to and from the suburbs more and more bearable, especially if the traveller could afford to delay the journey until after the crowded workmen's trains had departed.

The inter-war period also saw the development of today's road network. The historic arteries into the capital continued to be the principal bearers of traffic, but as road traffic (both private and commercial) increased, so too did the need for widened and scientifically designed roads. The 1920s saw the emergence of the modern system of numbering roads: thus the Dover Road became the A2, and Watling Street – or the Edgware Road as it is known in London – became the A5. Something of the romance of the road may have been lost, but the new numbers were a powerful symbol of the modernization and improvement of the capital's roads. Major new routes were built. Best known are Western Avenue and the Great West Road, which ran westwards over Middlesex's still-virgin acres. The memorably jazzy factories (fig. 103) that lined these routes exploited the superb transport amenities enjoyed by London's outer northern and western fringes.

104

The North Circular Road under construction at Stonebridge Park, August 1931

LONDON BOROUGH OF BRENT

The construction of this arterial ring road cut devastating swathes through the leafy fields of Middlesex. Here, hedges are already grubbed up and trees felled in preparation for the earth-moving and foundation-laying works.

105

The North Circular Road near Willesden, June 1934

LONDON BOROUGH OF BRENT

The completed dual carriageway, refreshingly free of traffic, was soon lined with factories and houses eager to exploit the road's convenience. Only in the 1950s was increasingly heavy traffic to spoil the dream of speed and convenience.

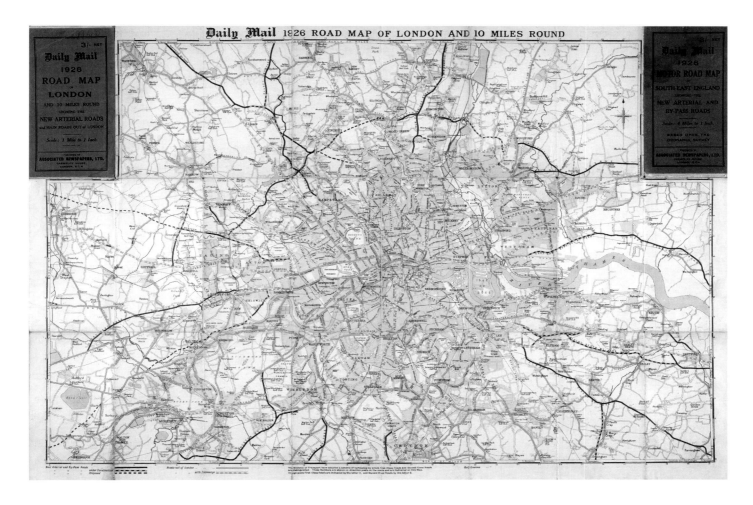

The Watford Bypass (now the Hendon and Watford Way) and the New Cambridge Road (now better known as the southern stretches of the A10) were similarly laid out in the early 1920s, at which time, too, the North Circular Road was commenced (figs. 104–05). New arterial roads pumped traffic in and out of the nation's political, commercial and cultural heart. The Londoner of today can only dream of a lost golden age when motor traffic was relatively slight and swift (fig. 106).

The improvements in public and road transport made Greater London possible. Development overwhelmed the countryside and banished rural industries beyond the fringes of the capital. Middlesex had once been given over to market gardening: in 1885 over one-seventh of the country's entire garden produce came from the county, a remarkable proportion for such a small area. Between 1870 and 1930 the acreage of Middlesex land under grass fell by half, and the number of cattle fell by three-quarters. Farming was thus being displaced as an economic activity in the heart of the Thames Basin.[6] Acre upon acre of depressed agricultural land, previously too distant from the heart of the capital to be viable for development, was brought into London's web by the improved routes. Middlesex had long lost its woodland: according to a Forestry Commission Census of 1924, a mere 0.9% of the county was under woodland, and only

106

Daily Mail 1926 road map of London and 10 miles round

The emerging network of arterial roads is clearly shown on this road map, intended for the private motorist. The planning for these new roads was carried out just after World War I. Like the extensions to the London Underground network, these roads greatly encouraged development in London's outer suburbs.

the Orkney Islands had fewer trees. Such villages as Hornchurch, Ruislip and Morden were still detached communities in 1918. Great swathes of Middlesex, stretching from Hounslow out to Ickenham and up to Edgware awaited the arrival of the developer. By the time gas masks had been issued and war had once again been declared on Germany, these swathes would be covered in hundreds of thousands of new houses. More people than ever before would think of themselves as living in the capital, and the commuter challenged the Cockney for the title of the Typical Londoner.

The suburb tries to strike a balance between work and recuperation, proximity and retreat, town and countryside. J.B. Priestley, in the introduction to *The Beauty of Britain* (1935), wrote that there was 'a great deal to be said' for the suburb: 'nearly all Englishmen are at heart country gentlemen. The suburban villa enables the salesman or the clerk, out of hours, to be almost a country gentleman', even if these very suburbs did bite great chunks out of the countryside 'in the greediest fashion'. Modern eyes perhaps tend to draw too sharp a distinction between the country and the town. We see them as opposites, and tend to find the parts that blur this distinction muddling, neither one thing nor the other. The champion of the suburb takes just the opposite view. London was an undeniably crowded, dirty, busy and, in many parts, elderly city by 1914. Old buildings did not invariably possess the cachet that they now enjoy. George Orwell's novel *Keep the Aspidistra Flying* (1936) depicted an inner city that was run-down and grimy. The suburbs, on the other hand, were fresh. Houses and whole streets were new; the human density was much reduced and clean air, trees and sheer room to breathe were to be had in abundance. This combination of the country's appeal with the town's amenities had long constituted a sizeable part of the charm of the suburb.

How did the inter-war suburb preserve any sense of this rural appeal? True countryside was ever further away from London, and it became necessary to travel as far afield as Harefield, Epping Forest or Kenley Common to find it; at least the highly developed transport infrastructure was able to carry the Londoner outwards to these recreational purlieus. Pockets of former agricultural land continued to be purchased by local authorities to become public parks, such as the Clitterhouse Recreation Ground in Cricklewood, or the Lordship Lane Recreation Ground in Tottenham, preserved reminders of Middlesex's disappearing rural past. The latter was of exceptional interest. Opened in 1932, the Lordship Recreation Ground stood on former farming land and was laid out by the borough engineer. A paddle-boat pond, tennis courts and a bandstand were added as civic amenities and constructed using direct labour as a way of alleviating local unemployment. In 1938 the recreation ground acquired rather a special addition.[7] The Lordship Lane Model Traffic Area was laid out like a small road system, in which children on bicycles or in toy cars – available for hire by the quarter-hour – could familiarize themselves with road conditions. It sported roads, traffic lights and signs, and crossings with reduced versions of the new 'Belisha beacons'. Even a miniature telephone kiosk was installed so that, in the event of a miniature accident, juvenile passers-by could acquire the habit of informing the police. This remarkable scheme, which sought to prepare the youngest occupants of the suburbs for the dangers of the fast and busy world that was developing around them, was opened by the Minister of Transport, E.L. Burgin.

The more sensitively laid-out developments retained mature trees, and the historic cores of such villages as Carshalton, Ickenham and Finchley retained their distinct and venerable identities. Other ancient parishes, such as Edgware, were all but swamped by the new housing that came in the wake of the Edgware branch of the Northern Line. Medieval church towers and well-wooded parochial graveyards, village greens, Jacobean manor houses and Georgian pubs formed islands amid the tide of suburban development. Since they tended to occupy the highest ground, especially along the ridges of north-west London, these historic villages continue to dominate the geographical as well as historical topography of Middlesex. Their picturesque appeal was heightened by the quantity of modern development that lapped around their edges. Local authorities purchased numerous historic houses with their grounds to form pockets of green space, each with a historic core that offered a new amenity to the rising populations of the outer boroughs: thus Bexley Urban District Council acquired Danson Park in 1924 as 'a magnificent defence against the remorseless advance of the brick and mortar brigades from London' and opened a teashop inside. Middlesex County Council purchased Chiswick House in 1928, and Eastbury Manor House was taken on by the National Trust in conjunction with Barking District Council in 1936; nearby Valence House survived in the midst of the vast Becontree Estate. Many large houses around London were regarded as outmoded piles that would never find buyers; nonetheless, the land attached to them would readily attract developers eager to build on these estates. It is greatly to the credit of the many local authorities that these historic enclaves were purchased with public monies and preserved for the recreational enjoyment of inter-war and subsequent generations.[8]

London's outward growth at times seemed to have no limits, prompting the desire to preserve countryside within reach of London as an amenity for the capital. Tudor and Stuart proclamations against building 'in the skirtes' of the city had proved ineffectual in limiting growth: inter-war governmental and municipal decrees were to be more successful. In 1927 the Greater London Regional Planning Committee was established. One of the questions it was asked to consider was whether London should 'be provided with something which might be called an agricultural belt, as has often been suggested, so that it would form a dividing line between Greater London as it is and the satellites or fresh developments that might take place at a greater distance'. Advising the committee was no less an authority on the planning of cities than Raymond Unwin, who stressed that recreational rather than agricultural ground was of the greatest use to London. Herbert Morrison was instrumental in advancing an LCC scheme in 1935 that sought to 'establish a green belt or girdle of open space lands, not necessarily continuous, but as readily accessible from the completely urbanized area of London as possible'. In 1938 the Green Belt (London and Home Counties) Act was passed (fig. 107), which began to

The *Green Belt Exhibition*, April 1939

The LCC held an exhibition at Charing Cross Station devoted to their efforts at safeguarding the capital's outlying natural assets, such as Burnham Beeches and Nonsuch Park. The exhibition (including this montage panel) was prepared by students at the LCC's art schools. Not until 1962 was the Green Belt finally firmly tightened.

grant protection for London's rural perimeter, protection that was only finally secured with the Act of 1959.[9]

Another reminder of earlier times was to be found in the architectural style of many suburban houses. The majority of houses continued to be built in the Thames Valley's native materials of brick and tile, with many continuing the late Victorian predilection for half-timbering. Nowhere did this desire to perpetuate the local vernacular style manifest itself more clearly than in the peculiar structures designed by the Belfast-born architect Ernest George Trobridge (1884–1942) and built in the expanding hamlet of Kingsbury, north-east of Wembley. Trobridge's patent system of building wooden houses made a remarkably successful debut at the 1920 Daily Mail Ideal Home Exhibition (itself a reflection of the new mass demand for private houses). It used unseasoned elm – then, unlike today, plentiful – to produce 'rural cottages in which ancient construction is modified to meet modern needs'.[10] Trobridge designed a

sequence of exceptional suburban houses that formed the *ne plus ultra* of suburban rustic escapism.

Tile-hung gables, pebble-dashed or nogged brick panels, leaded windows and pronounced chimney-stacks were all deployed on new dwellings to create a sense of continuity and tradition, factors so vital for the idea of the home. Osbert Lancaster's sharply observed survey of architecture, *Pillar to Post* (1938), gave us the expression 'Stockbroker Tudor' (fig. 108). Bogus antiquity ('from the depths of some old iron-bound chest were audible the dulcet tones of Mr Bing Crosby or the old-world strains of Mr Duke Ellington') was sniggered at since it represented an utter rejection of material progress. The idiom worked its way down the range of house types so that ordinary speculative housing, too, could sport reminders of the mythical cottage of England's illustrious past: 'the passer-by is a little unnerved at being suddenly confronted with a hundred and fifty accurate reproductions of Anne Hathaway's cottage, each complete with central heating and garage'.[11] These houses were not accurate reproductions at all, of course, but simply combined modern house-building methods with the odd echo of a

108

'Stockbroker Tudor', from *Pillar to Post* (1938) by Osbert Lancaster

Lancaster's celebrated lampoon of the bourgeois suburb. The thatched garage encapsulates the age's attempt to have the best of both worlds: telephone pylons, aeroplanes and cars sit uncomfortably alongside an 'olde worlde' seat.

109

Hanger Hill Garden Estate, North Ealing

LONDON BOROUGH OF EALING

The Hanger Hill Garden Estate was developed by a private company between 1928 and 1936. Rigorous covenants (and conservation area designation) have ensured that this fine enclave of half-timbering has remained in pristine condition.

110

Kerry House, Kerry Avenue, Stanmore

LONDON BOROUGH OF HARROW

A bold example of the transitional sort of suburban house: the brick, the hipped and tiled roof with dormers and the symmetrical design are all traditional but the curved metal windows and angular profile show a more modern influence at work. This house was built in 1937; its architect is unknown.

distant vernacular past (figs. 109–11). Contemporary domestic architecture in Hitler's Germany took this return to a pre-industrial age far more seriously. There, National Socialist ideology placed great stress on 'Blood and Soil', on the mystical link that connected the German with his homeland. He needed to be housed in buildings that drew on tradition and that used local materials: thus half-timbering was a popular and officially encouraged architectural style there also. There is the world of differences between the Tudorbethan semi in 'Metroland' and the Teutonic idyll of the Nazi state. Yet there is something in common, too. In an age of economic uncertainty and enormous cultural change, security and comfort may be sought through a return to the perceived values of ages past. Greater London was being utterly transformed: the countryside was disappearing, new roads and rail links were speeding up the pace of life and the commercialization of modern urban life had arrived for good. Small wonder that house-buyers were attracted to a reassuring and secure sort of residential architecture. The intelligentsia

A suburban sitting room, Harrow, 1930s

LONDON BOROUGH OF HARROW

Not everything in 'Metroland' was jazzy: here, exposed timbers, a brick fireplace with niches and solid wooden furniture created a cosy haven, in which tradition kept the modern world at bay.

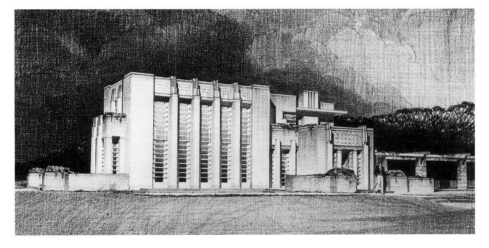

112

The White House, Hyver Hill
by D.E. Harrington, 1935

LONDON BOROUGH OF BARNET

An exceptional edge-of-town house, drawing heavily on Frank Lloyd Wright, designed for a cameraman who had worked in Hollywood. Few edge-of-town houses approached this in terms of avant-garde individuality.

might denounce 'the false art and pretentious vulgarity of the Tudor fake' and champion the 'potentially beautiful' properties of functional materials such as steel and concrete (fig. 112),[12] but these charges failed to deter the house-buyer from pursuing his homely ideal.

There were more house-buyers during this period than ever before. Building societies flourished as more and more professional and clerical workers abandoned the rented sector. J.M. Richards thought that the suburban dweller's 'first instinct' was 'his craving for economic security' and deplored 'the success of the Building Societies in persuading the suburban dweller how desirable it is for him to own his own home ...

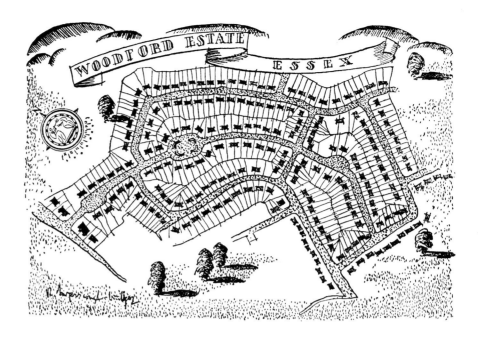

113

Layout of the Woodford Estate

LONDON BOROUGH OF REDBRIDGE

A stylish plan by R. Myerscough-Walker of one of the many estates built by Laing's in outer London between the wars: this estate stands on hilly ground just south of Woodford Green, centred around Forest Approach. The winding street pattern and variety of open spaces prevented monotony creeping in to a large development of near-identical brick semis. (From Ernest Betham (ed.), House Building, 1934–1936, *London ca. 1936)*

which can have no result but to bind the owner more firmly to the economic machine of which he is the victim rather than the operator'.[13] Others thought otherwise, and invested in bricks and mortar. Thousands of houses were available for between £400 and £1000, and developers were often prepared to offer mortgages at seductive rates.

Architects of the inter-war years grew very concerned at their dwindling involvement in the residential sector, since builders and developers seemed increasingly to be able to do without them. Developers were accused of 'jerry-building' and of erecting vulgar houses, while builders accused architects of being irrelevant to the modern building process and costly besides.[14] The great house-building firms such as John Laing's of Mill Hill, T.F. Nash, Harry Neal's of Northwood and Richard Costain's constructed some bespoke one-off developments, but most of their output was formulaic and, in bulk, repetitive. Estate layout was therefore of great importance: monotony could be averted through winding roads, planting and open spaces, the grouping of houses, variation of house types, materials and style (fig. 113).

The architect Gordon Allen, author of *The Smaller House of Today* (1926), advised builders on purchasers' taste in house styles: 'What the average purchaser wants as regards the elevations of his house', wrote Allen in 1934, 'is a question of psychology rather than of art. He is probably uncertain, although much influenced by a pleasing exterior. His judgment has been affected by being told that the fussy villa is evidence of bad taste, and also by his experience that houses spattered with 'features' are restless in appearance and expensive in upkeep ... he desires his home to look different from his neighbour's, and, above all, unlike the municipal house, owing to his sense of social dignity' (fig. 114).[15] This sense of pride in the ownership of a new house (for many fami-

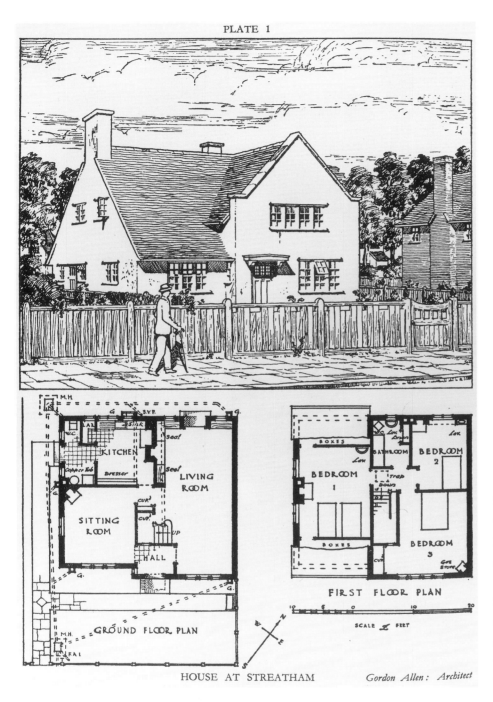

PLATE 1

SITTING ROOM

KITCHEN

LIVING ROOM

HALL

GROUND FLOOR PLAN

BEDROOM 1

BATHROOM

BEDROOM 2

BEDROOM 3

BOXES

FIRST FLOOR PLAN

SCALE OF FEET

HOUSE AT STREATHAM   *Gordon Allen : Architect*

114

**House at Streatham designed by
Gordon Allen**

LONDON BOROUGH OF LAMBETH

An illustration from Ernest Betham (ed.), House
Building, 1934–1936, *London ca. 1936, showing
the layout of a smart suburban house, still very
much in the Arts and Crafts tradition. Allen was
a specialist in such work, and was the author of
the influential book* The Smaller House of
Today *(1926).*

lies, for the first time ever) permeated the suburb and contributes significantly to our perception of the inter-war period as a time of contented domesticity. As J.M. Richards wryly observed, 'Ewbank'd inside and Atco'd out, the English suburban residence and the garden which is an integral part of it stand trim and lovingly cared for in the mild sunshine … it is each individual Englishman's idea of his home, except for the cosmopolitan rich, a minority of freaks and intellectuals and the very poor'.[16]

115

Vernon Court, Hendon Way, Cricklewood

LONDON BOROUGH OF BARNET

A late appearance of half-timbering distinguishes this apartment block built around 1930 on an extension of the Finchley Road. Amy Johnson, the celebrated aviator, lived here, as it was handy for Hendon Aerodrome.

The semi dominates our perception of the inter-war suburb, but another sort of dwelling was also increasing in popularity at this time. This was the apartment block, generally located on one of the arterial roads leading out of town. The inter-war period saw the emergence of a new housing market: busy professionals, generally young and affluent, who, instead of a family home, sought a *pied à terre* with easy access to the city centre. Amy Johnson, the celebrated aviator, lived in a neo-Tudor block (fig. 115) on the Finchley Road, handy for town yet handier still for Hendon Aerodrome. Frederick Gibberd's Pullman Court on Streatham Hill was an early instance of inner suburban development: a self-consciously modernist group of airy slabs, close to the road to Brighton and the south coast, and efficiently planned inside. Such schemes often swept aside earlier suburban villas set in extensive grounds, which offered tempting prospects for the developer. Such new blocks generally contained serviced apartments, which commanded reasonably high rents. Nevilles Court (fig. 116), Dollis Hill Lane, built in

1935, contained flats that were initially let for £120 a year: less than a decade renting there would buy one a house in Wembley outright. Such blocks were prestigious affairs, aimed at the aspirant and discerning, and were designed in an accordingly up-to-date idiom: the Modern Movement's messages of dynamic efficiency and gleaming brightness were perfect for such a market (fig. 117). The other principal form of inner suburban development in this period was the council estate: slum clearance programmes required the rehousing of tens of thousands, and huge estates such as the LCC's White City Estate, or the Guinness Trust's Stamford Hill Estate, arose in the 1930s. These, in contrast to the private apartment blocks, were almost invariably designed in a heavy neo-Georgian style and built in dark brick. Thus were the inner edges and not just the outer reaches of the capital affected by inter-war growth.

The London suburb was served by a diverse range of amenities. As they grew, the outer boroughs erected imposing town halls to reflect their new status: Wembley Town

116

Nevilles Court, Dollis Hill Lane,

under construction, 1935

LONDON BOROUGH OF BRENT

One of the wave of apartment blocks that was built around London's inner ring of suburbs, containing serviced flats for middle-class occupants. Blocks such as this were conveniently sited close to major roads and combined stylish modernity with efficiently planned flats.

117

Highpoint 1, North Hill, Highgate

LONDON BOROUGH OF HARINGEY

Lubetkin and Tecton's radical block of flats was completed in 1935. Inspired by Le Corbusier's vision for a new way of living, it was intended as a prototype for modern urban buildings: cutting down on suburban sprawl by concentrating dwellings vertically. The flats enjoy commanding views and are light and airy: these had long been vital factors in explaining the allure of the suburb.

118

New Malden Branch Library

ROYAL BOROUGH OF KINGSTON UPON
THAMES

*One of the finest of the numerous branch
libraries that were built in London's outer
suburbs between the wars: local authorities
were anxious to provide their rate-payers with
these oases of learning. This particular building,
by the Borough Engineer, A.R. Goldthorp, with
F.C. Otton as principal architectural assistant,
was opened in 1941 and has unusual carved
reliefs of the arts and sciences on its wedge-
shaped exterior.*

Hall (Clifford Strange, 1935–40) is among the finest, while Walthamstow Town Hall (P.D. Hepworth, 1937–42) is unsurpassed in monumentality. Robert Atkinson's Wallington Town Hall (1935) exemplifies the elegance that municipal architecture could attain. Public libraries such as those at Coulsdon (Gold and Aldridge, 1936) or New Malden (A.R. Goldthorp, the Borough Engineer, 1941; fig. 118) added valuable amenities while the ever-swelling population was served by an impressive programme of school building; Middlesex County Council in particular erected a number of Dutch-influenced brick schools, such as Greenford School (1937). London's defences, too, were substantially added to between the wars. Fear of aerial attack (and vast, sprawling London presented an irresistible target) led to a ring of First World War airfields on the outskirts of London being developed into important aerodromes. The names of Biggin Hill, Kenley, Hornchurch and Northolt were to become renowned during the summer of 1940. Never before had London's suburbs participated directly in events of such international moment as they did during the Battle of Britain.

National and local government-sponsored projects such as aerodromes, libraries, town halls, schools, parks and bypasses added significantly to the interest of London's suburbs. The exclusively residential character of the suburbs was further qualified by the continued building of churches. Two of the most remarkable churches to arrive in outer London between the wars were not even new buildings. One was nothing less than one of Wren's City churches, All Hallows, Lombard Street, which was demolished in 1938 and rebuilt on the arterial route to Twickenham. The other, St Andrew's, Wells Street, was an important Gothic Revival church of the mid-1840s by Daukes and Hamilton that was transplanted stone by stone to Kingsbury in 1933–34. Inner London's population had migrated outwards; now even its churches were following.

More worldly services were provided by the commercial sector. Many of the finest inter-war cinemas were built outside the Central London area. The Granada at Tooting, of 1931, with its fantastical Gothic interior by Theodore Komisarjevsky, provided a dream-house for this late Victorian dormitory suburb. Parades of shops sprang up along the arterial routes and at crossroads, picking up passing trade and forming new meeting-places for suburban residents: Clarence Court at Mill Hill on the Barnet Bypass, with its characteristic blue and green glazed roof-tiles and vaguely Georgian ornament, stands for dozens of similar developments. Exotic new pubs known as 'road houses' (fig. 119) sprang up on these same routes to service the growing numbers of motorists: like cinemas, they were often built in the picturesque styles of Tudor, Queen Anne or even Spanish Hacienda, and introduced further elements of fantasy into the outskirts of London. New suburbs could become alienating, unfriendly places, particularly for those left at home during the day, and amenities such as these helped to stave off loneliness.

Combinations of planning provision and accident, of local authority direction and entrepreneurial freedom, shaped the inter-war suburb. Aldous Huxley's *Brave New World* (1932) depicted a London of the future, a vast conurbation of rational planning, zoning, categorizing and control, as a means of satirizing totalitarianism:

Lenina looked down through the window in the floor between her feet. They were flying over the six kilometre zone of park-land that separated Central London from its first ring of satellite suburbs. The green was maggoty with fore-shortened life. Forests of Centrifugal Bumble-puppy towers gleamed between the trees. Near Shepherd's Bush two thousand Beta-Minus mixed doubles were playing Riemann-surface tennis. A double row of Escalator Fives Courts lined the main road from Notting-Hill to Willesden. In the Ealing stadium a Delta gymnastic display and community sing was in progress.[17]

In fact, Greater London withstood the enormous challenges of economic upheaval, technological change and huge population growth without over-rigorous control and direction from on high. Generally, the inter-war suburbs of the capital assumed their character through commercial development and amenities, leavened with a smaller yet crucial input of municipal building and supervision.

More subtle and affectionate than Huxley's, the satire of John Betjeman has captured the true flavour of the suburbs. Greater London of the inter-war period will forever be 'Metroland': that romantic fusion of vanishing countryside, domestic bliss, jazz-age entertainment, respectability and mortgages, where (thanks to an enlarged and efficient transport network) the Londoner no longer had to choose between Town and Country: in the suburb he could have both.

119

The Myllett Arms, Western Avenue, Perivale

LONDON BOROUGH OF EALING

One of the imposing 'road houses' built along London's arterial roads, which sought to entice the passing motorist in for refreshment. This pub (now cruelly disfigured by garish modern additions) was designed by E.P. Monson in 1935. The pub's name (elegantly depicted on this fine carved pub sign, sadly lost) comes from a local man, Henry Myllet (died 1500), whose brass is in the tiny church of Perivale near by.

NOTES
1. Mark Swenarton's book of this title (London 1981) remains the standard work on the subject.
2. E.C. Willatts, *The Land of Britain, Part 9: Middlesex and the London Region*, London 1937, p. 164.
3. H.W. Richardson and D.H. Aldcroft, *Building in the British Economy between the Wars*, London 1968, p. 302.
4. Alan A. Jackson, *Semi-Detached London*, 2nd edn, London 1991, p. 58. This is the essential introduction to the twentieth-century London suburb.
5. Willatts, *op. cit.*, p. 166.
6. Willatts, *op. cit.*, pp. 157–59.
7. Ruth Guilding, 'The Lordship Lane Model Traffic Area', *The London Gardener*, 2, 1997, pp. 18–22.
8. See Peter Mandler, *The Fall and Rise of the Stately Home*, London 1997, ch. 6.
9. See the Ministry of Housing and Local Government booklet *The Green Belts*, London 1962.
10. G.P. Smith, *Ernest George Trobridge*, Oxford 1982, offers an absorbing introduction to this architect's peculiar work.
11. Osbert Lancaster, *Pillar to Post*, London (John Murray) 1938, p. 62.
12. Sir Leslie Scott, 'Preservation of the Countryside', in *House Building, 1934–1936*, ed. Ernest Betham, London (National Federation of Building Trades Employers) *ca.* 1936, pp. 36–37. Scott was the legal adviser to the Campaign for the Preservation of Rural England.
13. J.M. Richards, *The Castles on the Ground: The Anatomy of Suburbia*, London 1946, p. 35.
14. Stanley C. Ramsey, 'Architectural Co-operation with Builders', in Betham (ed.), *op. cit.*, p. 113.
15. 'Building to Sell', in Betham (ed.), *op. cit.*, p. 149.
16. Richards, *op. cit.*, pp. 13–15.
17. Aldous Huxley, *Brave New World*, London 1932, pp. 72–73.

Chapter Four
The Road to Subtopia:
1940 to the present

ELAIN HARWOOD

We must articulate the wants, the frustrations of the individual by means of an architecture that has in it the needs of a different kind of city .... Our cities have slumped senseless and we have been irresponsible enough to let their sludge spread over the surrounding countryside.

Alison and Peter Smithson, 'Urban Reidentification' (1952–53)[1]

The continual outward expansion of London, hitherto unchallenged, was halted in 1939. This was the year in which the population of Greater London is estimated to have reached 8,615,050. Yet employment in central London peaked only in 1962, evidence of the growing significance of the long-distance commuter in the post-war years. The story of the suburb after 1945 is one not only of the expanded Greater London as defined from 1965 but also of the whole south-eastern region. Two factors in this are significant. One is the introduction of firm controls over London's growth. The other is the importance in the years 1945–79 of the local authorities as the chief housing supplier throughout most of the South East.

The War left London woefully short of accommodation. In 1951 the London County Council estimated that there were 250,000 families on the waiting-list in need of new homes. It hoped to provide these homes in five years, but recognized that its slum clearance policy and a rising population meant that more housing would continue to be required.

The Planning of Greater London

World War II had a profound impact on all aspects of domestic life. Under the Emergency Powers (Defence) Act instituted in May 1940 the economy of wartime Britain was subjected to a greater degree of state supervision than even Nazi Germany. By the end of 1941 Britain's was a command economy, with nationalization of munitions industries, a directed labour force and committee controls over agriculture and transport. In the midst of war, a community beset by privations looked not only for victory but also for a greater social justice as its reward. It expected a government that had been able to organize so effectively in wartime similarly to direct a peacetime economy to provide housing and community facilities. Planning was to have an important role in this 'people's peace'. The key document was *The County of London Plan*, commissioned in 1941 from J.H. Forshaw, the LCC's Chief Architect, and Patrick Abercrombie, Professor of Town Planning at University College London.[2] The following year its ideas were devel-

120

Parkleys Estate, Ham Common, Ham
LONDON BOROUGH OF RICHMOND
UPON THAMES
Designed by Eric Lyons for Span Developments Ltd and built in 1954–56, this was the first Span scheme, a series of two-storey ranges of flats set in courtyards, with some four-storey blocks to give interest. The site was a former nursery, the stock of which formed the basis for the lavish landscaping with which Lyons enveloped his simple blocks.

121

Haverhill, Suffolk

Originally a town with about 4000 inhabitants, it was developed by the LCC from 1955 into a town of about 33,000 people. The Clements Estate (1962–68), shown here, was characterized by the complete segregation of pedestrians and traffic.

oped in Abercrombie's *Greater London Plan*, the culmination of early twentieth-century thinking on the structure of London and the surrounding area.[3]

Some attempt had already been made to control the growth of London. As early as 1890 Lord Meath, first Chairman of the LCC's Parks and Open Spaces Committee, had proposed a series of open spaces linked by 'sylvan avenues'.[4] Similar ideas followed, combining Parisian ideas of a *périphérique* or ring road, Ebenezer Howard's desire to preserve agricultural land, and a concern for the health of Londoners by offering land for sports and walks within reasonable access of the centre by public transport. In 1927 a Regional Planning Committee was constituted, with Raymond Unwin as its technical adviser, who conceived a 'green girdle' surrounded by satellite towns. Delayed by the 'national financial condition', it was only in 1935 that the LCC voted £2 million towards the purchase of land identified as places of beauty or recreation within easy reach by public transport. By 1944 some forty square miles had been acquired, most of it north of the Thames but including areas of the North Downs, and Nonsuch Park in Surrey.[5]

Abercrombie's *Greater London Plan* distilled these ideas into a 'green zone', in which agricultural and recreational land would be protected and existing settlements checked. Within the zone there would be a 'suburban' ring to complement the urban rings Abercrombie had established in the earlier *County of London Plan*. This area, corresponding to the outer London boroughs, was to be developed to accommodate an average of 50 persons per acre (p.p.a.) while protecting areas within it where open countryside survived, particularly in Totteridge and Mill Hill. The leafier parts of inner London were to be developed for up to 70 p.p.a., with zones of 136 p.p.a. and 200 p.p.a. in the centre.

Fundamental to Abercrombie's plans was the displacement of some one million people beyond the green belt into New Towns (fig. 121). This figure was reduced to 311,000 in the *Administrative County of London Development Plan* of 1951, as many people had already left the LCC area of their own accord.[6] London's willingness to lose a large proportion of its population was in stark contrast to that of every other British city, where a large population was considered the basis of its power. It has been interpreted as a long-term move to secure the creation of an authority for Greater London, but as strong was the belief that too large and dense a city was inherently insanitary, both physically and morally. The garden suburb ideal had already been a key philosophy behind the LCC cottage estates and was a motivation for the wartime evacuation of London's children. Lewis Silkin, chairman of the LCC's Housing and later of its Town Planning Committees, took the idea with him when he became the first Minister of Town and Country Planning. He designated the first New Town, Stevenage, in November 1946, and seven more around London followed over the next three years – Harlow, Hemel Hempstead, Crawley, Bracknell, Basildon, Hatfield and Welwyn Garden City.[7]

The New Towns were the ultimate experiment in state planning in Britain, albeit founded on the most libertarian of principles. Yet their initial progress was slow. In desperation, the LCC went back to its inter-war policy of building estates beyond its boundary, often in the green belt that it was seeking to protect. Given the shortages of materials and low output elsewhere, the extent of the LCC's 'out-county' building in the years 1946–49 was remarkable, with over 31,000 houses built at Harold Hill, Aveley, Oxhey, Borehamwood, Debden, St Paul's Cray and Hainault. However, these estates were built with no extra facilities: no churches, no public houses and few shops. All the problems of Becontree stood to be repeated. Studying estates including Oxhey and Debden, sociologists such as Ruth Glass, and Michael Young and Peter Willmott aroused a first appreciation for the inner-city communities at the very moment of their dissolution.[8] Dispersal was nevertheless encouraged by subsequent government legislation. Most productive was the Town Development Act of 1952, which enabled large authorities to build their own New Towns and set up partnerships to expand existing towns with new housing and industry.

The 'out-county' estates were unpopular, too, with the architectural profession, for they were the work of the dynamic Valuer's Department under Cyril Walker, who, in November 1945, was made responsible for housing to ensure 'maximum output'. This frustrated the Architect's Department, which was rapidly being filled by keen young graduates with strong ideas on the aesthetics of public housing. After the appointment in 1947 of Robert Matthew as Chief Architect, tension mounted, and an exhibition on London housing in February 1949 led to a feud between the departments, conducted through the pages of the *Architects' Journal*. For journalists such as Ian Nairn, the 'out-county' estates epitomized the worst excesses of the 'creeping mildew that already circumscribes all of our towns' that he termed 'subtopia', a compound of suburbia and Utopia.[9] He was among the first to demand that new developments establish their own urban 'grain' and sense of place. Meanwhile, Matthew received the support of the Festival of Britain Architecture Committee to develop an estate without the valuers' interference, at Lansbury.

122

Silverdale, Dacres Estate, Sydenham

LONDON BOROUGH OF LEWISHAM

*A typical low-key brick terrace of the early
1970s.*

Public Housing

Public housing has come to have a poor reputation. Lack of maintenance through the
1980s, poor lettings management, and the reaction to the partial collapse of Ronan
Point, Newham, by a gas explosion in May 1968 have coloured perceptions not only of
local authority housing but also of the Modern Movement itself. In 1945 there was every
hope that simple buildings, designed with big windows and balconies or gardens, would
make for a healthier society. We can now distinguish the first post-war housing, with its
expensive space standards and finishes, from the system-built tower blocks built as part
of the 'numbers game' played in the 1960s. Much attractive housing of the 1970s
(fig. 122) awaits reassessment.

123

Downham Bungalow Estate,
Baudwin Road, Southend

LONDON BOROUGH OF LEWISHAM

*This is the largest surviving estate of 'prefabs'
in London, dating from 1945.*

Prefabrication

Building materials were rationed by licence until 1954. Chronic shortages of steel still recurred, however, and in 1961 the country was reduced to just three weeks' supply of bricks. Equally scarce were skilled bricklayers and carpenters. These difficulties were a convincing argument in favour of planned public housing, which, it was thought, could displace private developments entirely. Since local authorities had never built for the poorest people, the idea of middle-class public housing was not far fetched, while the model garden city movement had deliberately aimed at social integration through the building of mixed communities.

Shortages also forced authorities to experiment with less orthodox materials, and with prefabrication. Lord Portal, the Minister of Works, had a particular interest in sustaining wartime levels of employment, as he had chaired the Special Areas Reconstruction Association, founded in 1936. With the Building Research Station, his ministry built a small estate off Edward Road, Northolt, in 1944. In a series of standard-sized houses and flats, traditional brick construction was contrasted with poured no-fines concrete and concrete-block techniques, and a steel-and-brick house designed by Frederick Gibberd for the British Iron and Steel Federation also proved popular.[10] Better known is the prefabricated bungalow instituted under the Temporary Housing Programme in 1944. A model steel 'Portal bungalow' was exhibited outside the Tate Gallery in May 1944 but never went into production. Instead, eleven designs of a similar size (645 square feet), with two bedrooms and a standard kitchen and bathroom unit, were produced by private firms under licence from the government. They were supposed to last ten years, a reflection not on their prefabricated construction but on their reduced space standards and the temporary sites on which they stood; in practice, when the bungalows were passed to local authority ownership in 1967, several hundred remained in occupation. A total of 7865 bungalows were supplied to the LCC, including

124

Thamesmead

LONDON BOROUGH OF BEXLEY

The opening of 'one of Europe's largest and most technically advanced factories making forecast concrete structural units' in 1968. It was intended to produce enough units to build 850 dwellings a year without incurring overtime.

2563 for the 'out-county' estates, and the metropolitan boroughs received another 7361 between them.[11] The largest surviving group is the Downham Bungalow Estate in Southend (London Borough of Lewisham; fig. 123), where 187 'Uni-Seco' units were erected in 1945–47 along little streets named after the Knights of the Round Table. In 1961 the LCC instituted a second programme of emergency 'movable dwellings', to be built on empty redevelopment sites. Built to a similar size and standard as the 1944 bungalows but with a chunky timber frame and a flat roof, 276 of these units had been built by Calders Ltd by March 1963.[12] Most surviving prefabs in inner London are of this type.

In addition, the Ministry of Works could make grants of 'permanent' prefabricated houses from approved manufacturers. In May 1948 the LCC Housing Committee recorded that, of 1912 new permanent houses built that year, 1568 were of non-traditional construction. Otherwise ordinary 'semis' built in the late 1940s were often made of concrete, or incorporated light steel frames with asbestos-sheet cladding, while most had metal windows and sills.

Having once regained their grasp over housing, the LCC's architects were reluctant to let go again, so that London never contracted out very large building projects to private builders, as did most industrial cities. In the boroughs the situation was more varied. As other industries responded to the impetus of new technology, so the clamour grew for the building trade to become more sophisticated, too. When, at the 1963 Labour Party conference, Harold Wilson spoke of new housing 'built with the white heat of technology', he immortalized a dream cherished by many designers and local councillors since the War. Shoreditch Metropolitan Borough built a remarkable number of flats using proprietary prefabricated systems, a policy continued by the London Borough of Hackney after 1965. Edmonton developed its own Direct Labour Organisation for building large numbers of tall blocks, rejecting architectural niceties in favour of plentiful modern homes that offered many people a bathroom and inside lavatory for the first time.[13]

After ten years of debate, London's government was finally reorganized in 1965, with the formation of thirty-two enlarged local authorities responsible for their own planning and housing policies. A building boom followed, in part a backlash against the LCC's previous rigidity over planning and loan sanction, as authorities stamped a personal identity on their slivver of the city. Many turned to prefabrication. Willesden Metropolitan Borough, long frustrated for land, was gifted a site at Stonebridge Park in its merger with Wembley to form the new London Borough of Brent, and it developed the Chalkhill area with low-rise, high-density, deck-access blocks (demolished 1998–99). Both Southwark and Lambeth combined large system-built sites with smaller developments of brick. The principal tasks left to the Greater London Council were the development of housing in 'friendly' authorities with inexperienced housing departments, such as Tower Hamlets and Hounslow, and the building of large new suburbs, at Grahame Park and Thamesmead, on tracts of land given up by the government. The GLC broke with earlier traditions in designing Thamesmead to be system-built for speed, erecting a special factory on the site to manufacture precast units (fig. 124). The first area, Binsey Walk (see figs. 134–37), was erected in situ, however; subsequent delays and rising costs saw the abandonment of the project and the demolition of the factory.

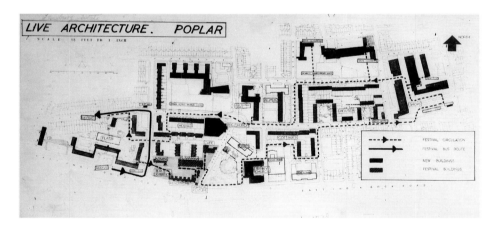

125

Live Architecture and Town Planning **exhibition, Lansbury, Poplar**

LONDON BOROUGH OF TOWER HAMLETS
The exhibition, which formed part of the Festival of Britain, received widespread publicity and served as a model for suburban developments in outer London and the New Towns. The plan shown here, of 1951, depicts a suggested route through the exhibition for visitors.

Mixed Development

In Stepney and Poplar a Comprehensive Development Area was declared in 1947. Here the LCC first experimented with separating residential and industrial areas into zones, and divided the area into eleven 'neighbourhoods', each with its own primary schools and a small shopping centre. Neighbourhood 'no. 9', later named after George Lansbury, the longtime local councillor who went on to become leader of the Labour Party, became the Live Architecture and Town Planning exhibition of the Festival of Britain (fig. 125). In July 1948 Frederick Gibberd proposed that the Festival's Architecture Council build a real suburb that could then be used to solve the housing need. The site was suggested by Robert Matthew because it was thought to be accessible from the main South Bank exhibition site by boat and because he 'had so far withstood pressure

126

Woodberry Down Estate, Stoke Newington

LONDON BOROUGH OF HACKNEY

This was the LCC's showcase estate of the 1940s, designed during the War and completed in 1954. The view from the tall blocks shows the maisonettes, houses and, in the middle distance, the first post-war health centre in London. Behind it is the distinctive tower of the Stoke Newington Pumping Station.

127

Ashdale House, Woodberry Down Estate, Stoke Newington

LONDON BOROUGH OF HACKNEY

Built in 1950–52, this is one of four eight-storey slab blocks that were the first tall blocks with lifts to be built by the LCC.

from the Valuer's Department to develop high density flats in isolation'. He hoped that the Festival's co-operation would ensure that a real neighbourhood with a range of social facilities was built.[14]

That only 86,000 people visited the Lansbury exhibition between May and October 1951 was accounted a failure. The chief landmarks, a clock tower and the Roman Catholic church, remained as foundations until the show was over. However, Yorke, Rosenberg and Mardall's primary school was admired for its modernity, show homes designed by the LCC and Geoffrey Jellicoe could be inspected, and Gibberd's shopping area was the first pedestrian precinct to be built in Britain. By May 1951 enough existed for Lansbury to serve as a model for the first phases of the New Towns. More important for London, Lansbury was a pioneering achievement of the concept of mixed development, the integration of houses and flats of varying sizes with shops and services to form a suburb that was a real community.[15]

Just one other suburb in London demonstrated the principles of mixed development at that time. This was Woodberry Down in Stoke Newington, where the LCC had started to buy up large Victorian houses in the late 1930s. Forshaw planned the neighbourhood while working on the *County of London Plan* in 1943, with a real centre containing a library, shops, schools and health centre (fig. 126). Most of the site was filled with rows of five-storey blocks, similar to those built across the LCC area from 1934 onwards but given lifts and a short return spur, which acted as a shield to the busy Seven Sisters Road. On the more sheltered south side of the road, however, Forshaw proposed a number of family houses with gardens, and four eight-storey blocks of flats built of concrete to ensure that the exceptionally high density of 178 p.p.a was reached (fig. 127). By providing a mixture of houses and flats it was hoped that there would be

appropriate provision for the entire community, and later schemes were to develop this idea further by including small bungalows for the elderly. Diversity, moreover, enabled a site to be planned more flexibly and helped the overall composition to be more picturesque – an important concept in the 1940s and a singularly British contribution to ideas on town planning.[16]

In 1950 Matthew organized a new Housing Division under J. Whitfield Lewis, with a team of some 250 young architects working in small groups, many fresh from the Architectural Association and/or with wartime experience of building under severe restrictions. It was to be the cutting edge of British architecture for much of the 1950s.

The one area within the London boundary where there was opportunity for building was Roehampton, where a handful of substantial eighteenth-century villas still stood in landscaped grounds. There were also a few streets of very large Victorian houses, many of them dilapidated or derelict but with mature gardens that deserved better than a sward of Valuer's flats, as had been proposed in 1947. By the time Whitfield Lewis took office this fate had already befallen the largest site, called Ashburton. He therefore turned to the smallest site, now known as the Ackroydon Estate (figs. 128 and 130), where Colin Lucas designed a slim eleven-storey 'point block', so called from the German *punkthaus* – although Swedish models (*punkthus*) from the 1940s were more directly influential. With just three flats per floor it occupied little more land than the Victorian villa it replaced, thus allowing the landscape to be preserved. But the three blocks built in 1951–54 to this pattern were expensive. At Portsmouth Road, later named Alton East, a more sturdy design of four flats per floor was devised, which was also used at the Fitzhugh Estate off

128

Oatlands Court, Ackroydon Estate, Wimbledon

LONDON BOROUGH OF WANDSWORTH

Oatlands Court was the first point block to be built on the Ackroydon Estate.

129

Alton Estate, Roehampton

LONDON BOROUGH OF WANDSWORTH

The Alton Estate is the best known of the large-scale LCC developments, most of it dating from 1952 to 1960. This aerial photograph of the estate shows Alton West (1954–62) in the foreground, including the five parallel slab blocks (1954–58) on the left, and Alton East (1952–55) in the distance to the right.

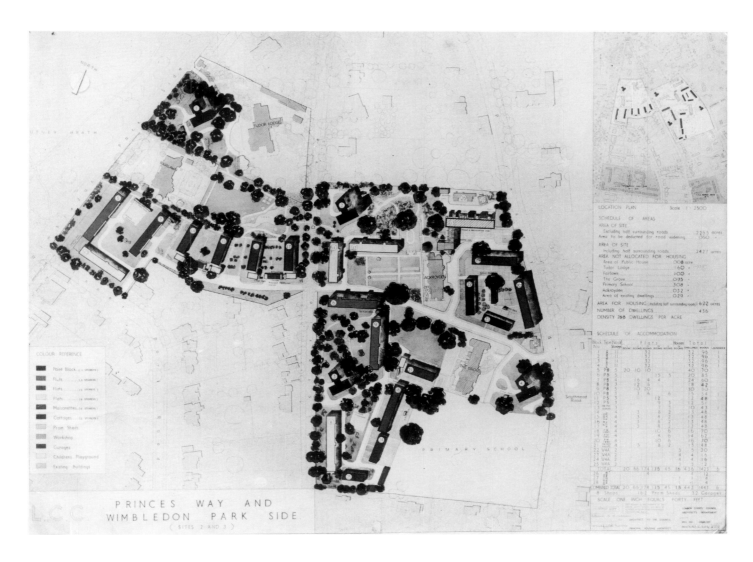

PRINCES WAY AND
WIMBLEDON PARK SIDE
(SITES 2 AND 3)

Wandsworth Common (1953–55) and in the later phases of Lansbury (1955). The Alton East team epitomized a new approach in post-war reconstruction, which looked at the needs of the user and tried to give a personal touch through attention to detail, landscaping and colour. They placed ten point blocks at the top of the sloping site to give them greater emphasis, while below were aligned blocks of four-storey maisonettes and terraced houses set in picturesque curves and culs-de-sac. The predominance of conifers among the surviving Victorian planting and the importation of a few rocks enhanced the similarity with the landscape of Stockholm suburbs such as Vällingby. The picturesque revival is often said to have culminated in the Festival of Britain held in 1951, with its attention to patterned surfaces and small-scale landscape planning. Alton East, designed the same year, incorporates many of these qualities in the far trickier task of public housing.

But by the time Alton East was completed in late 1955 tastes had changed in favour of its neighbour, the area originally known as Roehampton Lane (now Alton West; figs. 129 and 131). This was the largest and most open of the sites and included three eighteenth-

130

Plan of the Ackroydon Estate, Wimbledon, of 1950

LONDON BOROUGH OF WANDSWORTH

This was the first estate to be developed by the LCC's Architect's Department in the post-war period (1954–55), and where the point block was pioneered as a way of preserving a mature landscape attributed to Joseph Paxton.

131

Deanbury Avenue, Alton West, Alton
Estate, Roehampton

LONDON BOROUGH OF WANDSWORTH

The five slab blocks of Alton West (four of which
are shown here) were built in 1954–58. Their
hillside setting and open layout set these blocks
apart from similar but more urban developments
built elsewhere in London at this time.

century estates. The team here was also very different in character, including a slightly younger group more interested in form and structure than picturesque effect: Bill Howell, John Killick, John Partridge and Stanley Amis, who later formed a private practice. The broader landscape suited their ideas. They began work in 1951 with the presumption that a maximum amount of parkland should be left open for amenity and landscape value, and that as many tenants as possible should have views over Richmond Park. That summer, Howell and Partridge had seen Le Corbusier's Unité d'Habitation at Marseilles. They realized that a slim slab, one flat deep, would allow everyone a view of Richmond Park, and proposed five slabs set parallel to the ridge of Downshire Field, the most open area of land. However, the Minister of Housing, Harold Macmillan, objected to this 'continuous wall' overlooking a royal park. The orientation of these blocks was therefore changed to give the present massing into the slope of the hill, gaining dramatically in architectural power at the expense of the residents' preferred views. Permission to start on site was granted in 1954 and the main portion of the estate was finished by late 1958.

Alton West repeats the ingredients of Alton East, but on a far larger scale and to a more rigorously modern design. All the units were clad in storey-high precast panels, then an innovation. In addition to the slabs of maisonettes there are two groups of point blocks, regularized into perfect squares with inset rather than projecting balconies. There are also one-room bungalows for old-age pensioners, set in rows staggered to fit around the existing trees and to afford Mount Clare a continued prominence in the view. Indeed, what makes Alton West the ultimate in mixed development was the way that the three eighteenth-century houses, Mount Clare, Downshire House and Manresa House, were retained as part of the estate, the first two connected to the common heating system and adapted as much-needed teacher-training facilities, the last remaining a Jesuit college.

Though not the first high slabs built by the LCC, those at Alton marked a refinement of those built elsewhere because of their precisely precast panels and neat detailing. Yet it was the setting of the blocks into the side of Downshire Field that was crucial to their success, for it put their base of Corbusian-inspired stilts or *pilotis*, an often overplayed conceit of the period, to genuine practical use and impact. The result was 'one really magnificent effect, far and away the most majestic in London' in what was described as 'probably the finest low-cost housing development in the world'.[17]

Traffic in Towns

Pedestrian and vehicle segregation was an important concept in the 1960s. Car ownership in Britain doubled between 1949 and 1957, and trebled between 1949 and 1961. In 1962 as many as 4287 children under ten were killed on the roads. Ernest Marples, the Minister of Transport, commissioned a study of roads and traffic in the urban environment from a committee chaired by Colin Buchanan. His report was published in 1963 as *Traffic in Towns*, the definitive guide to contemporary ideas not only on planning roads but also on the towns and suburbs around them.[18]

132, 133

Lanacre Avenue, Grahame Park, Edgware

LONDON BOROUGH OF BARNET

Grahame Park was a major new suburb, built by the GLC, the local authority and private developers on former Ministry of Defence land in 1969–76.

One solution to the increasing problem of noise from roads and railways was to build a long block with its back set against it. At Grahame Park (figs. 132–33), Edgware, built by the LCC and the London Borough of Barnet between 1969 and 1976, flats and maisonettes were set in a long spine with shops and a library, in part as a barrier to the nearby M1 motorway. At Thamesmead two conditions encouraged the segregation of roads and footpaths – the proximity of the proposed Ringway Two motorway, and a local flooding regulation which demanded that housing be built at least 8' 6" above sea

134, 135, 136, 137

Binsey Walk, Thamesmead South

LONDON BOROUGH OF BEXLEY

Thamesmead was the only New Town to be developed within Greater London. Thamesmead South (1969) demonstrates the underlying philosophy of the estate's plan, with pedestrian walkways and access to all flats set at first-floor level, with roads and car parking beneath.

level. The result was that housing and shops, connected by cycle routes and footpaths, were laid out on a first-floor podium, with car parking and roads beneath. Binsey Walk (1969) at Thamesmead South, the only area to be completed as planned, best demonstrates this philosophy (figs. 134–37). Long slabs were also a feature of the gargantuan landscape created north and south of Burgess Park, both by Camberwell and its successor, the London Borough of Southwark (1965–76), and subsequently also by the GLC's Architect's Department at Gloucester Grove (1971–77).

Low-Rise Building

The first alternatives to building high came in the mid-1950s. The attack was centred on the point block and the prevalence for surrounding it with a greensward at the expense of the traditional street pattern. There was concern, too, for the effects of repetitive blocks on the townscape. Sir Leslie Martin was appointed to the first Chair of Architecture at Cambridge in 1957 and began to formulate low-rise brick building in Cambridge and to study London planning. His team suggested a broad area of northern

Bloomsbury for a low-rise, high-density redevelopment that retained only its most formal elements, such as the crescent of Cartwright Gardens. When part of this area was proposed for redevelopment by the Foundling Estate with a 40-foot tower, Martin's studies offered an alternative, which was developed by his assistant Patrick Hodgkinson as seven-storey terraces of flats forming an 'A'-frame over shops and basement parking. Though devised as early as 1961, work on what became the Brunswick Centre did not begin until 1967.

The most significant low-rise, high-density scheme was Lillington Gardens in Pimlico, the subject of a competition in 1961, which was won by John Darbourne. The key phases of the scheme were completed by 1972. Darbourne and his partner, Geoffrey Darke, used red-brown, load-bearing brick to build multi-faceted and organically formed terraces of flats and maisonettes. After the regularity of the points and slabs of the 1950s, the contorted planning so evidently enjoyed by the architects at Lillington Gardens had a profound influence on lower-density suburban housing. Though imitative schemes abound, the most interesting remain those by Darbourne and Darke themselves, including the Marquess Estate (1970–77; partly demolished 1998), Islington; Camden Road (1971–73), Holloway; and Queen's Road (1978–81), Richmond. The idiom of small, tightly packed and organically planned brick units lent itself well to infill sites, as came increasingly to be exploited in the late 1960s and through the 1970s. Lambeth's Architect's Department produced a number of distinctive examples, for example off Clapham Manor Street (from 1969).

Meanwhile, the Howells, James Stirling and Colin St John Wilson also investigated alternative low-rise ideas, initially for rural housing. Howell's interest in terraced housing went back to a student project that he supervised at the Architectural Association as early as 1954, and can be seen at Alton and in a terrace (1954–56) built at South Hill Park, Hampstead, designed with his wife and Stanley Amis for themselves and friends. Howell, Killick, Partridge and Amis redefined their concept of the terrace in housing for the elderly and disabled at Stonegrove, Edgware, for the London Borough of Harrow, built around a village green in 1964–68. A simpler scheme set around a village green is a suburban development by Donald McMorran for the Corporation of the City of London, at Lammas Green, Sydenham Hill. Built in 1956–57, it consists of three terraces of houses around a square, sheltered from the main road by flats on the fourth side. These schemes marked a return to the traditional London terrace. It is significant that many of these architects had been students at the Architectural Association in Bedford Square, the finest of all London's Georgian neighbourhoods. Moreover, terraces were economical in both materials and land.

One private developer took up the challenge of the terrace *and* the London square. Eric Lyons (1912–80) and Geoffrey Townsend (1911–) revived both idioms, albeit in a loosely formed and highly picturesque manner and obscured by foliage. At a time when most private housing was speculative and mundane, Townsend's company, Span Developments Ltd, was recognized for having 'started (or rather re-started) what may

138

Hallgate, Cator Estate, Blackheath Park
LONDON BOROUGH OF GREENWICH
This is one of the most imposing of Span's interventions in the Cator Estate, which features the sculpture The Architect in Society *by Keith Godwin.*

well become a movement that could save Britain from a great deal of further suburban horror'.[19] Townsend was an architect turned developer, a move that obliged him to give up his membership of the Royal Institute of British Architects, but this background gave a unity of intention between architect and client that was rare in the speculative building field and a factor in the firm's aesthetic and commercial success. The firm also pioneered the endowment mortgage, and established the system of tenants' management companies, which remain a feature of all Span developments. Lyons was committed to higher densities than those usually permitted and regarded his buildings as essentially urban, no matter how leafy their setting (see fig. 120). This led to many confrontations with planning officers and local councillors, especially when infilling bomb-sites on the early nineteenth-century Cator Estate (fig. 138) in Blackheath. This is symbolized by Keith

139

Alexandra Road Estate, Swiss Cottage

LONDON BOROUGH OF CAMDEN

*This is the showcase estate of Camden's
schemes for low-rise, high-density housing,
built in 1972–78 to the designs of Neave
Brown of Camden's Architect's Department.
The continuous spine wall of the largest block,
inspired by the formal proportions of the
Georgian crescent, was conceived as a buffer
against noise from the adjacent railway.*

140, 141, 142

Lakeside, Castle Bar

LONDON BOROUGH OF EALING

This estate, also known as the Grange after the house that previously occupied the site, was developed by Wates from 1966, to include a mixture of housing styles set in the preserved landscape of the earlier house.

Godwin's sculpture there, at Hallgate, which depicts a man straining to prevent a lintel from crushing him and is entitled *The Architect in Society*.

Span's formula was much repeated, by Austin Vernon and Partners for housing on the Dulwich College Estate, and, most imaginatively, by the builders Wates. One of their best schemes is Lakeside (figs. 140–42), at Castle Bar, Ealing, built in 1966. This small, enclosed development comprises three-storey houses and a tall block of flats, set around a shared landscape garden and small pool preserved from the nineteenth-century house previously on the site.

The cul-de-sac, initiated with Asmuns Place, Hampstead Garden Suburb, was exported across the Atlantic to become a feature of Radburn, New Jersey, in 1928. The concept seems subsequently to have been more influential back in Britain than in the States, and was featured in *Traffic in Towns*. The idea was that every area, or 'super block', would have no main roads, but be served by short spurs for parking. Traffic could be thus confined, while pedestrian paths offered alternative through-routes for those on foot. The system lent itself to the informal, complex planning necessary on the awkward sites available in the post-war period and enabled the retention of existing landscaping.

The ultimate low-rise, high-density module is the single-storey 'L'-shaped house linked to its neighbour around a private patio. The idea began with Hugo Häring's Werkbungsiedlung housing at Lainz, Vienna, of 1932, and projects by Mies van der Rohe, Hannes Meyer and other Bauhaus staff. An early British example is Chamberlin, Powell and Bon's Vanbrugh Park development begun in 1962, where two-storey houses are combined with a single, short point block. In the early 1960s the Ministry of Housing and Local Government (MHLG) set up a Research and Development Group to explore user needs and the technical possibilities of low-rise, high-density housing. A model entitled the 'Adaptable House' was exhibited at the 1962 Ideal Homes Exhibition, and thirty-nine houses were built at West Ham to the standards for space, privacy and heating recommended by the Parker Morris Committee in 1961. The use of a weatherboarded timber frame with brick end walls, which was innovatory here, became a common practice from the later 1960s.[20]

The most influential model for compact terrace housing, however, was Siedlung Halen, a development of eighty-one houses outside Berne, Switzerland, by Atelier 5 and built in 1959–61. It is a dense, repetitive, largely three-storey scheme, arranged in two long, broken rows on a steep hillside, with a shared entrance between each row.[21] The low-rise, high-density terrace, often of maisonettes set one on top of another, was a distinctive idiom of the Camden Architect's Department. The first Borough Architect, Sidney Cook, considered himself an impresario of talents, gathering to him a remarkable roster of architects with established reputations, some directly employed, others, such as James Stirling, Frederick MacManus and Michael Neylan, brought in as consultants. Neave Brown had already designed a tight-knit terrace of houses for himself and friends, with living rooms on an upper floor and a children's semi-basement giving on to the garden. This upside-down planning and a mixture of private and shared gardens were

features repeated in his two extensive local authority schemes. Fleet Road II of 1972–76, now the Dunboyne Road Estate, is the closest to Siedlung Halen, with two-storey maisonettes and some flats set over a partially sunken car park, each unit having its own private patio space and sharing a large podium from which the upper maisonettes are entered. Brown's larger development for Camden, the Alexandra Road Estate (1972–78; fig. 139), is more clearly inspired by the traditional Georgian terrace, on which Brown lays strong emphasis.

Halen's treatment of regular units stepped down a hillside is followed more closely at Branch Hill (fig. 143), Hampstead, of 1974–78, by Gordon Benson and Alan Forsyth. The land was bought by Camden in 1965 with a fiercesomely restrictive covenant, that any development must be of two storeys and semi-detached. There are consequently narrow paths between each pair of houses. The gardens of one house form the roof of

143

Branch Hill, Hampstead

LONDON BOROUGH OF CAMDEN

This is the last of Camden's distinctive low-rise, high-density housing schemes, built to the designs of Benson and Forsyth in 1974–78.

144

Turnpike Link, Park Hill

LONDON BOROUGH OF CROYDON

Turnpike Link, built in 1966–68 to the designs of MacManus and Partners, forms part of the extensive Park Hill Estate, developed by Wates between 1962 and 1970 using a variety of architects.

the house below, with a small courtyard between lighting the lower level of the upper house. Though five storeys in all, the development is never more than two storeys high at any one point, and the view from the surrounding higher land is dominated by the gardens and a surrounding belt of trees. At Central Hill, Norwood, Rosemary Stjernstedt designed a stepped scheme for Lambeth Architect's Department. Built between 1967 and 1974 of white brick, 374 houses and flats were set in terraces, one above the other, arranged on the 1:6 slope so that each has a front door at ground level. The design is simpler but less homogeneous than the contemporary examples by Camden.

Atelier 5 designed one scheme of their own in London, for Wates in Croydon. Twenty-one houses and a semi-basement garage were constructed in 1968–69 to the designs of Anatole du Fresne – all that was realized of an extensive development of 147 homes. Three terraces are entered at their upper level through a small courtyard, while the bedrooms and a large windowless workroom are set below.[22] This is the most significant element of a carefully planned redevelopment by Wates at Park Hill, Croydon. While the earliest schemes there, including Hill Rise and Hillmere, by K.W. Bland and Austin Vernon, are terraces of tile-hung flats and houses in the

Span tradition, Turnpike Link (1966–68; fig. 144), a series of flats and maisonettes by F.G. MacManus and Partners, is a more dynamic example of perimeter planning. Like St Bernard's (fig. 145), the site is a low hill, with flats and maisonettes concealed from their related garaging by high walls and rich planting, and themselves protecting a large shared garden in the centre of the block, where stands a single short tower of flats.

Perimeter planning was a concept favoured by the London Borough of Merton in an imaginative series of housing schemes from the late 1960s to the mid-1970s. The Borough Architect, B.V. Ward, gathered an enterprising design team, which briefly (1967–69) included a young Richard MacCormac, to develop a series of moderately high-density estates faced in white enamel panels. There are three main schemes, all similar in concept. Three-storey houses incorporating garages are set in a continuous terrace, which wraps around each site and has flats at the sharpest corners. On one side are culs-de-sac; on the other are small private gardens, with a large communal greensward beyond. First was Pollards Hill (1968), a sequence of squares arranged in a Greek key formation. Even more successful is its successor, Watermeads (1974–77), a development of 100 p.p.a., the garden of which leads directly on to the River Wandle,

145

St Bernard's, Park Hill

LONDON BOROUGH OF CROYDON

Another scheme on the Park Hill Estate is
St Bernard's, consisting of twenty-one terraced
houses on a steep slope by Anatole du Fresne of
Atelier 5, the Swiss firm that pioneered inventive
planning on hillside sites in the late 1950s.

where a small lake was created. In their use of lush planting and acceptance of high densities, such schemes from the 1970s reveal a continuing debt to Span.

The London Borough of Hillingdon experimented with a greater variety of small schemes, ranging from expandable homes to single-person's flats, and including such unusual developments as Edward Cullinan's wide-frontage houses (1974–77) at Highgrove, Eastcote. This repeated the pattern of paired houses found at Branch Hill, but placed them back-to-back around and over central garages. Here and at Westmoreland Road, Bromley, for the Solon Housing Association, Cullinan's work exemplifies 1970s' styling, with a use of contrasting colours, balconies, trellises (features he himself termed 'sticks') in the manner of Gerrit Rietveld and contemporary Dutch architects such as Aldo van Eyck, while progressively introducing a greater formalism.[23] Highgrove is best known for its brilliant blue metal roofs. The boundaries between modernism and postmodern classicism are brokered by the work of Jeremy Dixon, previously one of Cullinan's associates, who designed another small housing association project, St Mark's Road (1976–80), Kensington. This is a real terrace – of family maisonettes set over small flats – that combines the spirit of early Victorian rows with square patterning and bright colour, an idiom that Dixon developed further in Docklands schemes.

Development since 1979

By 1979 public housing was moribund. The big local authority housing schemes conceived in the mid-1960s were finally completed, while the oil crisis and international monetary controls ensured that little new work was begun thereafter. The arrival in 1979 of a Conservative Government that imposed restrictions on capital expenditure saw the end of local authorities as the principal house builders. In 1981 the GLC was made to pass its housing stock to the boroughs.

There remained refurbishment projects. When, in 1943, the Ministry of Health first asked London's metropolitan boroughs to produce one-year and five-year plans for their housing needs, rehabilitation was seen as no more than a temporary measure. The restoration of mid-Victorian terraces around Lorrimore Square from 1955 as an integral part of the LCC's new Brandon Estate in Kensington was the first time that 'mixed development' was taken to include humble older dwellings. Then, in the 1960s, refurbishment was allied to the regeneration of such inner-city areas as Islington by middle-class incomers. In the 1980s this movement burgeoned eastwards.

The GLC's *Greater London Development Plan* of 1969 did not anticipate the closure of the London Docks and Surrey Docks a year later. A re-evaluation led to the publication of a strategic plan in 1976, but relatively little was done until 1981, when the Conservative Government vested control in the London Docklands Development Corporation.[24] With its flat, waterlogged sites and lack of transport infrastructure, Docklands can be seen as the natural successor of Thamesmead. Yet the pattern of planning and building is very different. In part this was due to the survival of a historic industrial landscape, which gives form to the new environment, in part because the

LDDC's task was to provide an infrastructure for a wide range of public and private builders rather than complete redevelopment. Much of Docklands repeats the formula of the City of London's Barbican, setting luxury flats around water (fig. 146), but here there is a stylistically restless mixture of converted or reconstructed warehouses and modern or postmodern infill. Narrow Street and Rotherhithe Street have renewed their old form as deep caverns from which views of the adjacent river are hidden, although in their hinterland the mix of local authority blocks and private terraces has become more open. If suburbs are defined as overwhelmingly residential areas with a distinct character and an isolation born of indifferent public transport, then large swathes of Docklands can truly be called suburban.

146

The Lakes, Norway Dock, Rotherhithe

LONDON BOROUGH OF SOUTHWARK

This private housing scheme, set in a crescent around what survives of Norway Dock close to the River Thames, was built in 1988–96 to designs by Shepheard, Epstein and Hunter.

THE ROAD TO SUBTOPIA

Beckton's one debt to London is the spoil from the basement of the new British Library at St Pancras, which has swelled its artificial ski-slope. Otherwise its amorphous greensward owes more to the decentralized plan of Milton Keynes and North American low-rise conurbations than to the native south-eastern garden city, let alone the proximity of the metropolis. Built since 1970 on land released by British Gas, redevelopment has sought to integrate isolated terraces of gasworkers' homes with dockers' cottages and local authority housing by means of new roads, the extension of the Docklands Light Railway and a district park. Most housing is for sale rather than rent, although there is a greater proportion of low-cost dwellings than in the rest of Docklands. Its centrepiece is not a public building or neat shopping precinct, but a supermarket and health centre, while the most lively meeting-place is the large Asda Savacentre set firmly in the adjoining industrial estate rather than among the houses. A similar store at Crossharbour performs a comparable function for the Isle of Dogs.

Ultimately, the suburb must be comfortable. It should be appropriate to our means and aspirations, and feel both psychologically and physically safe. Those of us who rail against it do so because it does nothing more; it offers no challenge, nor inspiration beyond the possibilities of *Homes and Gardens*. London seldom demonstrates the megalomaniacal aspirations of great social housing schemes similar to those that characterize the suburbs of northern cities. Save where wartime devastation was total (the Barbican) or undeveloped marshland was made available (Thamesmead, Beckton), schemes have been small or have been informed by existing buildings and landscapes. In the immediate post-war years this meant a deliberately picturesque composition of small-scale elements, to be superseded by grander concepts in the 1960s. The last twenty years have seen a revival of the *Beaux Arts* planning popular in the 1920s, with straight avenues and through axes – layouts that can be readily grasped by those rushing through, as well as by residents wanting convenience and simplicity. Options for housing may have become more complex, yet as with 'mixed development' there is a growing consistency across London in which 'urban' and 'suburban' are becoming increasingly blurred.

NOTES

1. Alison and Peter Smithson, 'Urban Reidentification', 1952–53, in *Ordinariness and Light*, London (Faber and Faber) 1970, pp. 18, 30.
2. J.H. Forshaw and Patrick Abercrombie, *The County of London Plan*, London (HMSO) 1943.
3. Patrick Abercrombie, *The Greater London Plan*, London (HMSO) 1945.
4. Lord Meath, 'A Green Girdle round London', *The Sphere*, no. 6, 1901, p. 64; David Thomas, *London's Green Belt*, London (Faber and Faber) 1970.
5. LCC Council Minutes, 1931–38.
6. *Administrative County of London Development Plan*, London (LCC) 1951.
7. Andrew Saint, '"Spread the People": The LCC's Dispersal Policy, 1889–1965', in *Politics and the People of London*, ed. Andrew Saint, London (Hambledon Press) 1989, p. 229.
8. Michael Young and Peter Willmott, *Family and Kinship in East London*, London (Routledge and Kegan Paul) 1957: contrasting Bethnal Green and Debden.
9. Ian Nairn, 'Outrage', *Architectural Review*, CXVII, no. 702, June 1955; reprinted London (Architectural Press) 1956.
10. *Demonstration Houses*, London (HMSO) 1944; *Architectural Design*, XIV, no. 2, February 1944, p. 26; no. 3, March 1944, p. 76; no. 10, October 1944, p. 233; no. 11, November 1944, p. 249.

11. LCC Housing Committee paper on the Temporary Housing Programme, 8 July 1948, from London Metropolitan Archives, LCC/MIN/7631.

12. LCC Council Minutes, 12 December 1961 and 31 March 1963.

13. Miles Glendinning and Stefan Muthesius, *Tower Block*, New Haven and London (Yale University Press) 1994, pp. 265–82.

14. PRO WORK 25/28 (A2/D4 1–6)

15. *Poplar, Blackwall and the Isle of Dogs* (Survey of London, XLIII), London (Athlone Press) 1994, pp. 212–35.

16. Nicholas Merthyr Day, 'The Role of the Architect in Post-War State Housing', unpublished PhD diss., University of Warwick, 1988, pp. 179–212.

17. Ian Nairn, *Modern Buildings in London*, London (London Transport) 1964, p. 62; G.E. Kidder Smith, *The New Architecture of Europe*, Cleveland OH (Meridian Books) 1961, p. 42.

18. *Traffic in Towns*, Reports of the Steering Group and Working Group appointed by the Minister of Transport, London (HMSO) 1963.

19. 'The Architect Returns to "Spec" Building', in *House and Garden*, 14, no. 129, October 1959, pp. 80–84.

20. Space standards were high in the 1940s but declined thereafter. Parker Morris's recommendations were commonly adopted: *Homes for Today and Tomorrow*, Report of the Parker Morris Committee, London (HMSO) 1961; *Official Architecture and Planning*, April 1964, p. 405; Ministry of Housing and Local Government, *Family Houses at West Ham*, London (HMSO) 1969.

21. Roger Sherwood, *Modern Housing Prototypes*, Cambridge MA (Harvard University Press) 1978, pp. 62–65.

22. 'Croydon Atelier 5', in *Architect's Journal*, 151, no. 24, 17 June 1970, pp. 1482–84.

23. Kenneth Powell, *Edward Cullinan Architects*, London (Academy Editions) 1995, pp. 12–16.

24. *Poplar, Blackwall and the Isle of Dogs* (Survey of London, XLIII), London (Athlone Press) 1994, pp. 19–20.

Chapter Five
The Place of Conservation

EDDIE BOOTH

Conventionally, protection has been given to the remarkable and, even more, to the monumental. It has taken a long time for the public, and then politicians, to accept that the ordinary can be worthwhile too. Yet the contribution of ordinary buildings to the *genius loci*, the spirit of the place, has long been recognized. Travel writers from the early nineteenth century understood the value of what we now call townscape. Thus the twisted timber-framed buildings outside the Cathedral Close at Salisbury or in the vicinity of York Minster (fig. 148) were appreciated as much for their own merits as for the way they enhanced the experience of visiting the awesome cathedral in their midst.

The relationship between a grandiloquent monument and its humbler cousins was certainly recognized and enjoyed by the British during the nineteenth century. More than anyone, painters depicted characteristic townscapes with their everyday buildings rich in identity and local colour, while *The Penny Magazine*, one of the earliest working-class weeklies, occasionally delighted its readers with accounts of cities in which the monumental and the ordinary happily co-existed. But the need for progress was also understood and promoted. Cities had to modernize or die, declared *The Builder* – the most influential professional journal of the day. The loss of picturesque buildings was the price to be paid for progress. Time and again its editor, George Godwin, enthused as the authentic townscapes of one city after another were removed in the interests of traffic, hygiene, civil administration and commerce. Ancient monuments might often be retained to punctuate a pleasure ground or vista, but their ordinary surroundings were transformed.

Towards the end of the nineteenth century, however, some dissenting voices began to be heard. William Morris, a founding figure of the modern conservation movement, wrote passionately about the charms of traditional townscapes and his Society for the Protection of Ancient Buildings (SPAB), established in 1877, strived to preserve the settings of historic buildings as well as their fabric. For Morris, however, history was essentially pre-1700. Everything later was lacking in art, its vitality sapped by mass-production, division of labour and speculation, the capitalist tools that had destroyed the beauty of architecture and, indeed, life. And this was how Morris saw London's Georgian and Edwardian suburbs. He knew them first hand, from the merchant suburb of Walthamstow, where he was born in 1834, to the stuccoed suburbs of Kensington, where many of his clients lived, and the early Georgian linear development overlooking the River Thames at Hammersmith, where he bought an eighteenth-century house.

For decades, the notion that whole historic townscapes might be preserved could not be taken seriously, let alone such late eighteenth- and early nineteenth-century suburbs as Islington and St John's Wood. Instead, the rise of the suburb coincided with

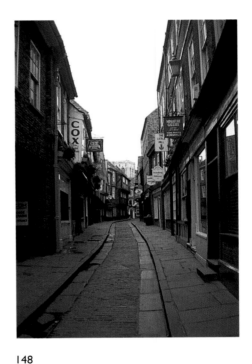

148

The Shambles, York

The picturesque qualities of lesser buildings give a context to the monumentality of the Minster.

147

No. 174 New North Road, Islington

LONDON BOROUGH OF ISLINGTON

Inappropriate stone cladding of a Georgian terrace building.

149

The Paragon, Blackheath

LONDON BOROUGH OF GREENWICH

Conservation areas are concerned with the relationship of building, pavement, kerb, carriageway and landscape, as well as with the buildings themselves.

150

The Paragon, Blackheath

LONDON BOROUGH OF GREENWICH

A distinctively random pattern of setts at the entrance to the crescent.

the consolidation of local government and the birth of modern town planning. With its origins in public health and sanitation, early by-law planning did much to reduce over-crowding and raise standards of daylight, ventilation and immunity from fire, although by comparison, as was noted by Raymond Unwin:

> ... the remarkable fact remains that there are growing up around our big towns vast districts, under these very by-laws, which, for dreariness and sheer ugliness it is difficult to match anywhere and, compared with which, many of the old unhealthy slums are, from the point of view of picturesqueness and beauty, infinitely more attractive.[1]

It was through the garden city movement that planning was brought together with architecture in a deliberate aesthetic, more reminiscent of the country than the town, reaching perfection in Parker and Unwin's Hampstead Garden Suburb, begun in 1908. It was also at the core of subsequent developments shaped by the recommendations of the Tudor Walters Committee of 1918, which set standards for three-bedroom houses with kitchen, bath and garden, and densities of no more than twelve houses to the acre, and which were fuelled by subsidies under the Housing and Town Planning Act of 1919.

Meanwhile, as the growth of town planning was stalled by war, the Georgian Group was formed out of a sub-committee of Morris's SPAB. This was a direct reaction to the demolition of Mecklenburgh Square, Waterloo Bridge and the Adam brothers' Adelphi, all major eighteenth-century structures that, in one way or another, can be associated with the suburbanization of the capital. The society's committee pushed for the retention of large groups of buildings in historic towns rather than just their monuments, and, while parliamentary debates leading to the 1947 Town and Country Planning Act entertained the possibility of designating streets, set pieces or even whole districts for retention, listing was in the end limited to individual buildings.

It was not until the Civic Amenities Act of 1967 that statutory protection was given to the conservation of entire districts. This was the brainchild of Lord Kennet, Parliamentary Secretary at the Ministry of Housing and Local Government in Harold Wilson's Government of 1966–70. Kennet had been impressed by the French system of *zones protégées*, which imposed restrictions within a radius of one kilometre of each *monument classé*, and more so by their *secteurs saufguardes*, which protected whole urban quarters. He collaborated with Duncan Sandys, founder of the Civic Trust, to promote a Private Member's Bill, which aimed, as Sandys said in the House, 'to preserve beauty, to create beauty and to remove ugliness ... it seeks to protect the character not only of buildings but also the area around them'[2] (figs. 149–50). While Sandys may have seen the emerging conservation areas as protection for the setting of listed buildings, Kennet recognized the group value of less distinguished buildings on a wider scale. He was later to say, 'I wanted the local authorities to designate many and large areas'.[3]

The Act used the following words, which are still in force today:

> Every local planning authority shall from time to time determine which parts of their
> area are areas of special architectural or historic interest the character of which it is
> desirable to preserve or enhance, and shall designate those areas as conservation
> areas.[4]

The accompanying Ministry circular turned principles of the Act into guidance. Although it was less than helpful on size – 'they may be large or small, from whole town centres to squares, terraces and smaller groups of buildings'[5] – it was clear that areas did not have to centre on listed buildings, but that 'pleasant groups of other buildings, open spaces, trees, a historic street pattern, a village green' were also important.

At the same time, the Ministry published *Historic Towns: Preservation and Change*, which was concerned with:

> ... an aspect of town planning that is now receiving more and more attention: the kind
> of planning which is needed in order to preserve, in a positive way, the good things
> our towns already possess. It is concerned not only with single old buildings, but also
> with the general visual qualities of historic towns.[6]

The Government also commissioned studies of four historic towns – Bath, Chester, Chichester and York – which, by their detailed analysis of problems and solutions, have formed the basis for modern urban conservation. Donald Insall's report on Chester, for instance, took account of post-1914 buildings as well as street surfaces and pavements, while all the reports acknowledged that there was a class of building worthy of conservation for what it contributed to the overall character of a place.

So, by the late 1960s the way was finally open to consider the protection and positive planning of whole historic districts, the only distinction of which was their particular character, and not whether they contained any individual buildings that might be considered outstanding. That, at least, was the theory.

In practice, early designations, made by county councils, tended to be tightly drawn around listed buildings and unambiguously historic centres. The first was in the

151

Sundew Avenue, Wormholt Estate, Shepherd's Bush

LONDON BOROUGH OF HAMMERSMITH AND FULHAM

A distinctive, peaceful character derives from ordinary buildings but with generous standards of space and layout.

Lincolnshire market town of Stamford and, in London, a Mayfair Conservation Area soon followed in December 1969. These were far from ordinary places, but the principle had been established. In 1982 responsibility for conservation areas passed to the district councils and designations became noticeably more liberal, embracing whole country parks, canals, industrial complexes … and suburbs.

London has over 800 of the nation's 9000 conservation areas. As a device to identify the more historically significant suburbs, the conservation area is most appropriate because, as is often the case, the whole concept matters more than the individual constituents (figs. 151–52). However, conservation areas initially had little statutory force, being more a statement of intent allowing local character to be taken into account in determining development decisions. It was important, therefore, that areas with significant individual buildings should continue to look to listing for protection even after they had been designated a conservation area: the Norman Shaw houses of Bedford Park, Turnham Green, exemplify this, being individually listed despite a conservation area having been designated there in the early 1970s. The mass listing of less distinguished buildings is not feasible and, now that controls have been introduced over the demolition of buildings, the felling of trees and the enforcement of urgent repairs, area designation is the practical answer to protection.

Protection, however, is only a part of conservation. It has taken thirty years to evolve current best practice in the management of historic areas. This can be found primarily in the government's Planning Policy Guidance PPG15 *Planning and the Historic Environment*, but there is no shortage of additional information published by English Heritage, the English Historic Towns Forum and the Royal Town Planning Institute.

The preliminary task for those wishing to designate a particular conservation area must be to locate its 'special architectural or historic interest'. In some cases there may at

152

Holland Park

ROYAL BOROUGH OF KENSINGTON
AND CHELSEA

*Uniform appearance can be part of the
essential character of a conservation area but
is difficult to maintain without strong planning
controls.*

first appear to be a contradiction between 'special' and 'ordinary', and it will be a matter of judgement whether the cumulative value of ordinary buildings amounts to an overall interest which is special and warrants designation.

The second step must be to establish a clearly definable boundary, which should follow the edges of property or physical features such as roads or streams. Often the cut-off will be readily apparent (where one property contributes to the special interest and the next is outside), but sometimes it will be necessary to consider whether marginal areas or buffer zones should be included.

Thirdly, the character of the conservation area must be defined so that the purpose of designation is understood. As PPG15 puts it:

> The more clearly the special architectural or historic interest that justifies designation is defined and recorded, the sounder will be the basis for local plan policies and development control decisions, as well as for the formulation of proposals for the preservation and enhancement of the character or appearance of the area.[7]

153

Tottenham High Road

LONDON BOROUGH OF HARINGEY

*'Character' means more than appearance: traffic
blight is as much an issue as the architectural
qualities one is seeking to preserve.*

While this assessment will include the history and development of the area and the appearance of buildings and spaces, it should also cover the less tangible elements of character such as activity, uses, noise or tranquillity, smells even, and those elements that may detract from the character (fig. 153). The English Heritage leaflet *Conservation Area Appraisals* (1997) is particularly helpful here.

Designation takes effect with the vote of the borough's relevant planning committee, on the advice of conservation staff, and although there is no requirement for public consultation, it clearly makes sense, especially in residential areas. In the past it was common for consultation to be a token trawl of local amenity societies, which, of course, already had a vested interest and were bound to agree. Now, however, it is usual for a wider public meeting to be held.

This may pose a further contradiction. Although most suburbs were planned entities with a high degree of uniformity, they also represent freedom from the constraints of the city, and the understandable (if not always appropriate) desire for individuals to personalize property can be seen as part of a natural evolution of the suburb (fig. 155). Conservation, on the other hand, is concerned with retaining local distinctiveness by preserving elements of the original form (figs. 156–58). This tension between individual freedom and collective control will determine the level of popular support for designation. It is also coloured by ownership and values. New freeholds created under the right-to-buy in the midst of public estates tend to assert their independence whereas private enclaves encourage mutual conformity in which a degree of personal sacrifice may well be an attractive price for the prospect of control over neighbours. This, no doubt, is at the heart of a number of recent conservation proposals put forward, not by obscure conservation professionals, but by the residents themselves, for instance at the Meadway Estate in Southgate.

The principal effect of designation is the requirement for permission, known as Conservation Area Consent, to be obtained for the demolition of any building. Exceptions are made for minor structures, including most boundary walls. Demolition does not, however, include alteration, although, until recently, local authorities were able to make use of a definition of 'building' (which included part of a building) to require consent for partial demolition. This enabled one High Court case to decide that the removal of tiles from a roof, in order to insert a dormer window, amounted to demolition, which therefore required consent. This apparent loophole was closed by the House of Lords in *Shimizu (UK) Ltd v. Westminster City Council* (1997), when the defini-

THE PLACE OF CONSERVATION

156

Queen's Park Estate (*top left*)

CITY OF WESTMINSTER

Cast-iron window guards are particular to the 1870s' estates of the Artizans, Labourers and General Dwellings Company.

157

Wallflower Street, Wormholt Estate, Shepherd's Bush (*top right*)

LONDON BOROUGH OF HAMMERSMITH AND FULHAM

Distinctiveness is provided by the gable turned towards the street and the detail of the tiled eaves.

tion was interpreted differently. Now, 'demolition' refers to the whole, or a substantial part, of a building, and 'partial demolition' no longer applies. This matters less for listed buildings, where alterations also require consent, but in conservation areas the effect is far reaching, as we shall see below.

Trees are commonly an integral part of the later suburbs and they give important punctuation to the formal terraces and squares of earlier developments. While planning legislation provides for the protection of individual trees with Tree Preservation Orders, all trees in designated areas (again with minor exceptions) are protected (fig. 154). Six weeks' notice must be given to the local authority of any intention 'to lop, top or fell', during which time a specific preservation order may be made.

Further controls include the power to serve Repairs Notices in cases where listed buildings are seriously dilapidated (fig. 159), and this can ultimately lead to compulsory purchase. Urgent works necessary for the preservation of unoccupied buildings, whether they be listed or unlisted buildings in a conservation area, may be undertaken by the local authority and the cost can be charged to the owner. There is also a little-used power to serve Amenity Notices in cases where the amenity of a neighbourhood is being adversely affected by the condition of land in the area. This power was originally intended to kerb overgrown gardens and the dumping of rubbish, but it clearly has more potential. On the south coast, for example, the former Hove Borough Council used it frequently to secure the repainting of flaking stucco façades.

These powers will seem draconian because they are essentially matters of last resort. It is important that they be used sparingly and with relevance if public support is to be maintained. Research has shown that, in the vast majority of cases, the threat of action is

158

Latchmere Estate, Battersea (*bottom left*)

LONDON BOROUGH OF WANDSWORTH

The survival of original detailing, such as these porches and doors, is increasingly vulnerable. English Heritage believes that all the best examples of historic suburbs should be designated conservation areas.

159

Nos. 810–812 Tottenham High Road (*bottom right*)

LONDON BOROUGH OF HARINGEY

Conservation strategies have to address the problem of buildings at risk with repairs action or grant aid.

160

Englefield Road, Kingsland

LONDON BOROUGH OF HACKNEY

Home owners replace their front doors for all manner of reasons, although, as with the two shown here, their choice is not always appropriate or in keeping with the period of the property.

161

Dover House Estate, Roehampton

LONDON BOROUGH OF WANDSWORTH

Gable hips formed with traditional 'bonnets'.

162

Dover House Estate, Roehampton

LONDON BOROUGH OF WANDSWORTH

Gable hips formed with modern concrete half-round ridge tiles.

sufficient to make things happen. The real problem, however, is the cumulative effect of small-scale change.

Alterations to buildings, as opposed to demolition, are not controlled by conservation area designation and, since the *Shimizu* case, the device of 'partial demolition' is no longer available. Planning permission is required for 'development', which includes works having a material affect on buildings. Although this would appear to control alterations, there are wide-ranging automatic dispensations from this requirement, known as 'permitted development', and these apply particularly to dwellings. Needless to say, it is domestic property that, almost by definition, forms the majority of buildings in the suburbs.

Permitted development allows householders to change windows, doors (fig. 160) and roof materials (figs. 161–62), to alter boundary walls and to extend houses. Each change may have little impact, but the effect in chorus can seriously erode the special

163, 164

Woodgrange Estate, Forest Gate

LONDON BOROUGH OF NEWHAM

Originally, these villas of the 1880s had a uniform appearance with elegant verandas (left), *but many have since been altered virtually beyond recognition* (right).

character of a conservation area and undermine the very reason for designating it (figs. 163–64). In theory, it has always been possible to remove permitted development rights, thereby making it necessary to obtain planning permission, even for minor changes, by seeking an Article 4 direction, but the procedure for this, involving approval by central government, has proved very cumbersome.

In 1992 the English Historic Towns Forum published a report, *Townscape in Trouble*, which demonstrated the damaging effects of permitted development and the absurdity of a regime that could control changes to shops and flats but not houses. As a result, the government introduced a simplified version of the Article 4 direction which local authorities could make themselves, but there are still problems. A direction cannot give blanket coverage of an area, as the properties have to be identified individually. This is a time-consuming exercise and boroughs have to know whether houses are in single occupation, because those converted into flats must be excluded. Unsurprisingly, there are still very few Article 4 directions and alterations therefore continue unabated, fuelled by a heavily marketed replacement industry (fig. 165).

At the same time English Heritage, through its *Framing Opinions* campaign, has challenged this industry by showing how traditional joinery details cannot be replicated in plastic or aluminium; how timber windows may be cheaper when the whole life cycle of

165

Queen's Park Estate

CITY OF WESTMINSTER

Top-hung plastic imitations of sliding sashes
(left) *debase the value of the original windows*
(right).

166

Highgate (*bottom left*)

LONDON BOROUGH OF CAMDEN

Survival of the details of street surfaces is as
valuable as retaining the materials themselves.

167

Hampstead Garden Suburb (*bottom middle*)

LONDON BOROUGH OF BARNET

A new gateway into the suburb uses traditional
features to slow traffic.

168

Highgate (*bottom right*)

LONDON BOROUGH OF CAMDEN

Traffic calming with minimum visual impact on
its surrounding landscape.

costs is considered; and how thermal, sound and draught insulation standards can be achieved without resorting to double-glazing.

Similar considerations apply to the spaces between buildings. Although the 1967 Act made it a requirement for local authorities to designate conservation areas and to enhance them through the use of their planning powers, as Lord Kennet later reflected: 'It did not bind them to use their highway and transport powers to the same end, an omission which I came to regret not having fought to rectify.'[8] With no formal connection between conservation and highway engineering, much has been lost: traditional materials, street furniture and often the distinctive relationship between carriageway, verge and footpath. Much has also arrived: over-large signs, cable-television control boxes, yellow lines, red lines and parked cars. Of course, suburban streets have to evolve with modern needs, to cope with increasing traffic and decreasing budgets, but there is often more than one way to achieve this (figs. 166–68).

After many years of advising on individual cases, English Heritage is now publishing the *London Streetscape Manual* to offer guidance on best practice and how this can become everyday practice. With good analysis of local traditions and forward planning,

169

Trinity Church Square

LONDON BOROUGH OF SOUTHWARK

*Cast-iron railings help to define the character of
this outstanding square of 1824–32.*

simple design can achieve high quality and reduce the accretion of clutter that seems to
afflict most streets. Less complexity can actually reduce costs. Signs can be co-ordinated
on fewer poles; reducing the number of materials makes maintenance easier; and where,
for instance, bound gravel is an appropriate surface, it is less than a tenth the cost of York
stone. The *Manual* is more of a process than a product and is accompanied by a series of
practical demonstration seminars throughout Greater London to ensure that the messages are received.

170

**Bedford Park Estate, Turnham Green,
Chiswick**

LONDON BOROUGHS OF EALING AND
HOUNSLOW

*In contrast to the above, white wooden railings
help to define the character of this development,
begun in the 1870s.*

The planning controls that come with conservation areas also bring sanctions in the
form of enforcement and ultimately prosecution, but this is a social regime of collective
consent whereby those who embrace the system of mutual policy will benefit from the
implied threat of controls over their neighbours. This is at the heart of the conformity
that gives the suburbs their reputation for comfortable respectability and, of course, for
which they are also despised. However, the reinforcement of local identity (figs. 169–70)
brings further benefits: better resources, higher standards of public investment, a mecha-
nism for residents to be more involved and, commonly, added value to property.

In addition to the financial implications of enhancing everyday managerial decisions,
such as tree surgery and street cleansing, some boroughs are able to provide grants for
building repairs and community action. On a larger scale, funding tends to come from
external agencies such as the Single Regeneration Budget, the Housing Corporation,
English Heritage, the Heritage Lottery Fund and even European sources.

The criteria for these grants are generally based on a mix of heritage merit and public
need, tending, therefore, to favour the more economically and socially deprived areas.
Details have recently shifted too frequently for analysis to be relevant here, but, in the
current round (1998–2001) of Conservation Area Partnerships, funded jointly by English

171

No. 145 Southgate Road, Islington

LONDON BOROUGH OF ISLINGTON

The inappropriate paintwork – let alone the insensitive replacement windows – that distinguishes this Victorian house from its neighbours can be avoided by the adoption of a coherent management strategy in areas of historic interest.

Heritage and the Heritage Lottery Fund, London has secured almost 20% of the national budget. The addition of further contributions from other partners, such as the boroughs and property owners themselves, means an investment in London's conservation areas of at least £33.5 million. Haringey Council has secured funding through these means for repairs and the reinstatement of original details at Muswell Hill.

From 1999 the Heritage Lottery Fund will take on much of the responsibility for conservation area funding with its new Townscape Heritage Initiative. Of only nine schemes in England, one is for the regeneration of the Lansbury Estate in Tower Hamlets, which was built as a housing demonstration project in conjunction with the Festival of Britain in 1951.

The key to successful conservation of historic areas is a coherent management strategy (figs. 171–72; see also fig. 147). In its review *Conservation in London* (1995), English Heritage set the agenda with recommendations to:

- *Promote greater awareness of the extent of the historic environment in London*
- *Expand the focus of conservation from single buildings to the wider setting of London*
- *Provide a policy framework for effective management of the historic resource*
- *Make full use of all the measures available*
- *Promote a multi-disciplinary approach, including highways and traffic agencies*
- *Record the condition of the historic environment*
- *Set environmental targets.*

While these points are gradually working their way into the development plans for each borough, their councils have additionally responded in different ways. For instance, Barnet, which already includes the pre-eminent Hampstead Garden Suburb, has recently designated conservation areas for the Railway Terraces at Cricklewood and the Edwardian shops of Golders Green town centre, and is now looking at estates from the late 1930s. Hillingdon and Ealing take care to involve communities by respectively publishing a conservation newspaper and holding a regular forum for amenity groups. Wandsworth has published *Do it in Style*, a guide to the sensitive care and repair of suburban houses, while Haringey has published a repair and conservation guide for the Tower Gardens Estate to explain the reasons for strong planning policies. Many other London boroughs – notably Westminster – also publish material on conservation, much of which is available without charge.

Local residents can, and often do, become actively involved in the process too. The Civic Trust will advise on setting up amenity groups that can pool resources to research the history of a district and identify areas of special interest. Borough councils can be lobbied to make designations and groups can assist by defining character, suggesting policy and putting forward ideas for enhancement. Most boroughs also encourage the formation of conservation area advisory committees to give them local views on planning proposals. But management is a balancing act and too much involvement is, of course, as great a danger as too little. Over-precious nannying by a local authority or local amenity group may destroy the freedom to remain anonymous, which, for some, is the virtue of the suburb.

So what of the future for the suburb? Housing is still being created, but not with that spirit of place, the *genius loci*. Indeed, there is mounting criticism of the volume house-builders for the unimaginative quality of their product. The Popular Housing Forum, led by Robert Adam, has emerged to challenge the ubiquity of designs that owe more to a salesman's thin view of history than to the hand of an architect. Also, the greenbelt and the M25 motorway have encouraged housing to leapfrog beyond the metropolis so that today's commuters are as likely to travel from Peterborough or Winchester as yesterday's were from the City's outskirts.

Instead, are we seeing the post-suburban suburb? A re-colonization of the centre is cetainly well under way, as the Docklands are reinvented as housing; as areas such as Spitalfields are regentrified (figs. 173–74); and as developers discover that inner-city factory shells are worth more as empty 'lofts' than they are when converted to flats. This is the suburban backwash that can only gather strength as the pressure to develop 'brownfield' sites continues. Meanwhile, the conservation issue to address is the inconsistency with which London's boroughs recognize and responded to the qualities of their existing suburbs.

172

The Ridings, Hanger Hill Estate, Ealing
LONDON BOROUGH OF EALING
A successful extension achieved by using the existing form and details and appropriate materials.

NOTES

1. Raymond Unwin, *Town Planning in Practice: An Introduction to the Art of Designing Cities and Suburbs*, London 1909, pp. 3–4.
2. John Delafons, *Politics and Preservation*, London (E. and F.N. Spon) 1997, p. 96.
3. Wayland Kennet, *Preservation*, London 1972, p. 66
4. Civic Ameneties Act 1967. This wording appears in Section 69 of the Planning (Listed Buildings and Conservation Areas) Act 1990.
5. Ministry of Housing and Local Government Circular 53/67, London (HMSO) 1967.
6. Ministry of Housing and Local Government, *Historic Towns: Preservation and Change*, London (HMSO) 1967.
7. Department of the Environment, *Planning Policy Guidance: Planning and the Historic Environment (PPG15)*, London (HMSO) 1994, paragraph 4.4.
8. Wayland Kennet, *op. cit.*, p. 65

173, 174

Parfett Street (*left*) and
Myrdle Street (*right*), Whitechapel
LONDON BOROUGH OF TOWER HAMLETS
Parfett Street during, and nearby Myrdle Street after, repairs funded under English Heritage's Conservation Area Partnership.

Enfield

Barnet

Harrow

Haringey   Waltham   Redbridge
            Forest   Havering

Hillingdon   Brent   Camden   Hackney
                      Islington
                                  Barking &
                                  Dagenham

Ealing   Hammersmith   Westminster   City   Tower   Newham
              & Fulham   Hamlets

                      Kensington   Southwark
                      & Chelsea
Hounslow   Greenwich

              Richmond upon   Wandsworth   Lambeth   Bexley
              Thames
                                              Lewisham

              Kingston   Merton
              upon
              Thames   Bromley

                      Sutton   Croydon

Gazetteer

This gazetteer does not claim to be comprehensive; rather, it includes developments, groups of buildings or, in some cases, individual properties that, for reasons such as innovation, embodiment of theoretical ideas or degree of survival in their original form, encapsulate some of the special qualities of London's suburban development in a given period.

GLC   Greater London Council (1965–86; successor to the LCC)
LCC   London County Council (1888–1965; precursor to the GLC)
LDDC   London Docklands Development Corporation (1981–98)
p.p.a.   persons per acre (a measurement of population density)

Only inner-London postcodes (beginning N, E, S or W) are given.
Entries are listed chronologically within each borough, to reflect the organization of the preceding chapters.

London Borough of

BARKING AND DAGENHAM

Between the Wars: 1914–1940

Becontree Estate, Dagenham

Begun in 1921, this enormous estate was the largest of all the LCC housing projects. Occupying no fewer than 277 acres in the area around Valence House (which was retained as a historic core, with its immediate grounds), the estate consisted of some 26,000 houses, primarily semi-detached, laid out around the wide expanses of Parsloes Park. The prevalent material is brick, with some rough-cast, and tiled roofs. Many of the semis are entered through shared arched openings; decorative features are sparingly applied. The sheer scale of this estate is daunting to behold. The estate is not a conservation area, although Valence House (a largely seventeenth-century manor with medieval origins) and St Mary's Church (Welch, Cachemaille-Day and Lander, 1934) are listed.

London Borough of

BARNET

Aristocratic to Middle Class: 1690–1840

Hadley Green Road, Monken Hadley

Londoners began to settle around the Green in
Monken Hadley in the early eighteenth century.
The surviving group of Georgian and early
nineteenth-century houses here (❍ pictured below)

and near the parish church retain something of the
village quality that was once common in London's
suburbs. Interestingly, this area was one of the first
conservation areas to be designated – in 1968 –
within the boundaries of the former GLC.

Infinite Variety: 1840–1914

Moss Hall Crescent, Finchley, N12

This small conservation area consists of nineteenth-
century villas, some of which have been converted
into flats.

Hampstead Garden Suburb, Golders Green, NW11

The jewel in the crown of London's suburbs,
Hampstead Garden Suburb represents a milestone
in the history of the planned estate. The brainchild
of Henrietta Barnett, 'the Suburb' (as it was called)
was developed by a trust after 1906 to a layout
designed by Raymond Unwin, fresh from building at

Letchworth Garden City. The crucial ideas were to
keep densities low; to set the houses in generous
front and back gardens divided by hedges rather
than walls; and to build the houses in asymmetrical
compositions rather than follow the rigid 'by-law'
building lines. Unwin also designed many of the
houses in Arts and Crafts rural vernacular styles.
The picturesque street and cul-de-sac planning
contrasts with the formal centre, which is the work
of Sir Edwin Lutyens: the Central Square, two
churches, the Institute and grand classical houses,
of 1908–14. The suburb contains buildings by major
Arts and Crafts architects including M.H. Baillie
Scott, Geoffrey Lucas, Courteney Crickmer and
Michael Bunney.

The northern and eastern areas are post-1914.
These later enclaves include Southwood Court
(❍ pictured right) and Bigwood Court (both Soutar,
1925), ranges of flats around three sides of a court

in a Wren-influenced style, erected originally for
ex-servicemen; and Hutchings Walk and Howard
Walk, containing well-preserved semis of 1935–36

with sun-trap windows by Crickmer. The whole
of Hampstead Garden Suburb is in a conservation
area with many listed buildings representing a range
of types and styles.

Between the Wars: 1914–1940

Finchley Garden Village (south-west of Church End), Finchley, N3

A development by the Finchley Co-Partnership begun in 1909 and designed on garden city principles. The core of the development is Village Road. The cottages and houses are in a rural vernacular style (rough-cast and gabled), and grouped in pairs around a central green.

Aeroville, Colindale, NW9

Built in 1918–19 by Herbert Matthews for the Grahame-White aircraft manufacturing company. The small estate is similar to Roe Green (see **London Borough of Brent**), another wartime housing development for aviation workers. A quadrangle of houses, collegiate in feel, borders a square resembling a parade-ground, with English Renaissance details such as a colonnade along the north side. Built in the standard vernacular materials of brick, tile and rough-cast, this was all that was erected of a larger scheme.

Watling Estate, Burnt Oak

A large estate of ca. 4000 houses with some flats, built by the LCC as one of its 'out-county' estates in 1926–30: only the Becontree Estate in Dagenham (see **London Borough of Barking and Dagenham**) exceeded it in size. Laid out on the garden city principle, it took advantage of

the Northern Line extension of the Underground and enabled a generously laid-out estate to be created. The houses are built in a variety of materials including brick, rough-cast, tile- and slate-hanging and weather-boarding (● *pictured above*). Neighbours in private estates allegedly referred to the estate as 'Little Moscow'. Designated a conservation area.

Edgware

Often described as *the* Underground suburb, Edgware developed rapidly following the arrival of the Northern Line extension in 1923. The station, in a restrained neo-Georgian, is by S.A. Heap. Near by are numerous shopping parades, a good Wren-style bank (Palmer and Holden, 1928) and the exceptional Railway Hotel (● *pictured above*), a mock-Tudor extravaganza of 1931 by A.E. Sewell. All about are streets of homogeneous semi-detached houses: half-timbered in Purcell Avenue, modern and green-tiled in Mowbray Road.

The Bishop's Avenue, Highgate, N2

This road continued to attract wealthy and celebrated residents such as Gracie Fields (whose own house has since been demolished). Notable inter-war survivals include Gable Lodge of 1927 by P.D. Hepworth, in a Cape Dutch style, and the bogus half-timbered pile Kenstead Hall. The road (also known as 'Millionaires' Row') now epitomizes the super-rich, edge-of-town suburb and is distinguished by a growing number of distinctly queer mock-classical piles set behind security gates.

The Road to Subtopia: 1940 to the present

Grahame Park, NW9

A collaboration of 1969–76 between the GLC, the local authority and private developers to build a large new neighbourhood on land released by the Ministry of Defence. One of the largest of the GLC's developments, it features a long spine of shops and maisonettes, built to shield the rest of the development from the nearby M1 motorway and to separate pedestrian and traffic areas. The scheme is reminiscent, on a smaller scale, of the LCC's unbuilt but much published design for Hook New Town, of 1961. The recent addition at Grahame Park of pitched roofs has disfigured the careful unity of dark brick elevations, pathways and retaining walls.

London Borough of
BEXLEY

Aristocratic to Middle Class: 1690–1840

Danson House

By the late eighteenth century Bexley in Kent was popular with City merchants. Danson was the grandest of the new suburban estates in the parish, extended in the 1760s and given a new Palladian house. In the 1920s the outlying lands of the estate were sold for redevelopment. Many of the streets adjacent to Danson Park take their form from the field patterns of the former estate.

Infinite Variety: 1840–1914

The Green, Sidcup

This conservation area is important precisely for its dearth of buildings: it is the broad green spaces of Sidcup that distinguishes it from many other

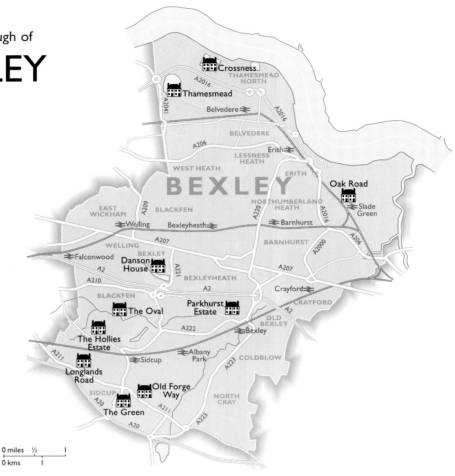

metropolitan suburbs. The open area of The Green continues to provide an informal recreation site and a venue for annual fêtes and fairs. It is the vegetation, as much as the late nineteenth-century cottages and Edwardian villas bordering The Green, that is prized in this part of Bexley: the colourful flowering cherries, hollies, hazels and horse-chestnuts, pines and Wellingtonia, as well as an avenue of London planes. The scenic qualities of the area (❍ *pictured above*) have long been recognized: Walsham's *Directory* of 1898 wrote of newly erected Sidcup homes: 'the style of architecture being varied, the monotonous

appearance common to many modern roads is obviated'. The area is considered 'fragile' and any proposals for new development are particularly well scrutinized.

Crossness, Erith

The Crossness Sewage Works were designed by Sir Joseph Bazalgette, chief engineer to the Metropolitan Board of Works, and his engineers, and completed in 1865. The works formed part of a system that would prevent any sewage from the metropolis being disposed of into the Thames near densely populated sites, hence the need to locate the works away from those areas and where the sewage could be released into the river immediately after high tide and carried downstream. A monument to Victorian engineering prowess, the Crossness Works occupy a site of 37 acres and include the splendid Beam Engine Pump House (listed Grade I), workshops and outbuildings,

workers' cottages, and a reservoir for the sewage. This important industrial complex, now open to visitors, is all contained within the Crossness Conservation Area.

Parkhurst Estate, Bexley Village

The Parkhurst Estate consists of large villas for the well-to-do built following the arrival of the railway in 1866. Examples of the earliest houses survive in Upton Road South with a variety of styles including castellation on no. 240. Development continued to the north-east in 1876 and was completed within a decade with semi-detached villas. The area is characterized by wide roads and elegant, detached houses with mature trees in long rear gardens, particularly in Parkhurst Road. Chimney-stacks and chimney-pots, gabled dormers and finials make an interesting and varied skyline (❍ *pictured opposite above*). Some façades have bay windows surmounted by pierced balustrades; others have patterned brickwork and central recessed porches. The estate forms the core of the Parkhurst Conservation Area.

Oak Road, Slade Green, Erith

A small estate of railway workers' cottages built by the South East and Chatham Railway Company in 1900. The cottages remained in railway ownership for many years and consequently have survived as an unusual example of a company-built estate of cottages worthy of protection. The cottages are set out in groups of four, the central ones in each group having paired entrances below a central porch, with the end houses having recessed entrances on the flank walls, creating the appearance of a single building with a central entrance. A corner pub near by, contemporary with the cottage estate, is the Railway Tavern, and is similar in character and style. The estate and the pub comprise the Oak Road Conservation Area.

Between the Wars: 1914–1940

Longlands Road, Sidcup

Late 1920s' semi-detached houses by the builders Cory and Cory: a good survival of speculative housing of its day with tile-hung bays, leaded windows and timber porches.

The Hollies Estate, Sidcup

Early 1930s by H. Smith and Co., builders of Eltham. An above-average enclave, centring on Willersley Avenue and Braundton Avenue consisting of gabled semis with prominent chimney-stacks. Designated a conservation area.

The Oval, Sidcup

An imposing development of 1933, consisting of a row of half-timbered houses with shops, with matching flats behind, set back from an oval green. This area characterizes the suburban tendency for shopping parades to form centres of local interest amid otherwise repetitive zones of housing. Designated a conservation area.

Old Forge Way, Sidcup

An unusual development of 1936, consisting of a cul-de-sac of cottages and houses (with garages) designed in a Wealden vernacular style by Kenneth Dalgleish (1887–1964). The intention was to create an organic extension to Sidcup High Street; an early

instance of a contextual approach to suburban development. Designated a conservation area.

The Road to Subtopia: 1940 to the present

Thamesmead, SE2

This is the only complete New Town development within Greater London. Proposed from the early 1960s, a master plan was produced by the GLC in 1967, but it was much altered as building fashions changed in the 1970s. Thamesmead South, the only

area to be completed as planned (1969; ◗ *pictured above*), demonstrates the underlying philosophy of the plan, with pedestrian walkways and access to all flats set at first-floor level because of the risk of flooding. The contrasts between the tall blocks of flats, the long slab of Binsey Walk and Southmere Lake can appear genuinely dramatic. In later phases system-built towers gave way to conventional brick houses, some by the GLC, others privately built.

London Borough of
BRENT

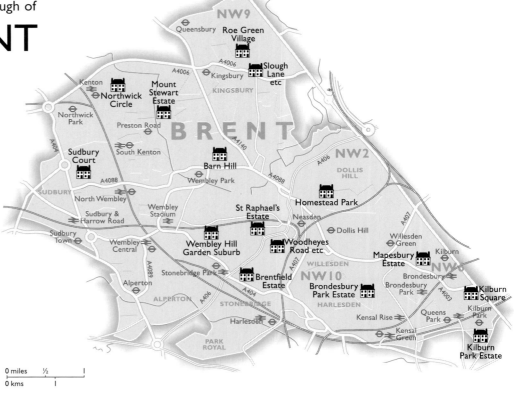

Infinite Variety: 1840–1914

Brondesbury Park Estate, NW2, NW6 and NW10
Typical of the development of the borough in the mid- to late nineteenth century. Heathfield Park (1883, ○ *pictured below*), Willesden Green, shows

the influence of Bedford Park, Turnham Green (see **London Borough of Ealing**), and the Norman Shaw school. Designated a conservation area.

Kilburn Park Estate, NW6
This area, comprising the North Kilburn and South Kilburn Conservation Areas, represents the typical development of the borough in the mid- to late nineteenth century: the work of several builders' firms for houses in a variety of styles with well-preserved details.

Mapesbury Estate, NW2
An estate of typical Victorian houses. Designated a conservation area.

Woodheyes Road and Gresham Road, NW10
A development of railway-workers' cottages (each cottage only one window wide), built in 1899 for the Great Central Railway. Designated a conservation area.

Between the Wars: 1914–1940

Roe Green Village, Kingsbury, NW9
Developed in 1916–20 by (Sir) Frank Baines of HM Office of Works. Based firmly on the Hampstead Garden Suburb prototype, this is an outstanding enclave of workers' houses erected in connection with the Aircraft Manufacturing Company factory at the adjoining Stag Lane aerodrome: this employed nearly 4500 people at the close of the War. Winding roads, a variety of materials (with slate and render predominating), a village green and old trees: it is difficult to believe that this was erected during a world war as part of a munitions programme. Designated a conservation area.

Brentfield Estate, Harlesden, NW10
Built in 1919–21 by F. Wilkinson, borough engineer of Willesden Council. An adaptation of the Parker and Unwin theme of grouped cottages. Centred around Conduit Way, these were the first municipal houses in the area, built in response to the Housing and Town Planning Act of 1919.

Northwick Circle, Kenton
One of the distinctive mock-Tudor estates developed by Captain E.G. Spencer-Churchill (a cousin of the former Prime Minister), begun in 1923 and built by Frederick and Charles Costin. The distinctive circus-like open space has a Masonic Centre in its midst: an unusual amenity for an outer suburb. Designated a conservation area.

Wembley Hill Garden Suburb, Wembley Hill
A continuation of Sir Audrey Neeld's garden city development, carried out by the builders Callow and Wright, and including houses designed by Oliver Hill in 1924 set amid tree-lined streets. This further development of the suburb coincided with the British Empire Exhibition of 1924–25.

Homestead Park, Dollis Hill, NW2
Built in 1926 by W.E. Sanders. An enclave of suburban properties in which the twenty traditionally detailed houses are laid out in Y-shaped groups and share a common service core: an unusual and influential concession to functionality. Designated a conservation area.

Slough Lane, Stag Lane and Buck Lane, Kingsbury, NW9

These winding roads, located just to the east of the carefully preserved fields of the Fryent Country Park, contain outstanding groups of timber cottages by E.G. Trobridge (1884–1942). No houses more clearly reveal the yearning for a lost rural past that characterized the inter-war London suburb. Heavy undulating roofs of thatch top low walls sheathed in ragged timber boarding. Such houses include nos. 134, 142, 148, 152–56 Slough Lane (some of which are listed Grade II); nos. 3–5, 43–45 Buck Lane; and nos. 345–351 Stag Lane (**ⵔ** *pictured top right*), all of 1921–30. Also in Buck Lane are Trobridge's stone blocks of flats of 1934–36 (such as Rochester Court and Whitecastle Mansions), which reveal his dalliance with castle architecture. The above-average late 1920s' pub, the Green Man, fittingly has a bar named the Trobridge. The jettied and weather-boarded parade of shops on Hay Lane (**ⵔ** *pictured bottom right*) is also remarkable. Partly designated a conservation area.

Sudbury Court, Wembley

An above-average estate of mock-Tudor houses, begun in 1929 by the developers Comben and Wakeling, enriched with a variety of vernacular features such as cat-slide roofs and brick nogging. Designated a conservation area.

Mount Stewart Estate, Preston Hill

A 1930s' estate by Frederick and Charles Costin: a representative group of mock-Tudor houses (compare Northwick Circle, Kenton; *see above*) by one of the leading developers of inter-war north-west London. Designated a conservation area.

Barn Hill, Wembley

The rising ground to the north of Forty Avenue, commanding a fine view over west London, was developed by the Haymills company from 1926 onwards. They employed the architectural practice of Welch, Cachemaille-Day and Lander and laid out a complex of undulating roads that reveals the transition from humble half-timbered bungalow to modern concrete box. The former are best seen on Barn Hill, the latter in Mayfield. Lawns Court consists of a row of six stark concrete blocks by the same architects, completed in 1934 with powerfully expressed stairs. Compare the Hanger Hill Estate (see **London Borough of Ealing**). Part designated a conservation area.

The Road to Subtopia: 1940 to the present

Kilburn Square, Kilburn High Road, NW6

Towers of council flats from 1964, with a two-level shopping centre facing the main road added in 1967–71 by Ardin and Brookes. The development is an unloved and under-maintained ensemble.

St Raphael's Estate, Besant Way, NW10

A development of *ca.* 1965 onwards by the London Borough of Brent, with three- and four-storey terraced maisonettes, the upper flats reached by long walkways. More pleasant is a smaller group of houses of the 1970s in the nearby Dorman Walk.

London Borough of
BROMLEY

Infinite Variety: 1840–1914

Bickley Park Road Estate, Bickley Park

Developed from 1861, but best known for houses designed by Ernest Newton, pupil of R. Norman Shaw and resident of Bickley, who built houses in and around Bickley Road, Page Heath Lane and Chislehurst Road (**o** *pictured below*) between 1885 and 1902. Good examples of Newton's houses can be seen at no. 13 Denbridge Road and at Bullers Wood near by. Other houses on the estate are by C.H.B. Quennell and Amos Faulkner.

Camden Park Road, Wilderness Road and Chislehurst Road, Chislehurst

Large detached housing in a crisp Vernacular Revival style, 1890–1914, by the builders Willetts, with designs by C.H.B. Quennell and Ernest Newton. A re-adoption of vernacular construction (timber framing) and materials (small red-clay tiles for roofs, and finely detailed red-brick chimney-shafts) for the houses set among trees and large-scale shrubberies. Near by is the Wilderness Road Estate developed by Willetts from 1893, with individual houses designed by key Arts and Crafts architects. Some listed buildings; all in extensive conservation areas.

Between the Wars: 1914–1940

Station Square, Petts Wood

A neo-Tudor set-piece close to the new station of Petts Wood, developed (like much of Petts Wood)

by Basil Scruby and Leonard Culliford. The shop-lined square was completed by 1930, and its centre was filled by the matching Daylight Inn (so named because William Willett first thought of putting the clocks back while riding near here in the 1880s). Designated a conservation area.

Biggin Hill Aerodrome

The aerodrome, famous as a fighter station in the Battle of Britain and after, was built largely in 1931–32. Its officers' mess and station HQ buildings (**o** *pictured below*), designed in a chaste

neo-Georgian, are representative of the public buildings erected throughout the suburbs at this date. A close of housing built for other ranks survives too. Designated a conservation area; the officers' mess is listed.

Mottingham Estate, Mottingham, SE9

An LCC 'out-county' cottage estate, begun with the acquisition of some 200 acres in 1931 and largely completed by 1935; over 2300 houses, designed in the usual restrained brick style of the LCC, were eventually built. The irregularity of street lay-outs and house design, and the generous provision of open spaces (such as the retention of Marvels Wood), created a varied, uncrowded enclave on the edge of the city. Part of the estate lies in the London Borough of Lewisham.

The Chenies, Petts Wood

A smart development of detached houses, built in the early 1930s by Noel Rees, laid out around a curving cul-de-sac (which kept traffic to a minimum). Most of the houses are neo-Tudor; others have a touch of the Arts and Crafts. A late but successful appearance of the garden suburb. Designated a conservation area.

Chislehurst Road, Petts Wood

Another garden suburb of the 1930s, developed by Basil Scruby and the architect Leonard Culliford. Birchwood Road has mainly half-timbered houses: Tudor House of 1930 is particularly good. Designated a conservation area.

The Road to Subtopia: 1940 to the present

West Oak, The Avenue, Beckenham

A small Span estate developed by Eric Lyons around 1960. It is a good site, sloping and particularly leafy, which was enhanced by Lyons to frame his tile-hung and weather-boarded terraces.

Greatwood, Yester Road, Chislehurst

A series of short, staggered, three-storey terraces of 1962 by Norman Sherratt, in charcoal-grey brick with white balconies. Close by is no. 13 Camden Park Road (Robert Byron, 1970), an inventive intrusion into the Willetts development (see Camden Park Road etc *above*). Beyond Beechcroft in Yester Road is a pair of houses (Goddard and Phillips, 1973) with dramatic cats-slide roofs.

Hayesford Park, Hayes

A low-rise private development of *ca.* 1962–65 by the Building Design Partnership. The influence of the garden city movement is evident, down to the naming of the principal road as Letchworth Drive. Detached houses are set in picturesque groups around central shops. The single block of flats has a particularly lushly landscaped courtyard. Proposed a conservation area in the early 1990s.

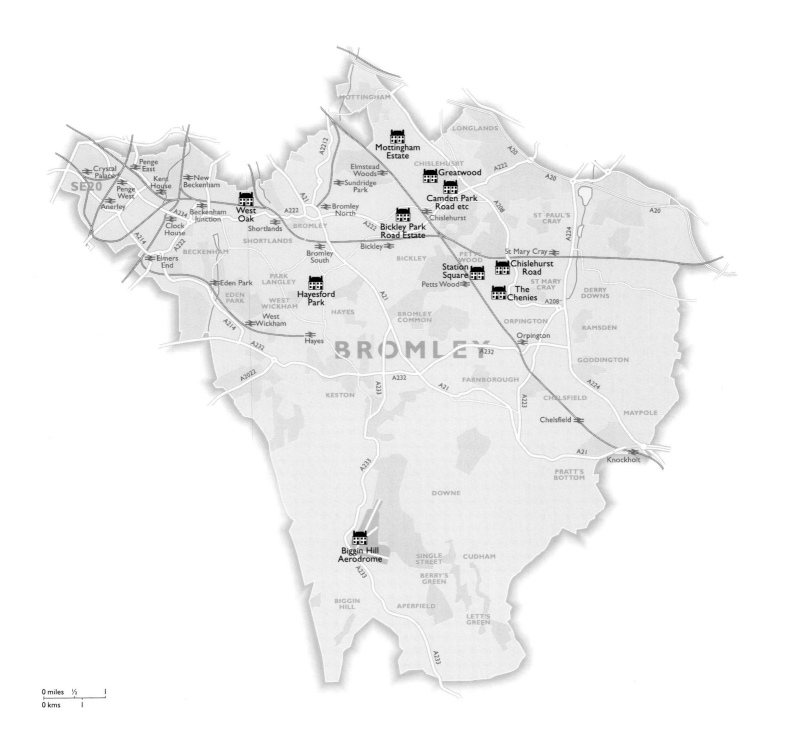

Crystal
Palace

Penge
East

Kent
House

New
Beckenham

MOTTINGHAM

LONGLANDS

Mottingham
Estate

A20

SE20

Penge
West

Anerley

Clock
House

A214

Beckenham
Junction

A234

A222

West
Oak

Shortlands

A21

A222

Bromley
North

BROMLEY

Elmstead
Woods

Sundridge
Park

CHISLEHURST

Greatwood

A222

A20

Camden Park
Road etc

A208

Bickley Park
Road Estate

Chislehurst

ST PAUL'S
CRAY

A20

Elmers
End

BECKENHAM

SHORTLANDS

A222

Bromley
South

Bickley

BICKLEY

PETTS
WOOD

St Mary Cray

A224

Eden Park

EDEN
PARK

PARK
LANGLEY

Hayesford
Park

Station
Square

Chislehurst
Road

ST MARY
CRAY

DERRY
DOWNS

WEST
WICKHAM

West
Wickham

HAYES

Petts Wood

The
Chenies

A208

A214

A232

Hayes

BROMLEY
COMMON

BROMLEY

A21

ORPINGTON

Orpington

RAMSDEN

GODDINGTON

A2022

KESTON

A232

A232

A233

A21

FARNBOROUGH

A223

CHELSFIELD

A224

MAYPOLE

Chelsfield

A21

Knockholt

A233

DOWNE

PRATT'S
BOTTOM

Biggin Hill
Aerodrome

SINGLE
STREET

CUDHAM

A233

BERRY'S
GREEN

BIGGIN
HILL

APERFIELD

LETT'S
GREEN

0 miles   ½

0 kms

London Borough of
CAMDEN

Victorian values. Although no strict covenants were contained with the leases, the whole estate had achieved a remarkable coherence by the time development was complete in the 1870s.

Infinite Variety: 1840–1914

Holly Village, Swains Lane, N6

A compact group of detached houses in an ornate Gothic style, set in grounds with mature trees. Designed in 1865 for Baroness Burdett-Coutts by Henry Darbishire. Some listed buildings; also designated a conservation area.

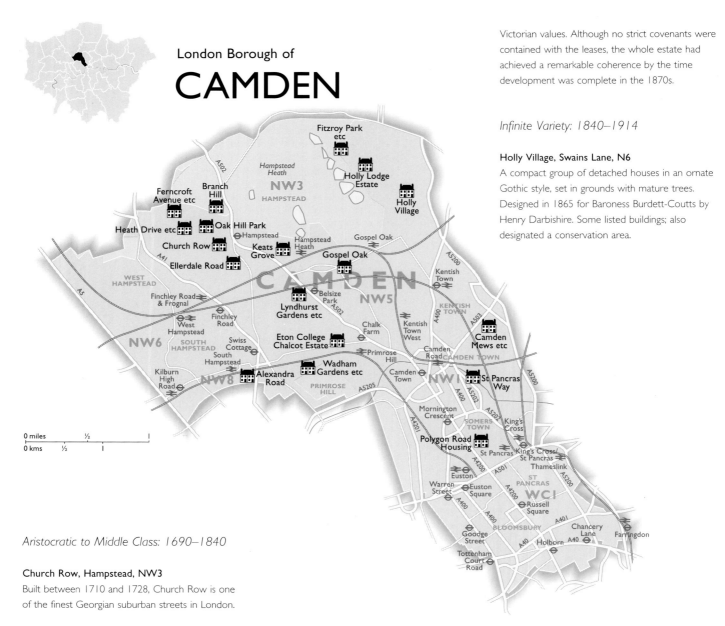

Aristocratic to Middle Class: 1690–1840

Church Row, Hampstead, NW3

Built between 1710 and 1728, Church Row is one of the finest Georgian suburban streets in London.

Keats Grove, Hampstead, NW3

Keats Grove, known originally as Downshire Hill and John Street, was developed from 1812 with smart villas by one William Coleman. The houses were designed by different hands, and there was a proprietary chapel at one end, giving the ensemble the right moral tone. Keats's friends, the Dilkes and the Browns, were among the first to build here. Keats himself lived in the house known as Lawn Bank from 1818 to 1820.

Regent's Park, NW1
See **City of Westminster**

Eton College Chalcot Estate, NW3

Encouraged by the success of the Eyre Estate in St John's Wood and by Nash's prestige development of the Crown Estates as Regent's Park, Eton College made plans for a complete villa quarter here, west of Haverstock Hill, in the late 1820s, but not much happened until the early 1840s when John Shaw jnr, the College Surveyor, re-drew the plans, reducing dramatically the size of individual plots. A variety of builders moved in, filling the streets around Adelaide Road with villas that have been said to embody middle-class

Lyndhurst Gardens, Wedderburn Road and Belsize Crescent; Eton Avenue and Strathray Gardens; Elsworthy Road, Wadham Gardens and Harley Road; NW3

Developments carried out between 1870 and 1910 by architects Harry Measures and Amos Faulkner and built by Willetts. Composed mainly of large detached houses in a variety of styles from Italianate to Vernacular Revival. Some listed buildings; most within a designated conservation area.

Ferncroft Avenue, Hollycroft Avenue and Rosecroft Avenue, NW3

Developments comprising substantial red-brick detached and semi-detached houses of 1895–1910 by C.H.B. Quennell. Some listed; all in a designated conservation area.

Wadham Gardens, south of Adelaide Road and the western end of Elsworthy Road, NW3

This area was developed after 1895. Large, detached houses are picturesquely grouped along curved roads. This is a Willetts development, mostly designed by Amos Faulkner, with a profusion of patterned tile-hanging and rough-cast, domed corner bays, gables and porches with shell hoods.

Heath Drive, Redington Gardens, Redington Road, Templewood Avenue and Templewood Gardens, NW3

Developed in high-quality materials in vernacular styles, 1905–20, by G.W. Hart and his architect C.H.B. Quennell, and others. Here the transition from Gothic eclecticism through Queen Anne to the precursors of neo-Georgian can be seen in the styles of these handsome detached houses. In Platt's Lane, no. 8 is Voysey's celebrated house of 1895 for his father, with sloping buttresses, rough-cast and little ornament. Designated conservation areas.

Ellerdale Road, NW3

Part of the Greenhill Estate developed from 1875 with grand Gothic villas, many by T.K. Green. Also includes R. Norman Shaw's own tall, asymmetrical house, no. 6, of 1874–76.

Between the Wars: 1914–1940

Holly Lodge Estate, Highgate, N6

Begun in 1923, this remarkable development of half-timbered houses and flats took its cue from Baroness Burdett-Coutts's Holly Village (see above) and was laid out on the sloping site of her estate. A select development, it mixed family houses with ranks of blocks of flats – also half-timbered – intended for 'lady workers', who were provided with a restaurant and social centre. Designated a conservation area.

The Road to Subtopia: 1940 to the present

St Pancras Way flats, NW1

These flats now seem a small and modest development, but they were one of the largest groups to be built in the initial phase of reconstruction led by the borough councils in the late 1940s. Built in 1947–50 to the designs of Norman and Dawbarn, they were awarded a Festival of Britain Merit Award. The six blocks are eye-catching in their massing but simple in their detailing, just brick and cheap corrugated balcony fronts. A similar group in Dalston, the Wilton Estate, is less homogeneous in its grouping.

Gospel Oak, NW5

A redevelopment area in the post-war period that attracted a number of interesting developments, the focus first of St Pancras Metropolitan Borough and then of the distinctive Camden housing idiom. The key components are Powell and Moya's Barrington Court and surrounding terraces (1952–54), originally brightly coloured; and Dunboyne Road (originally Fleet Road II), of 1969–76 to the designs of Neave Brown for Camden Architect's Department. A more delicate and intimate design by the architect of the Alexandra Road Estate (see below), with a mixture of private patios and semi-public squares that give access to the upper flats. Providing a neo-Georgian contrast near by are Farquharson and McMorran's Barnfield and Woodfield Flats for Hampstead Metropolitan Borough.

Oak Hill Park, Hampstead, NW3

Three towers, two lower blocks of flats and a single house of 1961–65, built in two phases by Michael Lyell Associates. They show how crisp and elegant the Modern Movement can be when expensive finishes (in this case marble) were used and the buildings are properly maintained. The landscaped grounds are particularly elegant.

Fitzroy Park and Millfield Lane, Highgate, N6

An area of largely one-off houses from the post-war period by a number of architects. Fitzroy Park is a leafy meander; the houses, interesting individually, become still more so as they can be enjoyed as a group. No. 6 was designed by Erhard Lorenz (1962) for the engineer Ove Arup. Nos. 7 and 7a are by June Park (1957) for herself and her architect husband, Cyril Mardall, and for her

mother. No. 8 is by Higgins and Ney (1966), an unusual luxury house for the period. Adjoining are two closes of houses, The Hexagon by Leonard Michaels (1960) and Highfields Grove (late 1970s). There are also houses by C.G. Stillman and Stephen Gardiner (1952).

Camden Mews and Murray Mews, Camden Town, NW1

An area of artists' houses which became fashionable in the early 1960s. Camden Mews is most noted for no. 62, by Edward Cullinan, built for himself and his wife in 1962–65. Also by Cullinan is no. 16 Murray Street, built in 1983 for a disabled client. Nos. 15–19 Murray Mews is the first scheme by Team 4 (including Norman Foster and Richard Rogers), of 1964–65. No. 22 (1970–71) is by Tom Kay. Best of all are Cliff Road Studios (1968 and 1972) by Georgie Wolton: the affinity with the work by Team 4 is striking.

Alexandra Road Estate, NW8

Two terraces of flats, and a third of houses separated by a small park. The longest and highest terrace, shielding the area from the adjacent railway, is claimed to be the longest in Europe. Built in 1972–78 to the designs of Neave Brown, it is the flagship of the London Borough of Camden's enterprising policy of low-rise, high-density housing developments and among the first post-war public housing in Britain to be listed. Listed Grade II*; conservation area designated to include adjoining hostels by Evans and Shalev.

Branch Hill, NW3

Built in 1974–78 by Gordon Benson and Alan Forsyth for the London Borough of Camden. The last and among the most successful of Camden's low-rise housing schemes. The sloping site and restrictive covenants inspired a series of paired units that step down the hillside, with rooftop gardens.

Polygon Road Housing, NW1

Low-rise, high-density flats of 1976 in striking red brick by the London Borough of Camden with Roman Halter Associates and James Gowan.

City of London

See London Borough of Islington and the City of London

London Borough of
CROYDON

Infinite Variety: 1840–1914

The Waldrons and Bramley Hill

A picturesque development dating from the 1850s and laid out with winding roads and semi-detached or detached Italianate mansions. One group is arranged around an informal crescent facing an island with trees. In Bramley Hill is a small group of villas in different styles. The Waldrons is in a designated conservation area; Bramley Hill is not.

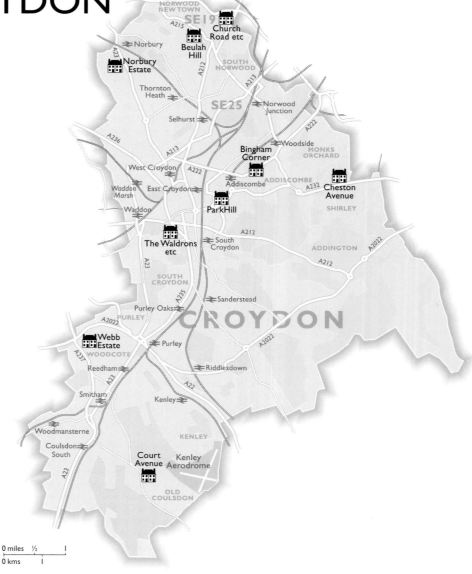

Beulah Hill, Upper Norwood, SE19

Some substantial middle-class houses from the 1860s to 1880s, when land from the Beulah Spa Estate was sold off in plots. The most quirky, no. 54 Beulah Hill (**⊙** *pictured above*), is by builder–architect Sextus Dyball.

Norbury Estate, Norbury Road, SW16

The first cottage estate to be built by the LCC as a suburb i.e. beyond its boundaries. It is an undulating 30-acre site, developed from 1905 to the layout and designs of the Architects' Department. One of the four LCC developments that refined the planning and grouping of small suburban houses, becoming the model from which two-storey suburban public housing was developed nationally. A grid of roads lined with houses in a mixture of brick and rough-cast with slate roofs, with some shops but no pubs. The later parts around Isham Road (1919–21) reflect the influence of Hampstead Garden Suburb, with winding roads and asymmetrical groups of houses.

Webb Estate, Woodcote Village, Purley

Developed from 1888 by William Webb, a local estate agent and keen horticulturist. Webb published his thoughts on housing development in *Gardens First* (1919), in which he emphasized the importance of integrating buildings with landscape: landscape features were laid before the houses were built. Following the creation of

the green and its surroundings, the roads of the estate were gradually developed, usually to incorporate a specific planting scheme. Rose Walk (❍ *pictured top left*), Silver Lane (with rows of silver birch) and so on, were planted up alongside the new roads and the houses were built only when the landscape had partially matured, from 1901. The houses themselves are mostly half-timbered. After World War I the Promenade de Verdun (❍ *pictured top right*) was laid out as a tribute to French sacrifices on the Western Front: a row of poplars was planted in French soil, especially brought over, and an obelisk was erected. It is perhaps the most funereal of suburban developments. Designated a conservation area.

Between the Wars: 1914–1940

Court Avenue, Bradmore Green

A characterful enclave of half-timbered houses of the late 1920s, some with castellated brick porches, mullioned windows with leaded lights and other picturesque devices from the speculative builder's repertory. Designated a local area of special character.

Bingham Corner, Lower Addiscombe Road, Addiscombe

An exceptionally ambitious parade of half-timbered shops, built in 1932, located among the suburban stretches of inter-war Croydon.

Cheston Avenue, Shirley

A late 1930s' development of modern brick semis featuring curved corners, metal windows and the odd decorative sun-ray. Designated a local area of special character.

The Road to Subtopia: 1940 to the present

Church Road/Westow Hill, Upper Norwood, SE19

Some good public housing of 1956 in Sylvan Hill by Riches and Blythin, and tight-knit private housing of 1975–81 by Clifford Davies Partnership for Barratts. They form a group with the Central Hill development just over the border in the **London Borough of Lambeth**.

Park Hill, Croydon

An extensive development on the Church Commissioners Estate by Wates, dating mainly from 1962–70 and using a variety of architects. Hill Rise (1962–63) by Wates's in-house architect K.W. Bland, repeats many ideas first explored by

Span Developments Ltd. Later groups of flats and houses include work by outside architects, including F.G. MacManus and Partners at Turnpike Link (1966–68; ❍ *pictured above*) and – most remarkably – St Bernard's, consisting of twenty-one terraced houses on a steep slope by Anatole du Fresne of Atelier 5, the Swiss firm that pioneered inventive planning on hillside sites in the late 1950s.

London Borough of

EALING

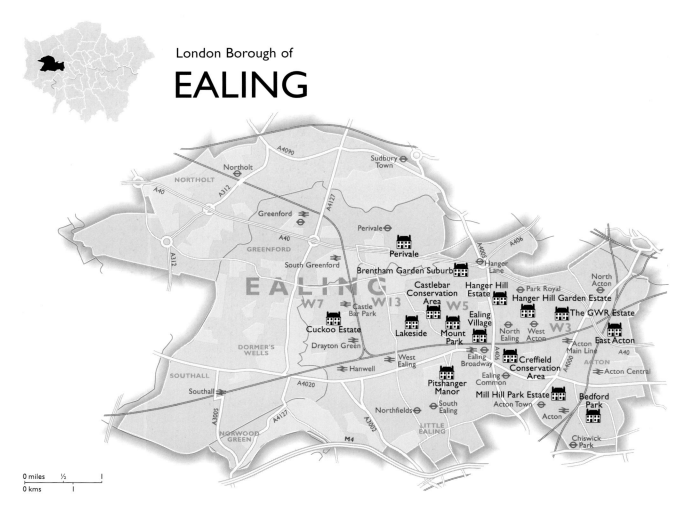

0 miles ½

0 kms

Aristocratic to Middle-Class: 1690–1840

Pitshanger Manor, Ealing Green, W5

Designed by the architect Sir John Soane as his own suburban retreat, and expanding an earlier house built by his master George Dance the younger, Pitshanger is one of the finest and most interesting late Georgian houses in London. The south wing is all that remains of the earlier house and it boasts interiors with fine Adam-style plasterwork. Soanes addition, completed in 1803, is a grandiose affair, its centrepiece adorned by four giant columns with statues on top. Soane sold it in 1811 to move back into town, taking the Lincolns Inn Fields site that now houses Sir John Soane's Museum.

Infinite Variety: 1840–1914

Bedford Park, Turnham Green (also partly in the London Borough of Hounslow), W4

London's famous artistic estate developed by the speculator Jonathan Carr after 1875 for the burgeoning bourgeoisie. Medium-to-large detached and semi-detached houses with front and rear gardens designed by architects E.W. Godwin, Richard Norman Shaw and E.J. May, and later Maurice Adams and William Wilson. Between them, these architects provided a stock of about thirty prototype designs for detached and semi-detached houses that were built throughout the estate. It was Shaw who created the architectural character of Bedford Park, which, by the end of the 1870s, became known as the 'Queen Anne style' – the style of the aesthetic movement – characterized by red brick, tile-hung gables, tall chimneys and white-painted bay windows (❍ *pictured right*). A

novelty was the lack of basements and rear extensions. The layout comprises straight, tree-lined roads with community buildings – church, pub, and club – and communal open spaces that preserved existing mature trees. Designated a conservation area, with many listed buildings.

Brentham Garden Suburb, south of Western Avenue, Pitshanger Lane, W5

A very early garden suburb (*i.e.* pre-dating Letchworth Garden City and Hampstead Garden Suburb), and surprisingly little known; built by a co-operative society, Ealing Tenants, from 1901 to 1915. Parker and Unwin were involved from 1907. They supplied the layout of meandering roads, culs-de sac, angled corners, as well as the Vernacular Revival architecture of hipped and tiled roofs, gables, rendered walls and varied fenestration with casements. Other housing is by F. Cavendish Pearson (Meadvale Road (◐ *pictured top left and left*), Ludlow Road (◐ *pictured bottom left*) and Neville Road). Church by E. Shearman (1916), and flamboyant contemporary shopping arcade (1909) by S.H. Burdward. G. Lister Sutcliffe designed the houses in Brentham Way, Fowler's Walk and Denison Road, and the handsome Arts and Crafts Brentham Institute (◐ *pictured above*), completed in 1911. Some buildings listed; designated a conservation area.

Castlebar Conservation Area, W5 and W13

Some late nineteenth-century villas, *e.g.* Wyke House (1891) with a tall octagonal viewing-tower.

Creffield Conservation Area: Creffield Road, Freeland Road, Inglis Road and Wolverton Gardens to the west; Layer Gardens, Montague Gardens and Western Gardens to the east; W3 and W5

Large detached houses of the 1890s in red brick with quality 'tuck pointing', moulded brick and terracotta panels, in a variety of styles. The houses have recessed porches, often with white-painted decorative stone lintels and keystones contrasting with the red brickwork, or decorative timber porches with tiled roofs. Much stained glass in leaded lights, showing Art Nouveau influence. The houses have generous front gardens.

Mill Hill Park Estate, South Acton, W3

The development of the Mill Hill Park Estate was begun in the late 1870s by the builder William Willett (1856–1914) and completed by 1895. Perhaps because of the proximity of the working-class South Acton area with its piggeries and laundries, the estate did not have the success of the nearby Bedford Park development (see **London Borough of Hounslow**). The quality of building is nevertheless characteristically high, with large paired villas incorporating elaborate stucco work on the door and window surrounds. Heathfield Road and Avenue Gardens bend and converge to form a large crescent lined with houses of red brick, with moulded and patterned brickwork and gabled slate roofs. Later houses in Heathfield Road show an Arts and Crafts influence in the use of render, Art Nouveau stained glass in the door and patterned tiles on the garden paths.

Mount Park, east of Castlebar Road to Eaton Rise, W5

Henry de Bono Austin initiated a large planned estate of superior middle-class housing, but few houses were built by the time he went bankrupt in 1872. When a train link was provided with the Ealing extension of the Metropolitan Line in 1879 and main drainage in the 1880s, the plan was taken up by the Wood family, well-established Ealing landowners. By 1906 they had built over 850 houses. The estate as developed by Wood eschewed Austin's rectilinear layout in favour of the picturesque style of suburban development. The detached houses have generous front and rear gardens. There is much variety in the architectural character of this area, some of it clearly influenced by R. Norman Shaw (e.g. no. 2 Blakesley Avenue by local architect E.R. Barrow (1906), and houses in Charlbury Grove).

Between the Wars: 1914–1940

East Acton, including The Long Drive, The Bye and The Green, W3

A group of experimental cottages erected in 1920–21 by the Ministry of Health as part of the 'Homes fit for Heroes' campaign. Low cost was a prime consideration, and these cottages were therefore built in a variety of concrete techniques. Nonetheless, attractive open spaces were provided in keeping with the houses' domestic scale.

The GWR Estate, West Acton, W3

A garden village development for railway workers, built in 1923–25 by T. Alwyn Lloyd, consisting of paired cottages in the usual mix of brick and render, set amid the extensive recreation grounds of the Great Western Railway and laid out around Noel Road.

Perivale, Greenford

Included for the remarkable buildings straddling the Western Avenue: Wallis, Gilbert and Partners' Hoover Factory (1931–35), the acme of jazzy Art Deco factories, together with the nearby canteen building of 1938; for the sadly altered 'road house', the Myllett Arms (1935), by E.B. Musman; and for the great arterial road itself, begun in 1921. The tiny weather-boarded St Mary's Church, just to the south, sits in a wooded enclave and is highly expressive of lost Middlesex. No other former village so reveals the changes wrought by the growth of the inter-war suburb.

Hanger Hill Estate, North Ealing, W3

A notable 1930s estate laid out mainly by Haymills (compare Barn Hill, Wembley; see **London Borough of Brent**), again using Welch, Cachemaille-Day and Lander as architects. These

long, curving streets contain a number of blocks of flats among the brick houses, which range in style from standard half-timbered semis (⊙*pictured above left*) to sleek modernist cubes with flat roofs and sun-rooms; one of the definitive inter-war suburban developments. Designated a conservation area.

Hanger Hill Garden Estate, North Ealing, W5

Developed in 1928–32 by Douglas Smith. A distinctive mock-Tudor development, extended to the west in 1933–36, and located to the south of the Hanger Hill Estate (*see above*). The flats are particularly impressive. Overall, an exceptionally well-preserved enclave. A conservation area, with an Article Four designation.

Cuckoo Estate, Hanwell, W7

Built in 1933–39 for the LCC. A spaciously planned, out-of-town cottage estate provided with a large community centre in the converted nineteenth-century school building. Designated a conservation area.

Ealing Village, Hanger Lane, North Ealing, W5

Developed in 1934–36 by R. Toms for the Bell Property Company. A remarkable enclave of five blocks of apartments, each white walled, with red-painted ornaments and crowned with green-tiled roofs (⊙*pictured top*): the acme of the Dutch Colonial style. This well-maintained estate is listed.

The Road to Subtopia: 1940 to the present

Lakeside, Castle Bar, W13

Also known as the Grange after the house previously on the site, this is a particularly pleasant development by Wates from 1966. Terraced houses (⊙*pictured above right*) and a single, quite tall block of flats are disposed carefully to preserve the mature landscape and lake from the earlier house. A second block of flats was added later. Wates are the most successful firm to have developed the idiom of simple massed housing and rich landscaping devised by Span, and indeed they took over the latter's over-ambitious New Ash Green project soon after Lakeside was completed. Designated a conservation area.

London Borough of

ENFIELD

Infinite Variety: 1840–1914

Bush Hill Park

Bush Hill Park station was opened in 1880 and
the railway line provided the classic physical social
divide in the housing development conceived a few
years earlier, in 1875, by R. Tayler Smith for the
Northern Estates Company. East of the tracks are
the pub, working-class terraces, Board school and
church; to the west the detached houses of
Wellington Road were to characterize the middle-
class quarter. Many of these houses have since
disappeared, but an important survival is no. 8
Private Road (A.H. Mackmurdo, 1883), which is
in an uncharacteristic classical style with terracotta
panels. The estate is designated a conservation area.

Crescent East and Crescent West, Hadley Wood

A development by the owner of the house called
Beech Hill Park, one Charles Jack, who laid out the
streets around the area of the Great Northern
Railway station, Hadley Wood, after it opened in
1885. The houses in Crescent East and Crescent
West are substantial, tile-hung buildings.

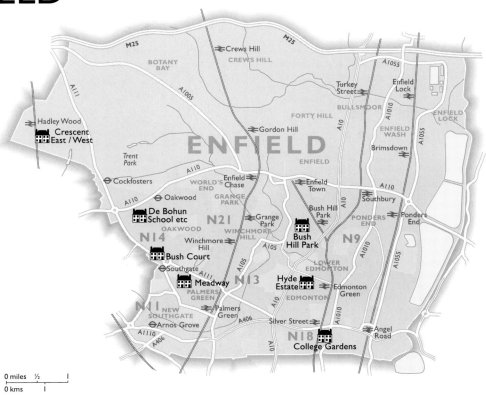

Between the Wars: 1914–1940

Hyde Estate, Edmonton, N9

A very early local authority estate of 1920, designed
by Niven and Wigglesworth on garden city
principles, consisting of rough-cast semis laid out
around small greens.

Bush Court, Crown Lane, Southgate, N14

An idiosyncratic block of flats, erected ca. 1936 by
Harwood Nash in the wake of the arrival of the
Piccadilly Line extension. A stepped composition
with a prominent central tower, representative
of the transitional phase of suburban domestic
architecture in its mixture of modernist flat roofs
and geometric starkness, alongside more traditional
features such as tile-hung bays and neo-Baroque
doors and arches.

De Bohun School and Health Centre and Library, Green Road, Southgate, N14

An outstanding group of municipal buildings
erected by the Middlesex County Council's
Architects' Department, led by W.T. Curtis and
H.W. Burchett. Both the school (1936, and
representative of the numerous 1930s schools
erected by the same body in London's outer
suburbs) and the health centre with library
(1938–39) are executed in a modernist brick
idiom, much influenced by contemporary Dutch
architecture. Their concrete construction is
expressed via flat roofs with strong horizontals
formed by the metal-framed windows. These were
the types of buildings that served the dynamically
expanding populace of Greater London. Both are
listed.

Meadway, Southgate, N14

A speculative development by the local firm of
Edmondson's, consisting of half-timbered houses
with many traditional vernacular touches, spaciously
laid out on rising ground just below Grovelands
Park. Opposite are the very different flats of
Ellington Court, designed in a spare, modern style
by Frederick Gibberd in 1937.

The Road to Subtopia: 1940 to the present

College Gardens, Edmonton, N18

A development comprising big slabs of maisonettes
by Edmonton Borough, strikingly brutal for their
date of 1956–61. Mainly of nine storeys, a
contrasting and still starker note is supplied by
a single tower of fourteen storeys.

London Borough of
GREENWICH

Aristocratic to Middle Class: 1690–1840

Croom's Hill, SE10

The Thames-side palace encouraged the development of Greenwich as a suburban resort from the sixteenth century. Croom's Hill gives as good an idea as any street in London of the succeeding generations of suburban housing, from the seventeenth to the nineteenth century.

Vanbrugh Castle, Westcombe Park Road, SE3

Built by the architect Sir John Vanbrugh for himself between 1718 and 1726, Vanbrugh Castle was designed to conjure up thoughts of the Middle Ages. While not the first private house ever to do so, the castle is on a more modest scale than the great Elizabethan houses in which the medieval past is evoked, such as Bolsover. It is also one of the first architect's houses meant as something of a demonstration piece. The original structure of 1719 was smaller than it is now. There were changes in Vanbrugh's day but also in the early part of the century and has more recently been divided up.

Blackheath Park, SE3

This former site of one of London's grandest Palladian piles, Wricklemarsh House (John James, 1723), was developed by John Cator as a smart villa quarter from 1783. There followed Michael Searles's spectacular development, The Paragon (1790–1807). Blackheath Park, Pond Road and Foxes Dale were laid out according to the comprehensive estate plan of 1806, and then filled with detached and semi-detached villas from 1819. Nos. 99–103 (odd) Blackheath Road are noteworthy, as are several houses in Lee Road.

Infinite Variety: 1840–1914

Blackheath Park Estate, south of Blackheath Station, SE3

Some mid-nineteenth-century villas survive in large gardens, as well as a good selection of nineteenth-century houses, including, on the north-west side of Blackheath Park, two by Aston Webb, dating from the 1890s.

Between the Wars: 1914–1940

Well Hall (or Progress) Estate, Eltham, SE9

The greatest of the government-built housing developments, erected in 1915 to accommodate munitions workers at Woolwich Arsenal. Over one thousand houses were constructed on this hilly site by (Sir) Frank Baines, who laid out the streets in a low-density, garden suburb manner, which was to prove highly influential with local authorities across the country after the Armistice. Given the wartime conditions, the estate is remarkably thoughtful in its variety of materials and in its subtle variations on the vernacular theme. Designated a conservation area.

Charlton Estate, Charlton, SE7

A 'Homes fit for Heroes' estate of municipal housing, designed by Alfred Roberts for Greenwich Council in 1920–21. The small-scale, rough-cast and tiled houses, centred around Fairfield Grove, follow the LCC tradition of plain but well-designed dwellings in the vernacular tradition.

Genesta Road, Plumstead, SE18

Amid the late nineteenth-century streets of Plumstead stands a row of four very unusual houses (**o** *pictured above*). Designed by Berthold Lubetkin and built in 1933–34, they constitute Britain's only terrace of advanced Modern Movement houses. Much admired in their day, they failed to find emulators. They are listed Grade II*.

The Road to Subtopia: 1940 to the present

Cator Estate, Blackheath Park, SE3

Within and behind the nineteenth-century villas (also partly in the London Borough of Lewisham) is the largest collection of Span developments, evolved from 1954 onwards by Eric Lyons (architect), Geoffrey Townsend (architect-turned-developer) and Leslie Bilsby (builder), who endeavoured to show that private housing could be as good as that done in the public sector. Their estates are remarkable not just for the sensitivity of the architecture and planning, but also for the luxuriant planting and the rigorous system of tenants' management committees and covenants that keep them in as good a condition as when first built. The journalist and architectural critic Ian Nairn wrote that 'if Eric Lyons is the modern Nash, then this is his Regent's Park'. Hallgate (**o** *pictured above*), one of the most striking blocks of flats, featuring Keith Godwin's sculpture *The Architect in Society* (1958–60), is listed, as are the Span flats along South Row (1959–61), just over the border in the London Borough of Lewisham. Also of interest, as well as the many fine listed nineteenth-century houses, are two private houses: no. 20 Blackheath Park, of 1957, by Peter Moro for himself; and no. 10 Blackheath Park, of 1968, by Patrick Gwynne for Leslie Bilsby, the builder responsible for constructing most of the surrounding Span housing. The Cator Estate is designated a conservation area.

Brooklands Park, SE3

Close to Span's Blackheath Park (*see above*) is an estate of similar density that also respects the landscape, but which is very different in style. Brooklands Park was developed by the LCC in 1958 with a mixture of point blocks and low terraces reminiscent of their work on the Alton Estate, Roehampton (*see* **London Borough of Wandsworth**).

Vanbrugh Park, SE3

As work on their Barbican development for the City of London began, Chamberlin, Powell and Bon designed this very different estate for Greenwich Metropolitan Borough. There is a single block of flats, its concrete frame boldly expressed but now somewhat spoilt by recladding. The rest of the housing is no more than two storeys high, with some units entered *via* broad walkways across garage roofs. The use of cheap concrete-block construction enabled money to be spent on the careful layout of hard surfaces.

Thamesmead, SE2

See **London Borough of Bexley**

London Borough of

HACKNEY

Aristocratic to Middle Class: 1690–1840

Clapton Square, E5

Developed from 1816, Clapton Square (**◗** *pictured opposite*) was one of the first in a series of middle-class enclaves that grew out of Hackney, an area that was overrun by modest terraces built for the 'middling sort'.

De Beauvoir Town, N1

The construction of the Regent's Park Canal persuaded the de Beauvoir family to develop their estate as speculative housing from 1821. The 130 acres conveyed to William Rhodes is said to have been the largest ever to have been put into the hands of a speculative builder. Initially Rhodes had grand ideas – four squares with an interesting grid of streets – but when fitful development on the fringes failed, de Beauvoir reclaimed the lease. The family then developed the area with short terraces and villas, adopting a spacious but by no means novel street plan. The centrepiece is the now partially destroyed De Beauvoir Square, where the houses are, unusually, in a late medieval style. The rest of the houses are Italianate in feeling. The estate was completed in the 1840s.

Infinite Variety: 1840–1914

Gore Road, Victoria Park, E9

A uniform, stucco-trimmed terrace of the 1870s overlooking the Victoria Park, one of the first and largest of the London parks of the nineteenth century, laid out by James Pennethorne and opened in 1845.

Bethune Road, N16

An unusual development of middle-class blocks of flats built from 1874 by Matthew Allen, in grey brick with artificial stone dressings, with tree-filled communal gardens.

Between the Wars: 1914–1940

Meynell Gardens, Victoria Park, E9

A development of largely semi-detached brick houses of 1932–33, designed by A. Savill in a variety of vernacular configurations and picturesquely laid out at the end of Well Street Common. Within a conservation area.

Stamford Hill, N16

A variety of large estates of public housing testify to the scale of slum clearance that was undertaken in this borough. The huge Guinness Estate (1932), of five-storey brick blocks, nine deep, owed much to the LCC's approach to design. The LCC's own Stamford Hill Estate (comprising some 353 flats by 1936) was indebted to Viennese influences in terms of its courtyard planning, steeply pitched roofs and concrete balconies.

The Road to Subtopia: 1940 to the present

Somerford Estate, Shacklewell Road, N16

This was the first post-war development designed
by Frederick Gibberd, for Hackney Metropolitan
Borough, and built in 1947. It is also the first
scheme consciously to experiment with a range of
houses, flats and maisonettes 'grouped in a series
of closes, each with its own character, and with
vistas across the site' to give 'unusual variety', as
Gibberd himself put it to the Festival of Britain
Architecture Committee. The result is perhaps
the first 'mixed development', though here of no
more than two and three storeys. The scheme
won a Festival of Britain Merit Award.

Woodberry Down Estate, Stoke Newington, N4

This was the LCC's showcase estate of the 1940s,
designed during the War and completed in 1954.
It was a consciously designed neighbourhood, with
impressively modelled blocks of flats contrasted
with brick terraced houses, as well as shops,
schools, a library and a health centre. Though
built at a higher density that limited the landscape
possibilities of the site, its picturesque qualities and
attempt to achieve a sense of place can now be
seen as anticipating the LCC's later work at the
Alton Estate, Roehampton (see **London Borough
of Wandsworth**).

Bentham Road, Hackney, E9

The same combination of tall slabs and lower
maisonettes as at the LCC's Alton Estate,
Roehampton (see **London Borough of
Wandsworth**), was first used here, in central
Hackney, in 1952–54. Without the dramatic open
landscape of Roehampton these blocks seem
unexceptional, although they are worthy of closer
attention.

The Beckers, Downs Road, Lower Clapton, E5

A development by Frederick Gibberd of 1956.
Taller and more varied than the Somerford Estate
(see *above*), the lower ranges with blue panels and
shallow pitched roofs are contrasted with two
eleven-storey point blocks.

London Borough of
HAMMERSMITH AND FULHAM

Infinite Variety: 1840–1914

Peterborough Estate, Fulham, SW6

Developed on the site of the Peterborough House, south of the New King's Road, from the 1890s by local builder James Nichols. The estate is bounded by the Wandsworth Bridge Road and Peterborough Road. The red-brick houses have strong details of shared gables decorated with heraldic lions on the apexes, half-gabled bays and terracotta panels.

West Kensington and Baron's Court, W6 and W14

West of North End Road the area of Baron's Court, Comeragh Road and Castletown Road was developed from the 1880s by W.H. Gibbs and Co., Kensington, and Earl's Court builders, with classy terraced houses of pale brick and stucco. West from Vereker Road the houses, of the 1890s, change to red-brick terraces influenced by the 'Queen Anne' and Aesthetic Movement styles. Around Baron's Court Underground Station (1905)

an artistic community settled and the streets give a nod to Bedford Park, Turnham Green (*see* **London Borough of Ealing**): Talgarth Studios (❍*pictured above*) and St Dunstan's Road, with St Dunstan's Studio (now the Hungarian Reform Church; 1891) by C.F.A. Voysey filling a corner site between terraces.

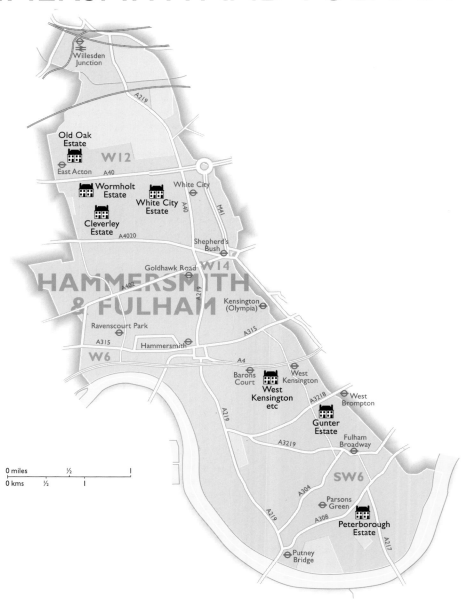

Gunter Estate, Fulham, SW6

A model estate of low terraced houses and some cottage flats and studios in the Arts and Crafts style, built by Walter Cave, surveyor to the estate, in 1900–04. The estate runs south of Lillie Road and east of North End Road, and includes Racton Road, Sedlescombe Road and Tamworth Road.

Old Oak Estate, East Acton, W12

This LCC cottage estate was begun in 1911 south-west of the railway, and completed at the north-east end in the 1920s. The development includes some picturesque Unwinian, serpentine, tree-lined roads within a more formal geometric layout, with small two-storey red-brick blocks of houses

(❍ *pictured top left*), each containing between four and eighteen dwellings. Some houses have tile- and slate-covered roofs, hipped dormers and prominent chimneys (❍ *pictured above*), and privet hedges around the front gardens. Designated a conservation area.

Between the Wars: 1914–1940

Wormholt Estate, North Hammersmith, W12
An early municipal garden city estate (1919–26) for Hammersmith Borough Council, overseen by Henry Hare. Generously laid-out and neatly detailed brick houses, offset by small greens and the whimsically baroque branch library of 1929. A good representative of the quality of estates built in the 'Homes fit for Heroes' campaign. Designated a conservation area.

Cleverley Estate, North Hammersmith, W12
Developed in 1928 by Victor Wilkins for the Peabody Trust. Like the similar estate in Fulham Palace Road, this an imposing development treated in a strong Wren-influenced Baroque idiom (❍ *pictured top right*), with bulls-eye windows and grand arched openings: few philanthropic estates can claim such grandeur. Designated a conservation area.

White City Estate, White City, W12
Built in 1938–39 for the LCC by the architects E.P. Wheeler, with F.R. Hioms and J.W. Hepburn. It is the largest LCC estate of the 1930s, occupying no fewer than 52 acres and housing around 11,000 persons. The five-storey blocks (❍ *pictured above*), repetitively ranked row upon row, consist of two main types: the '1934' type with continuous balconies, and the '1936' type with individual balconies to each flat.

London Borough of
HARINGEY

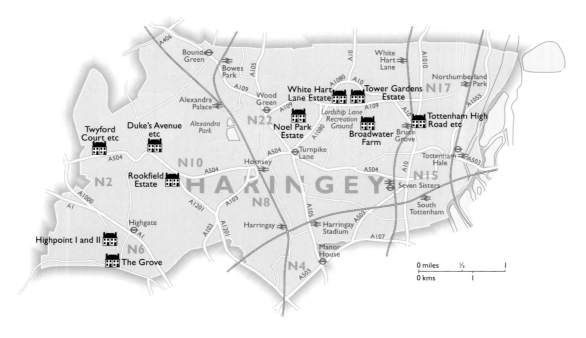

Aristocratic to Middle Class: 1690–1840

The Grove, Highgate, N6

Highgate Village began to see an influx of Londoners in the sixteenth century, and boasts several fine houses. Nos. 1–6 The Grove are rare survivals from the late seventeenth century, remarkable for being possibly the first set of speculatively built semi-detached houses in a London suburb. Semis were not unknown in the countryside by this date, but the form would not enjoy popularity among the well-heeled suburbanites until the late eighteenth century.

Tottenham High Road (nos. 483–485 and 810–812) and Bruce Grove, Tottenham, N17

From the early eighteenth century there were concentrations of suburban terraces in Tottenham High Road, which enjoyed good communications with the City. Nos. 483–485 and 810–812 are rare survivals of this type, although they are now much in need of repair. Towards the end of the eighteenth century and after the end of the

Continental wars, semis and villas were constructed in some of the lesser roads leading off Tottenham High Road, of which the houses at the east end of Bruce Grove are a good example.

Infinite Variety: 1840–1914

Noel Park Estate, Wood Green, N22

Developed from the 1880s by the Artizans', Labourers' and General Dwellings Company to designs by Rowland Plumbe. Straight roads of two-storey terraced housing in jolly Queen Anne style with polychromatic bricks and stone features crammed on to the tight façades. Designated a conservation area.

Duke's Avenue, Fortis Green Road, Prince's Avenue and Queen's Avenue, Muswell Hill, N10

A coherent, homogeneous Edwardian suburb for the middle classes, with shopping parades, churches and chapels (and, originally, an Athenaeum). The streets have good examples of the decorative

'Queen Anne' style (○ pictured above) derived from R. Norman Shaw. Much of the new building, from 1897, was carried out by the builders Edmondsons: red brick with vaguely Flemish Renaissance detail. There is some lavish decoration on the fronts of the substantial houses, such as those at the west end of Duke's Avenue.

Tower Gardens Estate, Tottenham, N17

An early LCC cottage estate, begun in 1903. It contains a mixture of Arts and Crafts-inspired cottages and terraces, with slate- and tile-hung

The remains of a remarkable model traffic scheme
of 1937, intended to educate the young in the
dangers of road-crossings. The miniature Belisha
beacons and police boxes have gone, but the road
layout and dwarf trees remain.

The Road to Subtopia: 1940 to the present

**Broadwater Farm, Mount Pleasant Road,
Tottenham, N17**

The London Borough of Haringey's most ambitious
housing project, planned in 1966 and completed in
1971, has been much modified since it gained
notoriety in the early 1980s but remains grim and
forbidding. It has all the austerity of a concrete
system-built estate without any relieving ingenuity
of planning or detailing. The centrepiece, Tangmere,
is particularly crude in its design. With 1063
households it can deservedly be counted as a
suburb, but it is the sort that unfairly gives modern
architecture a bad name.

gables, and a large open space, Tower Garden.
Designated a conservation area.

White Hart Lane Estate, Tottenham, N17

One of the first four cottage estates to the built
in the suburbs by the LCC. The earliest part, of
1903–13, is a grid of streets between Tower
Gardens and Risley Avenue, just north of Lordship
Lane, comprising two-storey terraced cottages with
slate and tile- hung gables, hipped roofs and bay
windows. The estate was extended after World
War I.

Rookfield Estate, Muswell Hill, N10

A pretty enclave of houses in the domestic
vernacular of Hampstead Garden Suburb: brick
and rendered walls, tiled roofs, white casement
windows and low privet hedges (○ *pictured three
times this page*). Built from 1901 to 1915 by
W.J. Collins and his sons Herbert and William.

Between the Wars: 1914–1940

**Twyford Court, Long Ridges and Twyford
Avenue, Fortis Green, N2**

A development, all of it by William Collins, of
neo-Georgian flats (1930 and 1933) alongside
Twyford Avenue (1935), a late example of the
garden suburb and characterized by the customary
tile-hung gabled roofs of the period. It is a late

and elegant development that capitalized on the
salubrious reputation of 'Healthy Hornsey'.

Highpoint I and II, North Hill, Highgate, N6

The outstanding Modern Movement residential
development of its day. Designed by Bertold
Lubetkin and Tecton, Highpoint I was built in
1933–35 and joined by Highpoint II in 1938. Built
for Sigmund Gestetner, these blocks mark the
arrival of advanced Continental thinking on the
urban environment in Britain. Le Corbusier's vision
of lofty towers in spacious, leafy settings was
realized spectacularly and with unsurpassed flair.
Their height and lofty hilltop site commanded
spectacular prospects and thus answered the
ageless requirements of the suburban retreat.
Recommended Grade I listing (awaiting outcome).

London Borough of

HARROW

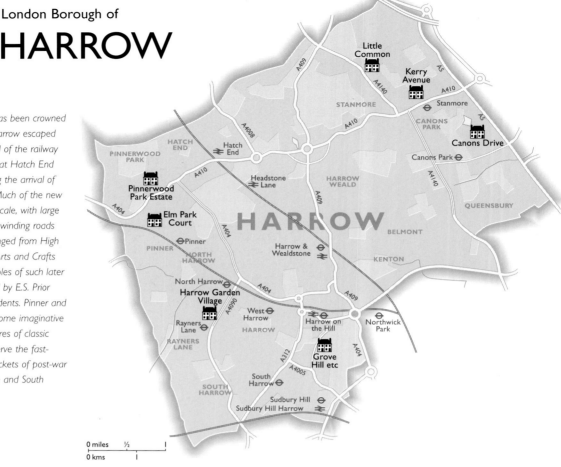

Distinguished by its steep hill, which has been crowned by a church since the Middle Ages, Harrow escaped suburban development until the arrival of the railway in 1837, with development beginning at Hatch End and becoming more intensive following the arrival of the Metropolitan Line in the 1880s. Much of the new development was still on a generous scale, with large houses set widely spaced apart along winding roads on the slopes of the hill. The styles ranged from High Victorian Gothic to Queen Anne and Arts and Crafts houses around 1900. The best examples of such later domestic building are houses designed by E.S. Prior and Arnold Mitchell, both Harrow residents. Pinner and Stanmore, on the flatter plain, boast some imaginative inter-war developments among the acres of classic semis, with churches and schools to serve the fast-expanding communities. There are pockets of post-war council or low-rent housing in Edgware and South Harrow.

Infinite Variety: 1840–1914

Little Common, Stanmore

Workers' cottages built between 1860 and 1870 in the Gothic Revival style.

Grove Hill, Harrow Park, Mount Park Estate, Peterborough Road, Roxborough Park and Sudbury Hill, Harrow on the Hill

Clothing the slopes of Harrow Hill, these areas of planned estates boast large detached Arts and Crafts houses of 1870–1905 (❍ *pictured opposite left*), designed by many architects including Arnold Mitchell, (particularly in Sudbury Hill and Grove Hill, including his own house, Grove Hill Cottage); E.S. Prior (nos. 60–66 Middle Road, 1887; ❍ *pictured opposite right*), and S. Pointon Taylor, who laid out an estate near Orley Farm School in consultation with Raymond Unwin (South Hill Estate, 1910). Many of the houses were inspired by R. Norman Shaw's Grim's Dyke, (1870–72) in Harrow Weald.

Between the Wars: 1914–1940

Harrow Garden Village, Rayners Lane, Harrow

Built by E.S. Reid in 1930–34 for the Metropolitan Railway Country Estates Co. Ltd. This development is one of the canonical expressions of 'Metroland'. Exceptionally fine public buildings enhance the estate, including the former Grosvenor Cinema in Alexandra Avenue (F.E. Bromige, 1936) and Rayners Lane Underground Station (Charles Holden with Reginald Uren, 1938); both are listed.

Elm Park Court, Pinner

A notable quadrant of apartment blocks, designed in 1936 by H.F. Webb in an idiosyncratic style that owes something to oriental architecture. The entrance arch, like the rest of the buildings, is roofed in vivid green glazed tiles. Each apartment has a jutting balcony, and is entered through a

modern main door. Compare nearby Pinner Court (1935) by H.J. Mark. Listed Grade II.

Pinnerwood Park Estate, Pinner

Built in 1931–39 for the Artizans', Labourers' and General Dwellings Company. A late example of the garden suburb, with rural touches provided by tile-hung brick houses of varying height and particularly by the rustic fencing. Designated a conservation area.

Canons Drive, Stanmore

A homogeneous development of smart mock-Tudor houses, begun in 1926 by A.J. Butcher in the grounds of the Duke of Chandos's great eighteenth-century residence: the lake and the basin survive as reminders of this vanished opulence, rather as they do at Wanstead. Designated a conservation area.

Kerry Avenue, Stanmore

Part of the Warren House Estate, developed in the mid-1930s. Dissatisfaction with the repetitious blandness of so much of London's suburbia prompted the landlord, the Irish baronet Sir John FitzGerald, to engage Gerald Lacoste to design six exceptional Modern Movement houses (now nos. 1–6 Kerry Avenue) in 1935. These combined geometrical austerity with a mix of materials to produce striking yet economical bespoke modern houses. These were joined by another exceptional house in 1937: no. 14, built by the New Zealand architect Reginald Uren for his own use. Designated a conservation area.

London Borough of
HAVERING

Infinite Variety: 1840–1914

Ardleigh Green Estate, Hornchurch
Emerson Park was developed from 1895 on the fringes of London and Essex by a Mr Carter, who intended to build country villas for City gentlemen. It became the Ardleigh Green Estate, with houses built by E.A. Coryn and, after 1919, by his son Allen Coryn, who had been clerk of works to Welwyn Garden City. Allen Coryn developed the neighbouring Great Nelmes Estate, with expensive, individually designed houses, into the 1930s. These estates are not in conservation areas and have suffered from alteration.

Gidea Park, Romford
The Gidea Park Garden Suburb was built in 1910–11 on the initiative of Liberal MPs Herbert Raphael, Charles McCurdy and Sir Tudor Walters, on the former Gidea Hall Estate, and served by a newly built station, Gidea Park. Gidea Park Ltd had close links with the Garden City Co. in which Raphael, McCurdy and Walters were all shareholders. A competition was held for designs of the houses, 'To demonstrate to housing and to public authorities, to builders and to the public generally, the improvement in modern housing and building due to scientific knowledge, the revival of the Arts and Crafts and the progress of the garden city movement, and by doing so to assist the raising of the standard of housing not only in the outer

metropolis but throughout Britain'. Over one hundred architects entered, including such luminaries as Barry Parker, Sir Raymond Unwin, M.H. Baillie Scott, T. Gordon Jackson Philip Tilden and Clough Williams-Ellis. The brief was for small, four-bedroom detached houses costing £500 (class I) and three-bedroom cottages costing £375 (class II). Stress was laid on convenient 'labour-saving' plans. Many of the houses were in the Tudor style, rough-cast and colour-washed (◑ *pictured left*) or half-timbered. The area was well landscaped and the plots were of good size. Baillie Scott's pair of fine Arts and Crafts houses at nos. 36 and 38 Reed Pond Walk (1911), a class I and II house side-by-side, are separately listed. Development continued into the 1930s; *see below*.

Between the Wars: 1914–1940

Collier Row, Romford
A Nash estate of 1937, principally of semi-detached brick houses laid out on the undulating land on London's north-easternmost fringes and characteristic of the great swathes of suburban development carried out by this firm in the area.

Gidea Park, Romford
Contained within the early twentieth-century development of Gidea Park (*see above*) are some remarkable interwar houses: a *Modern Homes* exhibition was held here in 1934 as part of a drive to inject greater architectural interest into the design of suburban houses. Thirty-five houses were built, mainly in Brook Road, just off the Eastern Avenue, in an advanced modernist brick style; many had flat roofs and were constructed of concrete. The winner of the competition associated with the exhibition was no. 64 Heath Drive, by Francis Skinner with Tecton: a Modern Movement box of reinforced concrete that cost a mere £900; listed Grade II. Designated a conservation area.

Gaynes Estate, Little Gaynes Gardens, Upminster
Several streets of exceptionally well-preserved semis of *ca.* 1930 (◑ *pictured above*), mainly half-timbered built on the site of the Esdaile family's large house; some ornamental features survive from the Georgian pleasure grounds in Parklands Park.

The Road to Subtopia: 1940 to the present

Harold Hill Estate, Romford
This is a particularly large and self-contained LCC 'out-county' estate of the late 1940s, built with a range of traditional brick and government-sponsored prefabricated houses by its Valuer's Department; 7631 houses were built, for some 25,000 people. Such 'prairie-style' suburbs were widely criticized for their lack of shops and social facilities, and for their distances from places of employment. However, the houses themselves have generally proved popular with families.

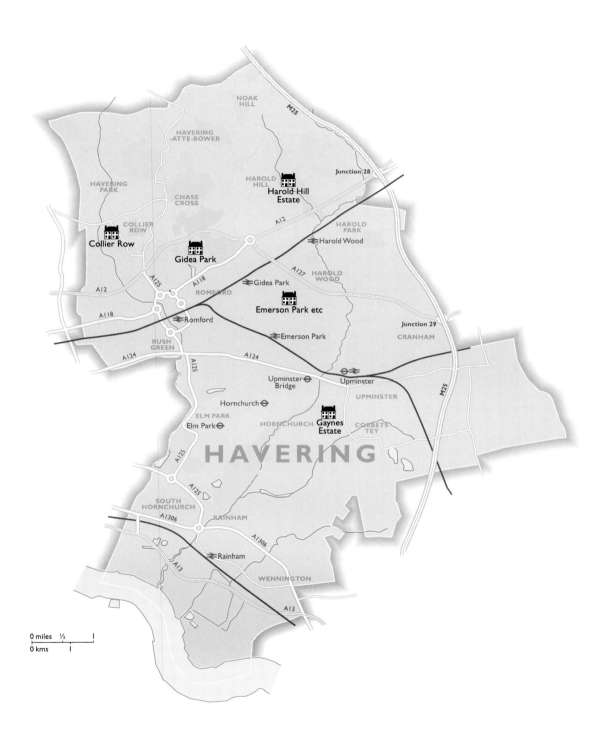

NOAK
HILL

HAVERING
-ATTE-BOWER

M25

Junction 28

HAVERING
PARK

CHASE
CROSS

HAROLD
HILL

Harold Hill
Estate

COLLIER
ROW

A12

HAROLD
PARK

Collier Row

Gidea Park

Harold Wood

A125

A118

A127

HAROLD
WOOD

A12

ROMFORD

Gidea Park

Emerson Park etc

A118

Romford

RUSH
GREEN

Emerson Park

Junction 29

CRANHAM

A124

A124

A125

Upminster
Bridge

Upminster

Hornchurch

UPMINSTER

M25

ELM PARK

HORNCHURCH

Gaynes
Estate

UPMINSTER

CORBETS
TEY

Elm Park

HAVERING

A125

A125

SOUTH
HORNCHURCH

A1306

RAINHAM

A1306

Rainham

A13

WENNINGTON

A13

0 miles   ½   I

0 kms   I

London Borough of

HILLINGDON

Infinite Variety: 1840–1914

Northwood and Eastbury Road Conservation Area

Development of Northwood came after the arrival of the Metropolitan railway in 1887, and the higher ground affording fine views to the south became popular for superior late Victorian and Edwardian houses. Frank Carew bought up the land surrounding the station and sold it off in building plots. The larger houses are in Dene Road, The Avenue and Carew Road. The houses were designed by C.H.B. Quennell, R.A. Briggs and Charles Harrison Townsend.

Manor Way Conservation Area, Ruislip

Suburban expansion from 1905 on land belonging to King's College, Cambridge. Manor Way was developed by the Ruislip Manor Cottage Society from 1911 with low-rental housing for the working classes, very much in the spirit of Hampstead Garden Suburb and indeed using the same architects: Soutar, Bunney, Crickmer, Hignett and Welch. The small houses, with pantile roofs and tile hanging, accommodated people who were to 'serve' the residents of a posher suburb planned for near by but never built.

Between the Wars: 1914–1940

Morford Way, Eastcote

A small enclave developed in the mid-1920s by the Telling Brothers; unusual for being designed in the Regency style as opposed to the mock-Tudor or vernacular styles that dominated speculative housing at this time.

Northwood Hills

Middlesex's northern heights were reached by the Tube in 1933. Some of the ensuing developments were in a progressive, semi-modern style, for example nos. 153–163 Northwood Way (Morgan and Edwards, 1934) and nos. 156–186 Joel Road (Robert de Burgh, 1934). Harry Neal and H. Peachey were the principal developers of this area.

Ruislip Manor

A particularly large speculative development of the late 1930s by Manor Homes, centred around Victoria Road. Near by, at nos. 97–101 Park Avenue, is a small group of white, flat-roofed, Modern Movement houses of 1936 by Connell, Ward and Lucas (listed Grade II).

The Road to Subtopia: 1940 to the present

Highgrove, High Road, Eastcote

A set of low-cost terraces by Edward Cullinan, built in 1974–77 for the London Borough of Hillingdon and noted for their blue roofs. The development exemplifies Hillingdon's commitment to good modern design in these years, which intelligently challenged preconceptions of public housing. The development comprises back-to-back units and garages separated at the sides by narrow passages in the manner of the contemporary Branch Hill (see **London Borough of Camden**).

Northwood and
Eastbury Road
Conservation Area

Northwood

Northwood
Hills

Northwood
Hills

HILL
END

HAREFIELD

SOUTH
HAREFIELD

EASTCOTE
VILLAGE

RUISLIP

Highgrove

Morford Way

Eastcote

Manor Way
Conservation
Area

Ruislip Manor

RUISLIP
GARDENS

Ruislip

West Ruislip

Ruislip
Manor

RUISLIP
MANOR

Ruislip Gardens

Ickenham

Ickenham

South
Ruislip

Northolt
Aerodrome

Hillingdon

UXBRIDGE

Uxbridge

NORTH
HILLINGDON

HILLINGDON

HILLINGDON

YEADING

HAYES
END

HAYES

YIEWSLEY

West Drayton

HAYES
TOWN

Hayes &
Harlington

WEST
DRAYTON

Junction 15   Junction 4B M4   Junction 4   M4   Junction 3

HARMONDSWORTH

HARLINGTON

SIPSON

A4   Junction 4A

LONGFORD

Heathrow
Terminals 1,2,3

London
Heathrow
Airport

Heathrow
Central

Junction 14

Hatton
Cross

Heathrow
Terminal 4

0 miles   ½   1

0 kms   1

London Borough of
HOUNSLOW

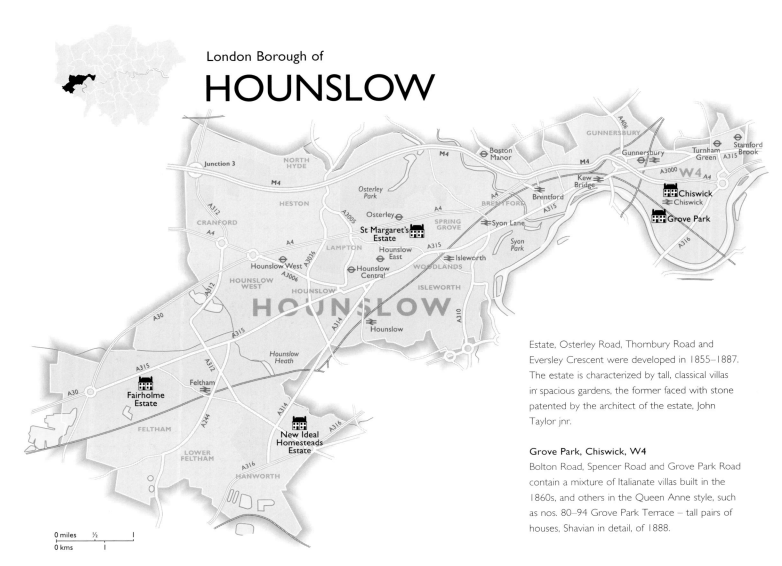

Estate, Osterley Road, Thornbury Road and
Eversley Crescent were developed in 1855–1887.
The estate is characterized by tall, classical villas
in spacious gardens, the former faced with stone
patented by the architect of the estate, John
Taylor jnr.

Grove Park, Chiswick, W4

Bolton Road, Spencer Road and Grove Park Road
contain a mixture of Italianate villas built in the
1860s, and others in the Queen Anne style, such
as nos. 80–94 Grove Park Terrace – tall pairs of
houses, Shavian in detail, of 1888.

Aristocratic to Middle Class: 1690–1840

Chiswick, W4

The growth of Chiswick was stimulated by the
river, which allowed easy access to the royal
residence at Kew near by. By the late seventeenth
century the old village had 230 houses, half of
which had hearths, a sure sign of the prosperity
which the Court brought. The Londoners who
resorted here in the eighteenth century were
drawn by the association with royalty: the same
snob appeal explained the popularity of Richmond
and Greenwich. The building of Chiswick House
also attracted people of means to Chiswick, and
by the late eighteenth century land values were
exorbitant. In 1779 a half-acre plot which as
agricultural land was worth £5 elsewhere fetched

£2000 in Chiswick. The district was then thickly
populated with nobility. The riverside prospect was
almost urban in character, with a series of grand
residences. Further prosperous developments were
also found around Chiswick Mall, where there are
the most substantial suburban survivals.

Infinite Variety: 1840–1914

Bedford Park, Turnham Green, W4
See **London Borough of Ealing**

St Margaret's Estate, Isleworth
This estate was developed from 1854 by the
Conservative Land Society, with curving roads,
and houses varying in size and style; Spring Grove

Between the Wars: 1914–1940

New Ideal Homesteads Estate, Hanworth
A large and characteristic (if unspectacular)
development, begun in 1933, by one of the largest
speculative builders of the London area.

Fairholme Estate, Staines Road, East Bedfont
Built in 1934 by T. Cecil Howitt. A late (and
excellently maintained) example of the Arts
and Crafts-influenced garden city estate, planned
as a low-rent development of seventy-two houses
around a grassed quadrangle, complete with a
matching community centre. This remarkable,
philanthropic enclave is reminiscent of almshouses;
indeed, Howitt used similar designs for almshouses
in his native Nottingham.

London Borough of

ISLINGTON

and the City of London

Aristocratic to Middle Class: 1690–1840

Islington was the quintessential late Georgian and Regency suburb. Remarkably, it has survived largely untouched. There is a wide variety of suburban development to be found here: short runs of terraced housing built to modest proportions, gently curving crescents, squares, and long, unrelenting terraces. The area around Upper Street and north of the green captures both the charm and the monotony of London's outlying districts at the start of Queen Victoria's reign. This makes it difficult to single out any one development over another. Nevertheless, a few high points from the 1820s, 1830s and 1840s are worth noting: Highbury Place, N5; the Lloyd Baker Estate, WC1; and Lonsdale Square, N1; see below.

Highbury Place, N5

One of the first really smart suburban developments in Islington, the east side of Highbury Fields was laid out with semi-detached houses from 1774 by John Davies, a stockbroker, who lived in nearby Canonbury. The terms of the lease specified that Highbury Fields would remain open, thus adding to the value and exclusivity of the properties. The entrance from the south was originally gated.

Lloyd Baker Estate, Finsbury, WC1

The site of the Lloyd Baker Estate consisted of three large fields and was developed in the 1820s by the son of the owner, being completed in the 1830s (❍ *pictured above*). Its residents were modest middle-class merchants, genteel tradesmen and moderately successful professionals.

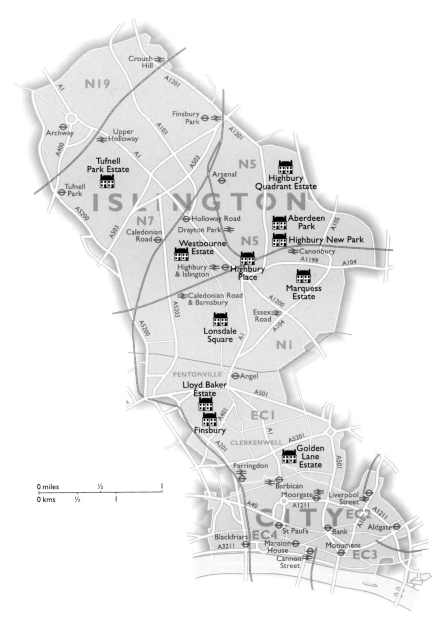

Lonsdale Square, N1

One of the first works by R.C. Carpenter, the architect who would become best known for his splendid churches, Lonsdale Square has all the charm of the cloister or the collegiate close and is a rare example of the Gothic style being used in a suburban speculative development in London (**○** *pictured right*).

Infinite Variety: 1840–1914

Tufnell Park Estate, N7

The Tufnell Park Estate was laid out by George Truefitt from the 1850s onwards, with large houses inventively varied in style, each with asymmetrical combinations of features, window heights and so on.

Aberdeen Park, N5

An estate developed from the early 1850s, with large, Italianate double villas. St Saviour's Church (William White, 1865–67) has a central octagonal tower and polychromatic brickwork, and is now used as artists' studios.

Highbury New Park, N5

An estate of eclectic villas of the 1850s. St Augustine's Church of 1869–70 is by Habershon and Brock. Habershon also designed the Presbyterian church in nearby Grosvenor Avenue, although only the façade remains.

The Road to Subtopia: 1940 to the present

Finsbury, EC1

In the 1930s the run-down Metropolitan Borough of Finsbury produced a model plan for its regeneration with sanitary low-cost housing and civic amenities, working with the incomparable modernists Lubetkin and Tecton. Before 1940 only a health centre, in Pine Street, was completed. Afterwards, the successor firm of Skinner and Lubetkin devised three schemes, of which the Spa Green Estate of 1946–50, built around a small park, is the finest. To the east, much larger blocks were built by Lubetkin's former assistant, C.L. Franck, including Brunswick Close, fourteen-storey flats, in 1956–58; King Square, up to nineteen storeys around a park, in 1959–63; and the Finsbury Estate, completed in 1968, which has one twenty-five-storey tower amid lower ranges of maisonettes.

Golden Lane Estate, City of London, EC1

The Golden Lane Estate is a residential oasis on the edge of the City (in the London Borough of Islington until 1994), built to the designs of Chamberlin, Powell and Bon in 1953–62. Blocks of various-sized flats are ingeniously massed around a series of landscaped courtyards, which make the most of the deep basements formerly on the site to give an interesting interplay of levels through which to walk. The estate is well blessed with social facilities, including shops, a pub, a club, a sports centre and a community centre. It and the adjoining Barbican, by the same architects, possess many characteristics of post-war suburban developments, albeit at a higher density. Listed Grade II.

Highbury Quadrant Estate, N5

An LCC estate of 1955–56, noted for its humane scale and warmth of materials. The development comprises low blocks of flats, pleasantly landscaped, with a clubroom and a sculpture, *The Neighbours*, by Siegfried Charoux. Highbury Quadrant brought out the idealism and social commitment of its young designers, who worked closely with the local community, particularly in the design of the clubroom; it was, with hindsight, the ultimate manifestation of the LCC's Swedish-inspired socialists, usually known as the 'herbivores'.

Marquess Estate, N1

At the very moment when high-rise system building was at its peak, Darbourne and Darke showed that a real domestic environment of brick, with small gardens and lush landscaping, could be created in local authority housing. The Marquess Estate (1970–77) was built in phases, incorporating some earlier council housing at its core, and with the landscaped New River Walk at its western boundary. Two-thirds of Darbourne and Darke's dwellings are family maisonettes with gardens, while the smaller flats above are reached from rooftop streets. In 1998 part of the estate was demolished to provide improved road access and security.

Westbourne Estate, Mackenzie Road, N7

A late example (1976–79) of the work of the Eric Lyons Partnership, who made their reputation designing private housing for Span. This scheme demonstrates the return to conventional streets and terraced houses, albeit on tight plans, as the 1970s progressed.

Royal Borough of

KENSINGTON AND CHELSEA

Aristocratic to Middle Class: 1690–1840

Chelsea, SW3

Chelsea was one of medieval London's grandest suburbs, known by the sixteenth century as the 'King of Villages'. Sir Thomas More moved to Chelsea in 1520; Henry VIII himself had a splendid home here. The list of noble residents is too long to cite. Less ostentatious suburban houses, short runs of terraces mostly, came in the eighteenth century on two main roads, Old Church Street and the King's Road. Henry Holland's Hans Place of 1777 was the first regular development on the model of London's West End estates, and thereafter the open fields between Chelsea and the centre were built over. By the mid-eighteenth century the area was no longer the quiet backwater that it had been, becoming an inner suburb. From this time it began to attract artists, writers and intellectuals more generally, establishing the Bohemian character that persists today, despite steep rises in land values. Traces of the old Georgian suburb survive in places along the King's Road, but the best collection of village homes is found in Cheyne Walk and Cheyne Row. Lindsey House (nos. 96–100 Cheyne Walk) is the only surviving great house from the old village.

Kensington Square, W8

The growth of Kensington was driven, like Greenwich and Richmond, by the presence of the Court, which, with the accession of George I, was in regular residence here. Even before then, in the late Tudor period, there were dignified suburban seats, including Holland House, Campden House and Nottingham House, all near the high road from London to Brentford. London residents came here after the Great Fire of 1666. Their influx persuaded Thomas Young to lay out Kensington Square in 1685 on the model of the new squares (Bloomsbury, St James's) laid out in the years following the Restoration. Kensington's popularity as a suburban retreat peaked between 1690 and 1710 (as also did Richmond's) but then fell out of favour

among the élite. By the 1760s London began to encroach and Young's square slipped down the social scale. Interestingly, the area's fortunes revived in the 1850s when it gained the reputation that it still has today.

Ladbroke Estate, W11

The Ladbroke Estate was one of the largest holdings in Kensington. Proposals to develop it as an elegant villa suburb were first put forward in

1821, but like many grand speculative schemes of the period (see also **London Borough of Lambeth**: Clapham Park Estate, SW4), its realization was delayed by the economic downturn of 1825. The initial private Act of Parliament obtained by J.W. Ladbroke allowed up to 5 acres of land for each house, and although these generous plots would quickly be whittled down, the idea of organizing the new streets around a great central circus with concentric avenues would remain a key feature of the plan drawn up by Ladbroke's surveyor, Thomas Allason (*see following entry*).

Infinite Variety: 1840–1914

Ladbroke Estate, W11

A coherent design of crescents and large communal gardens laid out according to a plan of 1823 by Thomas Allason (*see previous entry*) and built up from the 1840s to the 1860s by the speculative developer J.W. Ladbroke. There are shops and services at the west end of the estate, and a wide boulevard, Ladbroke Grove, as its spine. Many of the spacious houses were located in the south-west corner, designed by Allason with full-height bow windows; others with classical detailing are in Clarendon Road by William Reynolds, who was also responsible for Lansdowne Walk, Lansdowne Crescent and Lansdowne Road, each characterized by stucco-faced Italianate semi-detached houses. An elegant stucco terrace with bow-fronted houses in the middle in Lansdowne Crescent (nos. 19–38; 1860–62) is by Henry Wyat. The concentric crescents to the north date from the 1860s, and the central ones are separated by generous communal gardens. Ladbroke Grove boasts some large houses on the east side by Thomas Allom (nos. 36–40), who was also responsible for some of the finest work on the estate, in Stanley Crescent and Stanley Gardens. Designated a conservation area with a substantial number of listed buildings.

Norland Square and Royal Crescent, Norland Estate, W11

Laid out from the 1840s by Robert Cantwell with a classical crescent and a square, and some picturesque semi-detached villas, St Anne's Villas, of 1845–46. Designated a conservation area.

Kensington Palace Gardens, W8

Laid out in 1843 by Sir James Pennethorne and developed with huge villas from 1845 onwards by such eminent figures as Owen Jones and Sydney Smirke; and, at the southern end, Palace Green, with an important house by Philip Webb at no. 1, an early essay in the Queen Anne style. There is a fine sequence of houses at the north end of Palace Green dating from 1903 to 1912, some inspired by the seventeenth-century Dutch Baroque style, by Horace Field, J.J. Stevenson, E.J. May and others. In Kensington Palace Gardens are palatial houses of

1844–1865, mostly Italianate, but including the exotic house by Owen Jones, no. 24 (1845), with Moorish details such as the onion domes. Designated a conservation area.

The Boltons, SW10

Designed in 1850 and built in 1851–60, The Boltons (◐*pictured above*) is an almond-shaped estate stretching between the top of Tregunter Road to the south and Old Brompton Road to the north. The development comprises large, semi-detached, stucco-faced Italianate villas with generous front gardens by George Godwin jnr, surveyor to the Gunter Estate. Designated a conservation area.

Holland Park, W11

A development carved from the grounds of Holland House in 1860–79, comprising ninety identical detached villas in an exuberant Italianate style by Francis Radford. Holland Park Mews, of the same date, provided stables with accommodation above. There is a grand entrance gate to the mews at the west end. All the Holland Park villas and mews buildings are listed.

Collingham Gardens, SW5, and Harrington Gardens, SW7

Developed in the 1880s by Ernest George and Harold Peto in a rich variety of styles but

predominately a Flemish-inspired Queen Anne style. Designated a conservation area.

Between the Wars: 1914–1940

Kensal House, Ladbroke Grove, North Kensington, W10

A spectacular development (◐*pictured opposite top*) of 1936–37 by Maxwell Fry in this formerly industrial area on the edge of Victorian London, consisting of two slab blocks of reinforced concrete, and a nursery school. Built on the site of a demolished gas works by the Gas Light and Coke Company, the development was partly intended as a pioneering demonstration of how gas could be used in modern housing for heating and cooking. Listed Grade II*.

The Road to Subtopia: 1940 to the present

Cheltenham Estate, W10

Built in 1967–73 between the Grand Union Canal, Westway and Golborne Road, to the designs of Ernö Goldfinger, the Cheltenham Estate of houses, flats, an old people's home and a small park is dominated by the thirty-one-storey Trellick Tower – with its semi-detached lift tower, one of the most charismatic images of west London. The lower blocks and especially the terraces of houses repay close inspection; though in no way innovative for their late date, the attention to detail and quality of construction are exemplary. Trellick Tower was listed Grade II* in 1998.

World's End, Chelsea, SW10

A real neighbourhood of housing, a school and shops, with a suburban character despite its high density (270 p.p.a.). World's End was built between 1967 and 1977 to the designs of Eric Lyons, H.T. Cadbury-Brown, and Metcalfe and Cunningham as a rather complex series of red-brick towers and landscaped courtyards.

Woodsford Square, Addison Road, W14

An estate of 1968–74 by Fry, Drew and Partners for Wates. Though firmly in the Modern Movement tradition, this leafy development of four-storey terraces and communal greens is also indebted to the ideas of low-rise brick housing introduced by Darbourne and Darke.

St Mark's Road, W10

A pioneering housing association development (nos. 103–123) of 1976–80 by Jeremy Dixon. It is significant as the point where 1970s neo-vernacular formally became neo-Georgian. It also revived the traditional form of the terrace set tight against the street (⊙ pictured lower right), and was extremely influential, both in north London suburbs and in Docklands.

Royal Borough of

KINGSTON UPON THAMES

The core of the medieval borough (the royal charter dates from 1481) was around the market place, an area which even today retains a recognizably medieval street plan. There are not many survivals from this early period. By the late eighteenth century there were some smart villas on the edge of the old town, Nash's Southborough House in Surbiton being an exception. Kingston did not become a commuting suburb until the nineteenth century, largely because the railway passed it by, arriving in Surbiton in 1840. Portsmouth Road, by the river, was built up by the 1870s, along with surrounding streets. Kingston, by contrast, stayed a modest development.

Infinite Variety: 1840–1914

Coombe Lane and Beverley Lane, Coombe
A group of houses, designed by pioneering Arts and Crafts architect George Devey, of brick, stone, rough-cast and tiles, dating from of the 1860s.

Between the Wars: 1914–1940

Coombe
Numerous inter-war houses of note were built amid the late Victorian suburban villas here, such as Maxwell Fry's 'Miramonte' of 1936–37 in Warren Rise, a canonical Modern Movement house with the compulsory sun-room on top (listed Grade II) and the Sunspan houses at nos. 57, 65 and 69 Woodlands Avenue (○ pictured below) by Wells Coates and G. Pleydell Bouverie.

The Road to Subtopia: 1940 to the present

Coombe Hill Road, Coombe
Coombe was developed with grand houses towards the end of the nineteenth century, many of those by George Devey having stables and outbuildings, which have since been adapted to popular homes. New houses have since been built around them, and include buildings by Patrick Gwynne, Tayler and Green, and Alan and Sylvia Blanc. However, what was one of the richest areas of individual post-war houses has been gravely disfigured by the demolition, in 1995, of Ernö Goldfinger's 'Player House', and in 1998 of Patrick Gwynne's 'Junipers'. The conservation area is drawn tightly around the Victorian buildings.

London Borough of
LAMBETH

Aristocratic to Middle Class: 1690–1840

Clapham Common, SW4

The Common was levelled and planted in the late eighteenth century, when the area's reputation as a salubrious suburb was beginning to peak. Nothing survives of the earlier villas (of the sixteenth and seventeenth centuries) but there is an excellent group of Georgian and early Victorian houses comprising nos. 5–9, 11, 13–21 Clapham Common North Side. The latter, erected in about 1730 (❍ *pictured below*), are comparable to suburban terraces at Richmond (see **London Borough of Richmond upon Thames**: Montpelier Row), Hampstead (see **London Borough of Camden**: Church Row) and Greenwich (Dartmouth Row). There are some remains of this early period on the south side of the Common. (See also **London Borough of Wandsworth**: Clapham Common North Side)

Kennington Road and Kennington Park Road, SE11

Kennington Road was laid out after the opening of Westminster Bridge and still boasts an excellent collection of late Georgian suburban terraces. Nos. 123–133 (odd; 1773–75), on the east side, are particularly fine. Nos. 114–132 were built in 1787–90 by Michael Searles, who was responsible for the better-known Paragon in Blackheath (see **London Borough of Greenwich**: Blackheath Park). Nos. 140–162 of *ca.* 1795 are comparable in quality, as are nos. 61–167 in Kensington Park Road (in fact in the London Borough of Southwark), though these are later, of *ca.* 1790.

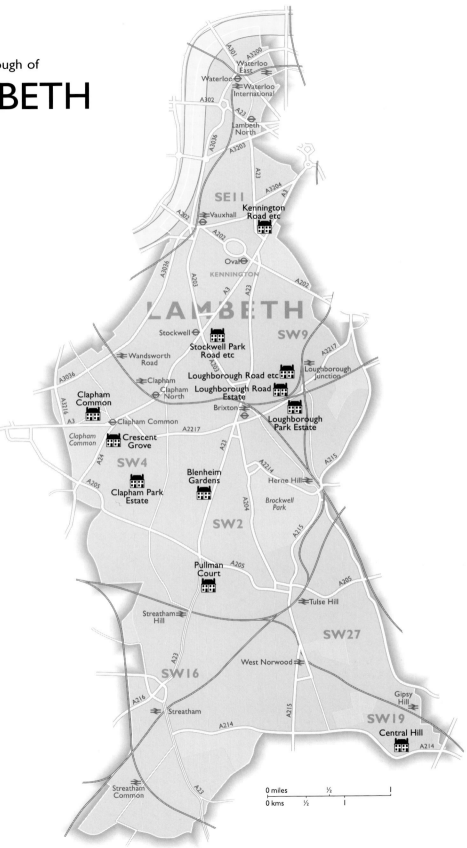

Crescent Grove, SW4

Francis Child developed this road in 1824. Identical houses at the Clapham Common end functioned as gateway buildings. The semi-detached houses on the left (◑ *pictured top left*) are a distant echo of The Paragon in Blackheath (*see* **London Borough of Greenwich**: Blackheath Park).

Clapham Park Estate, SW4

The great master builder Thomas Cubitt bought the estate in 1825, just as the London building world was beginning the steep slide from which it would not recover until Victoria came to the throne in 1837. Consequently, the estate was not completed until the 1850s and 1860s, by which time it was far and away the most fashionable suburb south of the river. Cubitt himself lived here; his house stood in Clarence Avenue, one of the main roads in the estate, along with Poynders Road, Atkins Road and King's Avenue, this last being where the only houses to survive from this time are to be found. As at Blackheath Park (*see* **London Borough of Greenwich**), there has been much infill and demolition over time.

Stockwell Park Road and Stockwell Park Crescent, SW9

These are lined with stuccoed villas and terraces of the 1830s (◑ *pictured top middle*), a rare survival of the sort of developments that were more commonplace in nearby Brixton.

Infinite Variety: 1840–1914

Loughborough Road and St John's Crescent, Loughborough Park, Brixton, SW9

A development of the 1840s and 1850s, with a range of houses, terraces and villas.

Between the Wars: 1914–1940

Pullman Court, Streatham Hill, Streatham, SW16

Built in 1933–36 to designs by Frederick Gibberd. A private venture, in its day it was the largest commercial development of blocks of flats in London before Costains built Dolphin Square in Pimlico in 1937 (*see* **City of Westminster**). The scheme comprises some 218 flats, in blocks varying from three to five floors, designed in an uncompromisingly modern idiom in reinforced concrete, with balconies and extensive glazing to take advantage of its hilly site. Listed Grade II.

Loughborough Park Estate, South Brixton, SW9

Edward Armstrong designed this 1939 estate, of almost four hundred flats in five-storey slabs of reinforced concrete, for the Guinness Trust in a modishly minimalist style. The buildings marked a clear departure from the heavier, brick-built, LCC-inspired blocks that the Trust (and others) had been using for such projects, and they were to prove influential.

The Road to Subtopia: 1940 to the present

Loughborough Road Estate, South Brixton, SW9

An early example of LCC high-rise slabs, of 1953–57, and comparable with those at Bentham Road, Hackney (*see* **London Borough of Hackney**), and the Alton Estate, Roehampton (*see* **London Borough of Wandsworth**). The strict rows of eleven-storey slabs make for quite a dramatic townscape, here unsoftened by landscaping and so giving an entirely different impression to the visitor.

Central Hill, SE19

Under Edward Hollamby, the London Borough of Lambeth enjoyed a fine reputation for its public housing in the late 1960s and 1970s. Specializing in low-rise, high-density developments, the most celebrated example is Central Hill (1964–67; ◑ *pictured top right*), designed by Rosemary Stjernstedt. On a steep slope are set tiers of terraced maisonettes, entered from above or below so that all have a front door at ground level. Although the group is less succinctly massed than the contemporary Camden housing, it is an interesting embodiment of the same ideals.

Blenheim Gardens, Brixton Hill, SW2

One of Lambeth's first large, low-rise, high-density developments of two-storey houses and flats from 1971–74, still within a geometric rather than a carefully informal layout. The pleasant landscaping makes for interesting comparisons with the pioneering Lillington Gardens, Pimlico (*see* **City of Westminster**).

London Borough of
LEWISHAM

Infinite Variety: 1840–1914

Sydenham, SE23 and SE26

After the opening of the exhibition halls at Crystal Palace, Upper Norwood, in 1851, the surrounding area of Upper Sydenham became a suburb of wealthy mansions, many owned by people associated with the exhibition of products of British trade and industry and of the Crystal Palace itself: Joseph Paxton, Owen Jones, Sir George Grove (secretary of the exhibition) and Samuel Phillips (author of the catalogues). Few of these grand houses remain although there are exceptions, for example in Sydenham Hill and Eliot Bank.

Sydenham Hill, SE23 and SE26

Some mansions survive here from the classy suburb built for those attracted to the area by the Crystal Palace. Examples are 'Sunnydene' and 'Ellerslie' (1868–70) by J.F. Bentley for W.R. Sutton, founder of the Sutton Housing Trust.

Brockley, SE4

Commodious villas neatly arranged along leafy streets, notably Wickham Road and Tressilian Road: tall terraces and pairs of houses of the 1870s, lavishly decorated.

Between the Wars: 1914–1940

Bellingham Estate, SE6

The Bellingham Estate, like the nearby Downham Estate (see following entry), is a large LCC 'out-county' estate, laid out on former agricultural land. Bellingham, begun in 1921, is the earlier of the two estates and consists of almost 2700 cottage-type houses laid out on a wedge-shaped site around a hexagonal green, an unusually formal arrangement, accentuated by the churches that face each other across the sward, as at Hampstead Garden Suburb.

Downham Estate, SE6

The Downham Estate, like the nearby Bellingham Estate (see previous entry), is a large LCC 'out-county' estate, which was built in 1924–38. With 7000 houses laid out along winding roads, it is much larger and more casually planned than the Bellingham Estate.

Mottingham Estate, Mottingham, SE9
See **London Borough of Bromley**

The Road to Subtopia: 1940 to the present

Downham Bungalow Estate, Baudwin Road, Southend, SE6

This is the largest surviving group in London of the 'temporary' bungalows erected following Winston Churchill's pledge to provide homes for heroes, and now usually referred to as 'prefabs'. There are 185 bungalows built in 1945 by Uni-Seco, a wartime firm of hut manufacturers, in little streets named after the Knights of the Round Table. Because they were detached, well planned and have large gardens, prefabs proved popular with residents and many have now been overclad rather than demolished.

Passfields, Daneswood Avenue, Catford, SE6

A handsome development of 1948–50 by Maxwell Fry and Jane Drew, innovative in its box-frame construction and displaying the better funding available in the 1940s. It won a Festival of Britain Merit Award in 1951 and was listed in 1998.

Lammas Green, Sydenham Hill, SE26

Donald McMorran built extensively for the City of London, including a number of housing developments in the suburbs. Lammas Green (1955–57) comprises a series of terraces around a village green, sheltered from the main road by blocks of flats and with a community hall. The slope of the hillside ensures that there are views of the Kent hills from most of the site, thus enhancing the semi-rural atmosphere of the development. Nos. 1–57 Lammas Green were listed Grade II in 1998.

Pepys Estate, Deptford, SE8

The seventeenth-century former Victualling Yard of the Royal Navy was developed with housing by the LCC in 1963–66. The Pepys Estate combines long blocks linked by high-level walkways with late eighteenth-century houses, which were imaginatively converted into sheltered housing and a community centre. The result has a drama rare in London housing.

London Borough of
MERTON

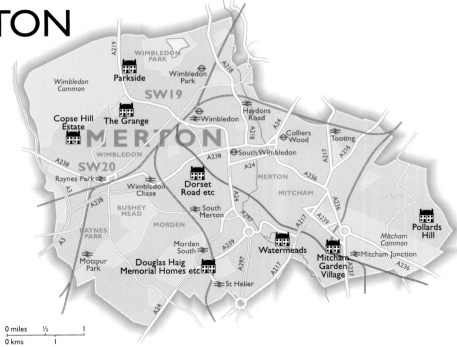

Infinite Variety: 1840–1914

The most affluent suburb in the borough is Wimbledon, which was developed in the nineteenth century and later, when reasonably grand houses, albeit varied in type and style, were scattered around the edges of Wimbledon Common (covering 1100 acres), and to the south along the Ridgway. Some of these have been casualties of later, more intensive developments of houses and flats. Some early Victorian housing here includes work by Roumieu, Ransome and Penrose; later examples include work by E.J. May, George and Yeates, T.G. Jackson, Baillie Scott and the local firm of Hubbard and Moore. Located near Merton parish church is the late Victorian middle-class suburb of Merton Park, created by the architects Quartermain and Brocklesby for the local landowner John Innes (of Innes compost). Meanwhile, the less pretentious streets of 'New Wimbledon' filled the area between Wimbledon Broadway and Kingston Road, and more suburban development spread south around the railway stations: Lower Merton, 1855; Merton, 1868; Raynes Park, 1870.

Much of the rest of Merton – around the villages of Mitcham and Morden – remained rural until the twentieth century, when development followed the extension of the Northern Line to Morden in 1926. The rural quality is retained by the good-sized open

spaces and parks in the borough, such as Morden Hall Park, Ravensbury Park and Mitcham Common.

The Grange, Lauriston Road, SW19

Handsome asymmetrical Arts and Crafts houses by various architects including T.G. Jackson (no. 1) and Sir Ernest George (no. 9).

Dorset Road, Melrose Road, Mostyn Road and Sheridan Road, Merton Park, SW19

An estate created by John Innes from the 1870s onwards, with planted avenues lined with houses for City gents in the Queen Anne Revival style by H.G. Quartermaine, built between 1880 and 1900, and Arts and Crafts-inspired cottages built between 1900 and 1911 by J.S. Brocklesby (in Melrose Road (❍ *pictured opposite left*), including Brocklesby's own house, no. 17 'Steep Roof').

Parkside, Wimbledon Common, SW19

An area rich in Arts and Crafts houses set along ample winding roads. Of particular note is no. 21 Calonne Road (1910; ○ *pictured top right*) – gabled and tile-hung – by M.H. Baillie Scott.

Between the Wars: 1914–1940

St Helier Estate, Sutton
See **London Borough of Sutton**

Mitcham Garden Village, Mitcham

A distinctive close of houses (1929–32) off the Carshalton Road, by Chart and Reading, picturesquely arranged and varied in design, sharing a common half-timbered style.

Housing for Disabled Ex-servicemen, Green Lane and Central Road, Morden

Two distinct and notable estates of houses for casualties of World War I. The earlier of these, the Douglas Haig Memorial Homes (1929–31) by Grey

Wornum, consists of a series of almshouse-like rows of neo-Georgian houses set amid green spaces, with portrait roundels of the Western Front commander; one of a number of such estates across the country, these were opened by the Prince of Wales. Near by are the houses and flats designed by Percy Morley-Horder in 1930 for the Housing Association for Officers' Families, in a collegiate style befitting this genteel organization aimed at helping officers' widows and families. Within a designated conservation area, but not listed.

The Road to Subtopia: 1940 to the present

Copse Hill Estate, Wimbledon, SW20

An early example of the influence of Span on a larger developer, Copse Hill was developed by Wimpey's team of in-house architects in 1961–62. The detailing is sharper and more clean-cut than Span's, the massing of houses and garages less successful.

Pollards Hill, Mitcham, SW16

This is the first of the London Borough of Merton's distinctive low-rise, high-density housing schemes, a deceptively simple layout of three-storey flats and houses set in a continuous thread, interwoven around closes for cars on one side and private gardens and open spaces on the other. Built between 1968 and 1971, the project architect was M. Kitchen; assistants included the young Richard MacCormac. The development is a prime example of perimeter planning, as expounded by Sir Leslie Martin and Lionel March a few years earlier.

Watermeads, Rawnsley Avenue, Mitcham

The concept of Pollards Hill (*see above*) was refined at Watermeads by R. Hodge and A. Bews in 1974–77. The concept of separating cars and play areas by means of a wall of housing is the same, as are the white enamel cladding panels, but the site is smaller. Communal gardens lead down to the River Wandle, which has been dammed to make a small lake and planted to make a charming foil to the simplicity of the housing.

London Borough of

NEWHAM

From the sixteenth century West Ham was a favoured resort for merchants and professionals in the City of London, as, to a lesser extent, was East Ham. Romford Road and Rancliffe Road were developed with merchant villas from the early nineteenth century; there are Georgian survivals, but in general the character of these areas is overwhelmingly late Victorian and twentieth century.

Nearby Stratford grew rapidly from 1700, with development concentrated on the high road through the old village. Plaistow, however, stayed relatively isolated until the late nineteenth century. The Cobham Estate near Whipps Cross (it survives only in the name of Cobham Road) was sold on from one City merchant to another from the early fourteenth century. From the late seventeenth century Forest House, close by, with its 50-acre estate, passed through a succession of owners who had connections with the Bank of England, as did the Great House Estate.

0 miles ½ 1
0 kms 1

Infinite Variety: 1840–1914

Woodgrange Estate, Forest Gate, E7

This area of around seven hundred properties was built in 1877–92. It was a speculative development by one of London's most prolific developers, Cameron Corbett. It is the most interesting of Corbett's seven estates. Built for the middle-class city commuter, reflections of station architecture are seen in wide glass canopies with cast-iron columns and valencing that decorate many of the houses (❍ *pictured below*). Cast-iron gates

and railings are another special feature. Some front elevations also have, unusually, two pairs of French doors. Although mostly terraced, small servants' annexes, set back from the building line, make the main houses appear detached. The estate was developed to one plan with shops and church, but no pub (Corbett was Baptist) and is distinguished from the extensive areas of Victorian housing in Newham by its sense of space and greenery, wide roads, deep front gardens and trees. Designated a conservation area in 1976

The Road to Subtopia: 1940 to the present

5m Housing, Ravenscroft Road, Canning Town, E16

A prototype housing scheme by the Ministry of Housing (1963), which experimented with Parker Morris standard houses at relatively high densities. Different units explored open-plan and flexible partitioning of the living areas, and were widely influential.

Beckton, E6

Beckton, though mostly post-war and suburban, owes its origin to the Gas, Light and Coke Company, which built their works here in 1860. The closure of the gasworks in 1970 led the local authority and subsequently the LDDC to develop the area with low-cost housing (❍ *pictured above*) A new park links the gas workers' cottages with Edwardian council housing and the new, largely private, schemes.

London Borough of

REDBRIDGE

Infinite Variety: 1840–1914

Barnados Village Homes, Horns Road, Barkingside, Ilford

Part of the Girls' Village Home built by Dr Barnado between 1875 and 1907. Seventeen two-storey cottages survive from the original sixty-five homes that were grouped around a green with school, hospital, church and laundry. The cottages have steep-pitch, double-gable roofs and are built of yellow stock brick with applied half-timbering.

The Drive, South Woodford

Late Victorian and Edwardian houses, each varied in design and scale, overlooking a green.

Empress Avenue, Woodford

A handsome sweep of medium-sized Edwardian houses in a long tree-lined street.

Between the Wars: 1914–1940

Mayfield, Goodmayes, Ilford

Also known as the Bungalow Estate, this area to the west of Goodmayes Lane consists of several streets of bungalows, with barge-boarded gables and bay windows, and was developed from the 1920s. The area is remarkable for its homogeneity: such large areas of cottages are rare in the inter-war suburbs of Greater London. Designated a conservation area.

Knighton Estate, Woodford Wells

An early 1930s estate on the edge of Epping Forest, developed by Southend-on-Sea Estates Ltd. Numerous detached houses of above-average quality, enriched with mock-Tudor features, including much half-timbering. The similar Monkhams Estate adjoins to the south-east.

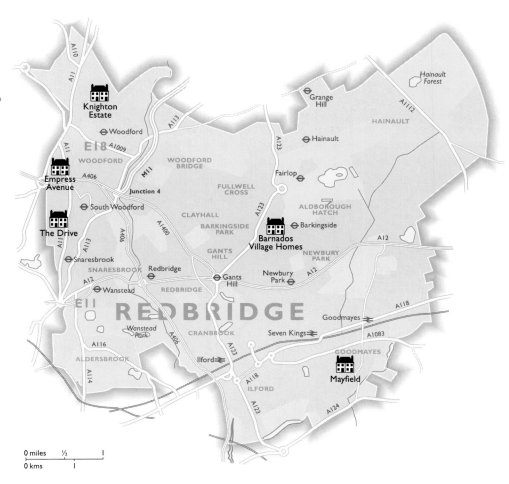

London Borough of

RICHMOND UPON THAMES

Aristocratic to Middle Class: 1690–1840

Richmond has been a prosperous suburb since the seventeenth century. Proximity to a Royal Park, mineral springs and ease of access (by river) all made its success something of a foregone conclusion. The area around the Green experienced a boom after 1690, a twenty-year period of rapid growth underwritten by London money and developed exactly as the new streets and squares in the West End, although on a smaller scale. A few speculators led the way: John Knapp, Nathaniel Rawlins, John Saunders and Vertue Radford. The last – an attorney and son-in-law of the Lord Chief Justice – moved to Richmond in 1688, only to demolish the house on the site and replace it with a handsome terrace of seven houses facing the Green (Old Palace Terrace, which survives). Michael Pew, the son of a brewer, speculated in larger houses in the late 1690s (nos. 1, 2 and 3 The Terrace), mortgaging one to finance the next. John Price, however, was the largest speculator, building houses to the northern end of the Green and on Little Green. Between 1710 and 1725 he put up six large mansions.

A second boom came in the 1750s and 1760s, when many villas were built on the river (e.g. Argyll House, 1761–65) and on the slopes of Richmond Hill. Less grand people began to settle in the 1820s, in rows of smaller villas. So-called New Richmond grew on the south side of Mortlake Road. Nearer the Hill was developed in the 1840s: Park Road, Park Villas, Queen's Road and Rothesay Villas in Friars Stile Road. There is more that survives in Richmond than can be detailed here, but among the most noteworthy developments are nos. 1–3, 6, 10–12 and 21–22 The Green (❍*pictured above right) and Maids of Honour Row. There is a smattering of good Georgian building on Sheen Road and Petersham Road. On Richmond Hill there is Ormond Terrace, The Rosary and The Hollies (an interesting semi-detached house where the two halves are joined at the rear wall), Church Terrace and The Terrace.*

Montpelier Row, Twickenham

Facing east towards Marble Hill Park, this elegant terrace was built in the 1720s as a speculative development by Captain John Grey, and is very similar in character to Syon Row (dated 1721). It is one of the best surviving examples of a suburban Georgian terrace in Greater London.

Infinite Variety: 1840–1914

The borough is particularly rich in Victorian and Edwardian suburban developments, especially for the affluent, in and around Barnes, Kew, Mortlake, Richmond, Strawberry Hill, Teddington and Twickenham.

Castelnau, Barnes, SW13

Twenty semi-detached classical villas designed and developed by William Laxton from 1842 for the Boileau family, whose ancestral home was Castelnau de la Garde, near Nîmes in southern France. Mature trees shade the deep front gardens.

The development continued into the 1860s with Italianate and Gothic villas along Lonsdale Road (❍*pictured above*), built as a result of the construction of Hammersmith Bridge.

Model Cottages, East Sheen, SW14

The first cottages were built along the pathway that is now known as Model Cottages by the Labourers' Friendly Society in 1853 and the last were completed around 1870. The cottages, pairs of two-storey buildings with small recessed wings

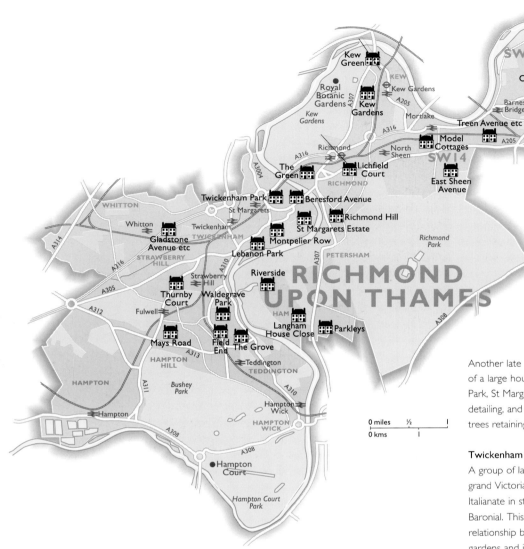

RICHMOND
UPON THAMES

Another late Victorian suburb built in the grounds of a large house is the development at Cambridge Park, St Margarets, of gault brick with Italianate detailing, and with a mixture conifer and deciduous trees retaining the park-like character.

Twickenham Park, Twickenham

A group of large middle-class houses make up this grand Victorian suburb of the 1870s, mostly Italianate in style with some Gothic and Scottish Baronial. This suburb demonstrates a successful relationship between buildings and planting, in gardens and in the street.

Kew Gardens, Kew

The architecture of the Kew Gardens Conservation Area is characterized by a plethora of examples of *fin-de-siècle* freestyle design, with rich and exuberant detailing in the ornamental barge-boarding, terracotta panels, gables, finials and turrets. Station Parade and Station Approach form a late Victorian shopping area adjoining Kew Gardens station. Dating from 1869, this is one of the few remaining original nineteenth-century stations on the North London line.

Waldegrave Park, Strawberry Hill

Sited on a gentle slope towards the river, large detached houses of the 1880s and 1890s are set in large mature landscaped gardens. Many have

for the entrances and sharing a large central stack, are set back from the path and have large front gardens; there are no rear gardens. Another example of workers' housing in the borough dating from the 1860s can be found at Blackmore's Grove, Teddington.

Kew Green, Kew

A variety of nineteenth-century houses, ranging from large villas around the Green to small cottages along the riverside. The Priory Estate (Priory Road and Gloucester Road) is characterized by Edwardian semi-detached and terraced houses in red and yellow brick with decorative details, in streets lined with mature trees.

The Green, Richmond

A fine group of symmetrical pairs of large, pedimented, mid-nineteenth-century villas front the north-west side of the Green; on the north side are two pairs of nineteenth-century Italianate villas.

St Margarets Estate, St Margarets

A residential estate developed form 1854, following the advent of the railway in the 1850s. The Conservative Land Society developed the park of St Margaret's House along principles later enshrined by the garden suburb movement, using the existing planting as a focus of the estates, and setting Gothic and Italianate villas in large plots defined by low brick walls and hedge-planting. Nineteenth-century industrial buildings are lined along the riverside in a pleasingly informal way.

distinctive brick, tile and stone detailing reminiscent of R. Norman Shaw's Bedford Park (see **London Borough of Ealing**). Of particular interest is the strong rhythm produced by the clay-tile roofscape, the prominent polygonal bays and corner entrances.

Lebanon Park, Twickenham

A distinctive area of large red-brick Edwardian houses with ornate features and substantial front gardens, all within a conservation area.

Treen Avenue, Rosslyn Avenue, Tudor Gardens and Priory Gardens, Barnes, SW13

A development of terraced houses of *ca.* 1910–13, bordered on the southern side by Beverley Brook. The brick and rough-cast houses, typical of the Edwardian development of Barnes, are at first glance identical but in fact contain subtle variations of layout and external period detail.

East Sheen Avenue, SW14

This street is a mixture of eclectic styles ranging from projecting half-timbered gables (**⊙** *pictured right*) to Indian-inspired domes. Many have balconies and porches. The houses are semi-detached set in large gardens with hedges and trees with a well-established suburban feel.

Between the Wars: 1914–1940

The Grove Teddington

A 1920s development carried out by the Royal Dutch Shell Company to provide their workers with housing: an enclave of cottages – built around a bowling green – which owes something of its appearance to the Continental origins of the firm that commissioned them. Designated a conservation area.

Gladstone Avenue and Rosecroft Gardens, Twickenham

A triangular development just south of the arterial Chertsey Road, consisting of single-storey semis of *ca.* 1930. Designated a conservation area.

Mays Road, Hampton Hill

A distinctive group of 1930s semis, firmly in the garden suburb tradition, arranged around a miniature square. The houses are distinguished by their vernacular flourishes such as prominent

chimney-stacks and timber-bracketed porches. Designated a conservation area.

Lichfield Court, Sheen Road, Richmond

Two giant blocks of flats of 1935, designed by Bertram Carter, in a self-consciously modern, ocean-liner style. Their mass dwarfs their Georgian neighbours: the inter-war suburb could be very intrusive. Within a conservation area.

Beresford Avenue, Twickenham

A mid-1930s cul-de-sac just south of the Thames, lined with modernistic rendered semis. Designated a conservation area.

The Road to Subtopia: 1940 to the present

Parkleys, Ham

This was the first major scheme by Span Developments Ltd, established by Geoffrey Townsend in 1954 with Eric Lyons as architect. Built on the site of a nursery, the gardener from which was retained by the estate, Parkleys exemplifies the Span combination of simply massed dwellings, carefully grouped around existing trees, and with lush planting. Townsend established the first residents' management committee here, a feature of every subsequent Span development and an insurance that all have remained in prestige

condition. The endowment mortgage for first-time buyers was also pioneered here. Originally split between Richmond and Kingston, the estate is now all in Richmond. Parkleys was listed Grade II in 1998.

Langham House Close, Ham

A small but pioneering example of the influence of Le Corbusier's Maison Jaoul in England is this small development of 1958 by James Stirling and James Gowan. It was one of the first developments of private flats to use a tough, wholly modern aesthetic of raw brickwork and exposed concrete. Listed Grade II in 1998.

Thurnby Court, Twickenham

A quadrangle of tile-hung Span flats similar to Parkleys, Ham (*see above*), dating from 1958.

Field End, Twickenham

A Span development of terraced houses of 1961, and one of the most wooded of all the Span schemes.

Riverside, Ham

A large and well-landscaped Wates development of 1961–68 that has all the ingredients but none of the intimacy of the nearby schemes by their mentors, Span.

London Borough of

SOUTHWARK

The land south of the River Thames, opposite the cities of London and Westminster, remained undeveloped for centuries largely because it was marshy. The problem was compounded by the lack of river crossings, London Bridge being the only one from Roman times to 1750. A thriving suburb developed at Southwark because this area was raised slightly above the surrounding tidal marshes; indeed, this is why the Romans chose it as their southern bridgehead.

Aristocratic to Middle Class 1690–1840

Kennington Park Road, SE11
See **London Borough of Lambeth**

College Road, Dulwich Common and Dulwich Village, SE21
College Road, Dulwich Common and particularly Dulwich Village boast a fine collection of eighteenth-century suburban dwellings. The last is especially interesting for retaining a village character.

Camberwell Grove and Grove Lane, SE5
Both roads were developed from the 1770s with terraces and semis. The eastern side of Camberwell Grove (at its northern end) offers a particularly good range of houses.

Trinity Church Square, SE1
This is comparable to contemporary estates in Islington, and features the particularly fine church of the Holy Trinity (1823–24; ○ *pictured below*)

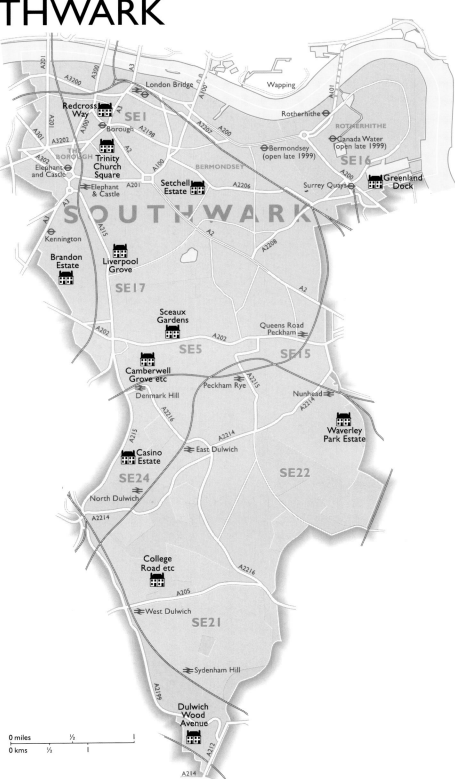

by Francis Bedford. The square, now marooned in an otherwise twentieth-century environment, illustrates particularly well the desire to couple suburban development with moral rectitude.

Infinite Variety: 1840–1914

Redcross Way, SE1

A group of cottages, a hall and a garden (◑ *pictured below*) planned by Octavia Hill and embodying her belief that the working classes deserved a healthy and decent environment instead of slums or overcrowded flats to live in. The cottages were

built between 1887 and 1890 by Elijah Hoole, with a pleasing jumble of gables and bays, overlooking Redcross Gardens. Redcross Hall (Hoole, 1888), with panels inside painted by Walter Crane in 1889, completes the group. There are more cottages, called Gable Cottages, to the south in Sudrey Street, designed by Hoole for the Revd T. Bastow in 1889 and arranged around a courtyard in the manner of almshouses. Designated a conservation area.

Waverley Park Estate, Ivydale Road, Peckham Rye, SE15

A classic two-up, two-down speculative development of 1884–1903 by Edward Yates.

Liverpool Grove, Portland Street, SE17

Three-storey cottage flats built by Cluttons in 1903–09 for the Ecclesiastical Commissioners under the guidance of Octavia Hill, with bay windows, gables and some variety of grouping. Designated a conservation area.

Between the Wars: 1914–1940

Casino (or Sunray) Estate, Herne Hill, SE24

A 'Homes fit for Heroes' estate of 1920–21, directed by the Ministry of Works under Sir Frank Baines, consisting of intimately scaled (if plain) houses around small greens. They were built using direct labour on behalf of Camberwell Borough Council. Adjoining are very different red-brick blocks of the later 1930s that take advantage of the fine hilltop setting.

The Road to Subtopia: 1940 to the present

Brandon Estate, Kennington, SE17

One of the most prestigious and innovative of the LCC's housing schemes, the Brandon Estate was designed by Edward Hollamby in 1955. The first phase was completed in 1962; it was subsequently extended. It was the first scheme to combine new (and, for their date, tall) blocks with the rehabilitation of Victorian terraces.

Dulwich Wood Avenue, SE19

The Dulwich College Estate now includes a number of interesting Wates estates, which have replaced large Victorian mansions but preserved their mature trees. All here are by Austin Vernon and Partners, architects to the College. Dulwich Wood Avenue contains groups of flats; there are terraces of houses in Woodhall Drive and Great Brownings.

Sceaux Gardens, Peckham, SE5

This was the showpiece of the extensive housing developments by F.O. Hayes for Camberwell Metropolitan Borough before 1965. It comprises two fourteen-storey slabs of maisonettes, with six-storey blocks (◑ *pictured below*) and bungalows in mature gardens. Near by, Hayes experimented with low-rise, high-density housing at an early date

(1957–63) on the Acorn Estate, Carlton Grove. Off the Old Kent Road is his similar Bonamy Estate of 1963–66, which rises to just four storeys.

Greenland Dock, SE16

The most suburban areas of redeveloped Docklands are to be found in the former Surrey Docks, of which Greenland Dock (◑ *pictured above*) is the finest survivor. Of a series of late 1980s private housing schemes, the most exciting is perhaps The Lakes, by Shepheard, Epstein and Hunter, of 1988–96, a crescent set around what survives of Norway Dock. Near by are further flats and maisonettes at Finland Quay of 1987–89 by Richard Reid; and the picturesque if fussy Swedish Quay by David Price and Gordon Cullen.

Setchell Estate, SE1

Built to the designs of Neylan and Ungless in 1972–78, this is one of the most deliberately 'villagey' groups of low-rise housing to have been built in inner London during the 1970s, characterized by steep pitched roofs and dark brickwork. Although it is nowhere more than three storeys, the high density of 136 p.p.a. is achieved. The layout follows the existing street pattern, but with closes for cars alternating with pedestrian walkways.

London Borough of

SUTTON

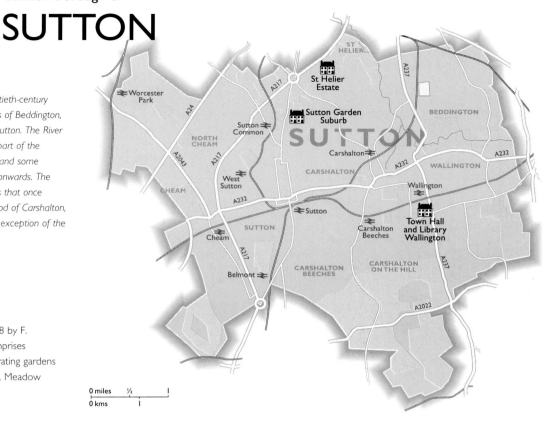

The borough of Sutton is largely twentieth-century suburban, built around the old villages of Beddington, Wallington, Carshalton, Cheam and Sutton. The River Wandle runs through the north-east part of the borough, and attracted rural retreats and some industry from the eighteenth century onwards. The many large eighteenth-century houses that once existed, especially in the neighbourhood of Carshalton, have left little trace, with the notable exception of the mansion Carshalton House.

Infinite Variety: 1840–1914

Sutton Garden Suburb

Developed between 1900 and 1918 by F. Cavendish Pearson, the suburb comprises Vernacular Revival housing incorporating gardens and open green spaces (Oak Close, Meadow Close, Horseshoe Green).

Between the Wars: 1914–1940

St Helier Estate, Sutton

Like the Becontree Estate (see **London Borough of Barking and Dagenham**), this is another of the very large LCC 'out-county' estates, begun in 1928 and laid out on customary garden suburb principles. Its designers were careful to provide it with more facilities, such as shops, a cinema and a large pub, than had the earlier, larger and bleaker Becontree Estate. Of the 825 acres used, 120 were given over to open spaces. Part of the estate lies in the London Borough of Merton.

Town Hall and Library, Wallington

Not so much a suburb as an excellent example of the new municipal centres that were constructed to serve boroughs with greatly enlarged populations. Wallington was a village until 1915, when (with Beddington) it became an urban district. Robert Atkinson designed this civic complex in 1933, and the town hall (later a court) was opened in 1935. Both buildings were designed in a Scandinavian-influenced style with neo-Georgian echoes. Neither is listed.

London Borough of

TOWER HAMLETS

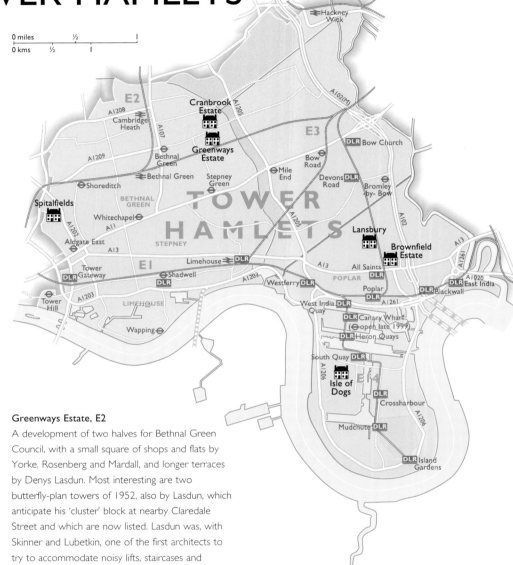

Aristocratic to Middle Class: 1690–1840

Spitalfields, E1

Spitalfields was developed as an industrial suburb from the mid-sixteenth century. Silk-weaving was established in the last years of the century by French Huguenots, and by the eighteenth century the local product was widely recognized for its excellence. The best collection of weavers' houses,

some of which retain their distinctive rooflights, are to be found in Fournier Street (◐ *pictured above*), erected from 1726. Good examples can also be found in Princelet Street, Wilkes Street, Folgate Street and Elder Street.

The Road to Subtopia: 1940 to the present

Lansbury, Poplar, E14

The *Live Architecture and Town Planning* exhibition of the Festival of Britain, developed hastily in 1949–51 by the LCC, Frederick Gibberd, Geoffrey Jellicoe and others. It is important as the first major neighbourhood scheme to have received widespread publicity after World War II and as a model for suburban developments in outer London and the New Towns thereafter. Its popularity is indicated by the widespread overcladding and window replacement that has occurred, a fervour that the newly declared conservation area status hopes to address. The principal public buildings are listed.

Greenways Estate, E2

A development of two halves for Bethnal Green Council, with a small square of shops and flats by Yorke, Rosenberg and Mardall, and longer terraces by Denys Lasdun. Most interesting are two butterfly-plan towers of 1952, also by Lasdun, which anticipate his 'cluster' block at nearby Claredale Street and which are now listed. Lasdun was, with Skinner and Lubetkin, one of the first architects to try to accommodate noisy lifts, staircases and services in a separate tower from the flats.

Cranbrook Estate, E2

The last and largest of three developments by Skinner, Bailey and Lubetkin for Bethnal Green Metropolitan Borough, the Cranbrook Estate, of 1955–66, combines tall point blocks with four-storey slabs (◐ *pictured left*) and old people's bungalows. It is the last and perhaps the most complex development by Berthold Lubetkin, an essay in axial planning that culminates in a circular *rond point* and a fence.

Brownfield Estate, E14

A development of two halves. To the west, low LCC flats continue (1955–62) the idiom of adjoining Lansbury (see above) at only a slightly greater height and density; to the east are buildings of the 1960s and a very different scale. The dominant feature is the dramatic concrete brutalism of Balfron Tower (1965–67) by Ernö Goldfinger, which is surrounded by a shop, pensioners' flats and two later medium-rise blocks in a similar idiom (Carradale House of 1967 and Glenkerry House of 1972, his last major work). Designated a conservation area; Balfron Tower (⊙ *pictured above*) is listed.

Isle of Dogs, E14

The island is quintessential Docklands, a mismatched combination of massive commercial development, luxury residential housing, refurbished council blocks and few facilities. The central Asda superstore seems to be the island's social focus. Though the best-known and most distinctive housing is in the former LDDC Enterprise Zone, the playful Cascades (Campbell, Zogolovitch, Wilkinson and Gough, 1985–88; ⊙ *pictured top right*) and colourful Heron Quay (Nicholas Lacey, Jobst and Hyett, 1981–89), the most suburban areas are the former residential districts to the south, at Milwall and Cubitt Town. Streets of substandard nineteenth-century housing were replaced by cottage estates in the inter-war period

(by Harley Heckford, Borough Surveyor), and subsequently by LCC/GLC point blocks and modern developments for both the public and private sectors. An early alternative to council housing was provided by Dr Michael Barraclough, who, in 1975, commissioned an idiosyncratic terrace from Stout and Litchfield, and followed this in 1985–90 with a self-build development designed by the same firm, Maconochie's Wharf, comprising terraces of sturdy cottages. Most suburban of all is Compass Point (⊙ *pictured lower right*), Saunders

Ness Road, where Jeremy Dixon has refined the idiom of the late Georgian paired villa and terrace.

London Borough of

WALTHAM FOREST

Walthamstow was renowned as an area where City men went to build large houses. The air was thought to be especially 'pure', a reputation underlined, no doubt, by the many fine gardens and estate parks. Houses here changed hands quite frequently, a sure sign of their suburban status, often with each new owner marking tenure by improvements to the property. The only survivor of this era is Walthamstow House in Shernhall Street, built in the 1770s.

Infinite Variety: 1840–1914

Leucha Road, E17

A street of terraced houses designed by John Dunn from 1895. Together with terraces of shops in St James Street, the area represents an attractive and largely original example of the earliest estate development by Sir Thomas Warner, founder of the Warner Estate Company, the building programme of which continued into the 1930s. The terraces in Leucha Road bear the distinctive 'W' on the fronts and were well built in red brick with slate roofs, gables and arched recesses and porches. The company also planted privet hedges and creepers in the front gardens and trees in the streets. Designated a conservation area.

Between the Wars: 1914–1940

Highams Estate, Chingford

The Warner family was responsible for developing much of Walthamstow. This estate, laid out on the site of the Highams Estate which had been landscaped by Humphrey Repton, aimed to be 'the most attractive residential estate north of the Thames' and was developed in 1930–36 around Charter Road by the architects William and Edward Hunt. Ten different sorts of houses were built; some were half-timbered. Designated an area of special character, but not a conservation area.

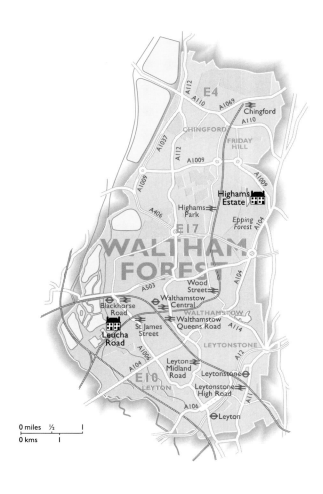

0 miles ½ 1
0 kms 1

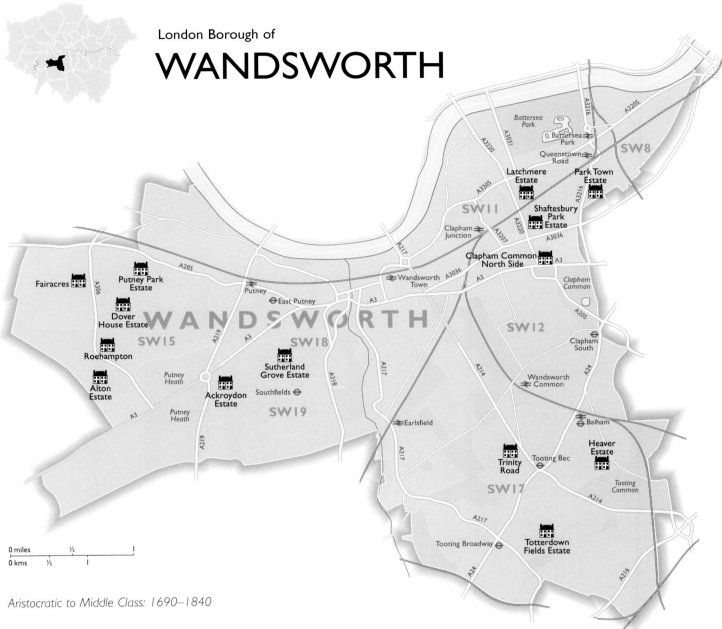

London Borough of
WANDSWORTH

Battersea
Park

Battersea
Park

Queenstown
Road

SW8

Latchmere
Estate

Park Town
Estate

SW11

Shaftesbury
Park
Estate

Clapham
Junction

Clapham Common
North Side

Clapham
Common

Fairacres

Putney Park
Estate

Putney

Wandsworth
Town

East Putney

Dover
House Estate

SW15

Roehampton

SW18

Sutherland
Grove Estate

Southfields

SW12

Clapham
South

Wandsworth
Common

Balham

Alton
Estate

Putney
Heath

Ackroydon
Estate

SW19

Putney
Heath

Heaver
Estate

Earlsfield

Trinity
Road

Tooting Bec

SW17

Tooting
Common

Tooting Broadway

Totterdown
Fields Estate

0 miles   ½   1
0 kms   ½   1

Aristocratic to Middle Class: 1690–1840

Roehampton, SW15

During the first half of the seventeenth century this once sleepy hamlet in Putney was transformed into an élite villa quarter. It had all the ingredients for success, including a perfect location and close association with royalty. A century later Daniel Lysons recorded many villas here, the most celebrated being Lord Bessborough's Parkstead, built to the designs of Sir William Chambers. One of the great survivors is Roehampton House (◗*pictured right*), designed by Thomas Archer and largely completed by 1710.

Infinite Variety: 1840–1914

The construction of the railways and opening of many stations from 1838 was the catalyst to the development of the open fields of Battersea and Clapham, which were progressively transformed into new housing estates; the strips and hedges of the fields later represented the boundaries of the new residential estates. Between 1840 and 1910 some 141 building estates were developed in the parish of Battersea, and the population increased from 6000 to 168,000. The developer Alfred Heaver made an enormous impact on the Battersea townscape with the construction of over four thousand houses in the area between 1880 and 1900. Many of these are in conservation areas, of which there are forty-four in the borough.

Clapham Common North Side, SW4

Most of the north side of the Common is typified by large, elegantly detailed red- or stock-brick late Victorian and Edwardian terraces, distinguished by balustraded balconies. (See also **London Borough of Lambeth**)

Park Town Estate, Battersea, SW8

By Philip Fowler and James Thomas Knowles from 1863. Unusually for a speculative development, Fowler and Knowles laid out the estate roads rather than rely on the lease purchasers to do so. The result is an unusual formal architectural layout, with the variety provided by the builders developing individual streets and plots within a roughly rhomboid area, and Queenstown Road as a central spine. Knowles reserved key sites for himself on which to erect such buildings as the centrepiece of the estate, St Philip's Church (1870) in St Philip Square. The surrounding houses in St Philip Street (1860–70; ⊙ *pictured above*) were also designed by Knowles and are the grandest Italianate houses on the estate, replicating the fashionable estates of Belgravia and Clapham Park. The apartment blocks in Queenstown Road were built in the French Empire style.

Shaftesbury Park Estate, Battersea, SW11

A consciously suburban estate to the south-east of Latchmere Road and abutting the railway, built by the Artizans', Labourers' and General Dwellings Company between 1873 and 1877 (i.e. contemporary with Bedford Park, Turnham Green (see **London Borough of Ealing**), and a

striking contrast). The estate comprises about 1200 two-storey houses with gardens, laid out in long, wide, tree-lined streets on a grid layout, designed by J.G.W. Buckle. They are of stock brick with red-brick dressings and pitched slate roofs. Gables towers and bays are used to break up the monotony of the long terraced frontages. The entrance to the estate in Grayshott Road is emphasized by two corner turrets on the end houses. Public houses were deliberately excluded. A designated and generally well-preserved conservation area; some groups of houses in Grayshott Road and Elsley Road are listed.

Trinity Road, SW17

West of Balham High Road, Crockerton Road, Dalebury Road and Trinity Road were developed between 1871 and 1890 by Alfred Heaver on the former Wandsworth Lodge Estate. The houses, in pairs or short terraces, are of red or yellow brick with porches and dormer windows, decorative cornices with nailhead string courses, stained glass in the doors, tessellated tiled paths and ornate cast-iron railings. Also in the southern stretch of Trinity Road is a fine police station of 1890 and Trinity Road LCC Fire Station of 1907.

Heaver Estate, Balham, SW17

Developed by Alfred Heaver, builder and speculator, and his architect, Charles Bentley, from 1890. The estate includes six streets off Ritherdon Road, comprising predominantly two- and three-storey houses, which vary from the substantial detached and semi-detached in Bedford Hill to long streets of terraces in Terrapin Road and Veronica Road. All houses are constructed of a warm orange- red hand-made brick to front façades, yellow for flank and rear walls. Slate or clay tiled roofs, panelled doors with stained glass. Designated a conservation area, but is struggling to retain its original character in the face of erosion of detail and insensitive alterations.

Putney Park Estate, West Putney, SW15

The Putney Park Estate – including Briar Walk and Woodborough Road – was developed in the 1890s and owes its strong architectural character to the fact that it was developed largely by a single builder, William Bishop, using just three or four designs. These include large detached houses in a free Arts and Crafts style with grand classical porch details, and built of high-quality materials: dark red brick,

stone dressing (from Bishop's own Ham quarries in Somerset) with some stone mullioned windows and tiled roofs.

Latchmere Estate, Battersea, SW11

A compact enclave of early public housing for the working classes off Latchmere Road: two-storey cottages in a grid of short streets lined with pollarded plane trees, built by Battersea Vestry in 1900–03. The houses are built in an identical style with similar materials, stock brick with red band course, moulded window heads in 'granolithic' concrete made with crushed granite, and slate roofs. There are projecting canopies over the doorways. A designated and well-preserved conservation area, although there are no individually listed buildings.

Totterdown Fields Estate, Tooting, SW17

The first of the LCC cottage estates, built in 1901–1911 by the Architect's Department under W.E. Riley, and influenced by the garden city principles and Arts and Crafts styles. Over one thousand two-storey cottages in groups are set in mostly straight streets either side of Franciscan Road. There is a variety of designs in four 'classes', each with front and rear gardens and using a mixture of rough-cast, tile-hanging, gables and bay windows. Designated a conservation area.

Between the Wars: 1914–1940

Dover House Estate, Roehampton, SW15

An 'out-county' estate built by the LCC from 1920 onwards, close to Putney Heath, consisting of over 1200 dwellings. The houses are laid out to a spacious and largely symmetrical plan, centred around Dover House Road, with a striking variety of different sorts of open spaces between buildings: crescents, closes, allotments, playgrounds and gardens. Putney Park House, on the former grounds of which the estate was built, was retained as a club house for tenants' use. Designated a conservation area.

Fairacres, Roehampton Lane, Roehampton, SW15

A complex of sixty-four flats designed by Minoprio and Spencely, completed in 1936. They are built of brick, but arranged on a sweeping crescent plan, with eight distinct blocks linked by stairs. The curved corners and metal windows lend the development an air of sleek modernity. Listed Grade II.

Sutherland Grove Estate, Southfields, SW18

A development of characteristic (if unexceptional) inter-war semis, many of which are half-timbered. Designated a conservation area.

The Road to Subtopia: 1940 to the present

Alton Estate, Roehampton, SW15

The most celebrated large-scale LCC development, mainly from 1952–60, in generous grounds but at a high density. Alton East (originally Portsmouth Road, 1952–55) is a mixed development of houses, maisonettes and flats in a Swedish style. Alton West (Roehampton Lane, 1954–62) is slightly later and tougher in its idiom, and includes the five slab blocks (1954–58) set into the side of the hill that are the most famous image of the development. Such slabs are found in more urban settings elsewhere, notably at the Loughborough Park Estate (see **London Borough of Lambeth**) and in Bentham Road, Hackney (see **London Borough of Hackney**), but the open layout and the hillside setting give the Alton slabs a unique quality that sets them above the rest. Alton West contains within it the listed eighteenth-century Mount Clare, Downshire House and Manresa House. The five slab blocks of the Alton Estate were listed Grade II* in 1998; ten further blocks and the bungalows were listed Grade II.

Ackroydon Estate, Wimbledon, SW19

The first estate to be developed by the LCC's Architect's Department in the post-war period (1951–54), and where the point block was pioneered as a way of preserving a mature landscape attributed to Joseph Paxton. The largest Victorian house on the site was retained as a school for the blind, while around it were gathered maisonettes. The first point block, Oatlands Court, was followed by two similar T-shaped points on the (later) eastern part of the estate, where the landscape is more open. Originally known as Wimbledon Parkside (the estate includes Princes Way, Victoria Drive and Inner Park Road, to the east of the northern tip of Wimbledon Common), the present name is often misspelt.

City of
WESTMINSTER

Westminster in the Middle Ages was separate from the City of London., having been established by the building of the collegiate church of St Peter, later Westminster Abbey. Even before the Abbey's precursor was built, Edward the Confessor moved his main royal residence here from the City of London so that, from the beginning, the district was an administrative centre of sorts. It was never really a suburb, although it spawned several, notably the Strand, which was lined with great houses by the sixteenth century. It was Henry VIII who encouraged large building schemes west of the City of London, by concentrating his administrative power on Westminster. Parliament was here and also the royal courts of law. Henry also formed parks at St James's Palace and Hyde Park. The building of regular streets around the Palace and Abbey did not begin until the late seventeenth and early eighteenth centuries, when the parish of St Margaret's was developed on the London leasehold model. Houses here were not suburban, being desirable mostly for their proximity to Parliament and the courts, and many of the residents had houses elsewhere, in proper suburbs.

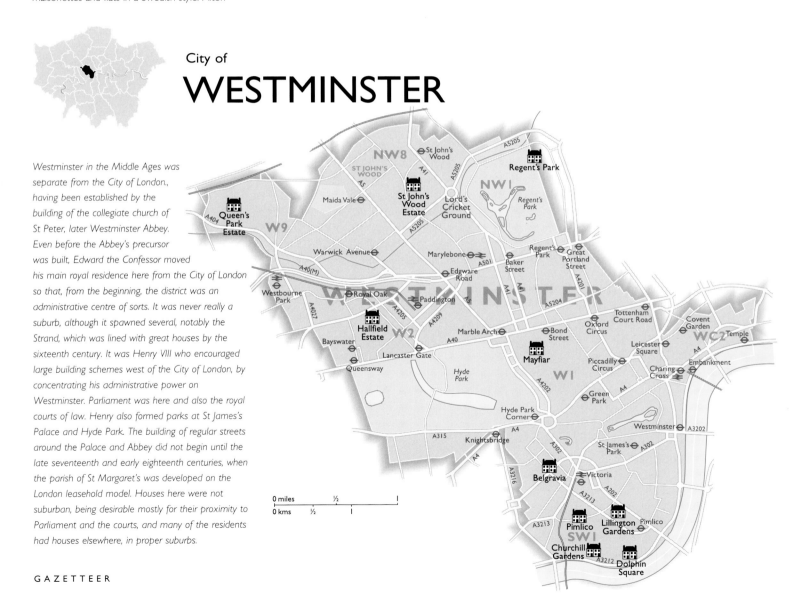

Aristocratic to Middle Class: 1690–1840

Mayfair, W1

The development of Mayfair, which takes its name from a fair held near the site of what is today Shepherds Market, began with the large mansions built in the 1660s. Denser speculative development of a very high quality followed, but in a fitful way. In the early eighteenth century Clifford Street, New Bond Street and Conduit Street were laid out, as well as the first houses in Hanover Square. Grosvenor Square was built in 1725, and Berkeley Square, which had actually been laid out much earlier, in 1675 (predating Kensington Square; *see* **Royal Borough of Kensington and Chelsea**), was filled in with houses during the 1730s. By the 1780s the area, a significant part of which belonged to the Grosvenor Estate, was built. Some houses survive from this first, protected phase of development, but much had been redeveloped, as the original ninety-nine-year leases expired. Mayfair is the sort of development that eludes easy classification. Was it suburb or town? For many of the very original grand inhabitants, Hanover Square would have been their primary town address, and leaving town meant going to a county house out of the 'season'. The high concentration of great wealth makes Mayfair a special case.

St John's Wood Estate, NW8

Even before Nash had projected his innovative scheme for the Regent's Park, St John's Wood was being developed with groups of modest villas laid out according to picturesque principles. The first scheme for the Eyre Estate dates to the mid-1790s and called for a grand circus girded with semi-detached houses. Only the semis were built, lining the roads north and south of the canal, the architecture a pleasant mix of Italianate and Gothic. When leases fell due in the 1920s and 1930s the estate took the opportunity to redevelop these modest houses with flats. More demolition followed, leaving only a few areas of late Georgian and Regency terraces, including Randolph Avenue (○ *pictured top right*)

Regent's Park, NW1

With building encroaching from the south in the 1790s, the 500 acres owned by the Crown Estates on the site of what would become Regent's Park was looking increasingly profitable. So when the farm leases fell due in 1811 a competition was held

to come up with a design for the estate. John Nash's winning design broke completely with the pattern of West End development, taking its cue from the park's curious shape. He scattered more than fifty villas along two concentric circles, leaving grand terraces around the edges. Only a fraction of the villas were ever constructed but the terraces were completed as planned by 1828. Nash did eventually design a villa quarter laid out on picturesque principles at the north-east corner of the Crown Estate in Park Villages East and West, executed from the late 1820s. This land had proved hard to lease so the architect took the

leases himself and built pretty houses calculated to evoke rustic associations. Park Village East was destroyed when the Euston railway cutting was enlarged in 1906. What remains, however, is a spectacular illustration of the ideals of the Romantic suburb.

Belgravia and Pimlico, SW1

A century after the Grosvenors developed Mayfair, they decided to do something with their Pimlico holdings. In the 1820s estate surveyor Thomas Cubitt, the grand man of the London building world, began to lay out Belgravia, later moving to

Pimlico. The star of the development, Belgrave Square itself (○ *pictured opposite bottom*), went to George Basevi, who built the four sides between 1826 and 1837. The architecture of the square has never really been admired by the *cognoscenti* and is best understood and appreciated as an uninspired version of Nash's winning Regent's Park Terrace formula. The rest of the area was developed from the 1830s to the 1860s. Pevsner observed that Eccleston Square and Warwick Square have much the look of Belgravia about them, seeming not to belong to Pimlico at all. Towards 1850 the character of development changed to the more recognizably Pimlico type as found in Bessborough Gardens, Bessborough Street, St George's Square, Winchester Street and Gloucester Street. This last has something of suburbia about it, and many of the houses would have been the primary residences of the commuting inhabitants. By mid-century, however, inner areas such as this were feeling the pressure of London's rapid growth. As for Belgravia, this was, like Mayfair, neither one thing nor the other. The scale and amplitude of its houses and spaces, its exclusivity, exude that sense of moral superiority which is one of the suburb's defining characteristics, but these houses were, for the most part, primary town residences, and so not suburban. Belgravia and Pimlico are transitional areas, caught on the cusp between the older Georgian model of suburban expansion and the railway-driven, outer London model.

Infinite Variety: 1840–1914

Queen's Park Estate, W10

Built between 1874 and 1885, Queen's Park was the largest of three suburban estates laid out by

the Artizans', Labourers' and General Dwellings Company. There is a gridded layout with long terraces of small two-storey houses by J.G.W. Buckle (of the Shaftesbury Park Estate; see **London Borough of Wandsworth**). Ornate porches and decorative brickwork enliven the terraces (○ *pictured left*). Rowland Plumbe designed the church and hall on Harrow Road. Designated a conservation area, with some listed buildings.

Between the Wars: 1914–1940

Dolphin Square, SW1

The *ne plus ultra* of large-scale developments of private flats, as found so often in the inner suburbs of inter-war London, epitomizing the domestic requirements of the professional classes for serviced, well-sited and efficiently run apartments. This vast development of 1937 (by the builders Costains, using Gordon Jeeves as architect) consists of some 1200 flats occupying a 7½-acre riverside site in Pimlico, with seven- to ten-storey brick ranges set around a courtyard in the customary (and, for this date, rather old-fashioned) manner. Dolphin Square was said to be the largest self-contained apartment complex in Europe at the time of its opening.

The Road to Subtopia: 1940 to the present

Churchill Gardens, Pimlico, SW1

Powell and Moya won Britain's first post-war housing competition in 1945 for a redevelopment then unprecedented in scale. Evolved over twenty years, replacing derelict dock areas and housing piecemeal, it featured Britain's first district heating system, fed by waste heat from Battersea Power Station. The first phase has large flats reached *via* distinctive glazed staircase towers; later, smaller flats with balcony access were preferred. The plan comprises large blocks with lower flats and houses at right-angles forming carefully landscaped courtyards, but the sweeping curve of the river and the principal estate road ensures that this grid is made fan-shaped and less formal. With shops and pubs, and incorporating a Victorian school, it was a pioneering example of mixed development at high density. Designated a conservation area; six blocks listed Grade II in 1998.

Hallfield Estate, Bayswater, W2

Designed in 1947 and built in 1950–55, this was the showpiece estate of Paddington Metropolitan Borough and the first public housing by Denys Lasdun, who took over the scheme when the Tecton partnership folded. It is similar to smaller housing schemes in Finsbury by ex-Tecton members, notably Spa Green by Skinner and Lubetkin, but the greater number of tall and low slab blocks, arranged in a loose grid similar to that of Churchill Gardens (*see previous entry*), gives a greater sense of place. This is reinforced by the abstract patterning of balcony fronts and end walls through the estate. It was one of the first schemes to combine housing with other facilities, here a fine school by Drake and Lasdun (1955). Designated a conservation area; school listed Grade II*.

Lillington Gardens, SW1

Like Churchill Gardens (*see above*), this was the subject of a competition from Westminster City Council, and in 1961 produced no less radical a solution (○ *pictured above*). Ideas on low-rise, high-density brick housing had been explored by CIAM in 1956 and by Sir Leslie Martin and his students subsequently, but Lillington Gardens (1964–72) was the first low-rise, high-density public scheme to be built. Its vibrant red brick, taking its cue from G.E. Street's church of St James the Less which the estate surrounds, its rich textures and complicated scissor plans transformed housing design over the next fifteen years. It is also an early example of perimeter planning, the blocks giving on to the street sheltering central communal gardens, an idea also subsequently explored by Leslie Martin and his team. Designated a conservation area; phases I and II were listed Grade II* in 1998.

Bibliography

P. Abercrombie, *The Greater London Plan*, London (HMSO) 1945

T. Affleck Greeves, *Bedford Park: The First Garden Suburb*, London 1975

Allison *et al.*, *The Value of Conservation? A Literature Review of the Economic and Social Value of the Cultural Built Heritage*, London (English Heritage) 1996

S. Beattie, *A Revolution in London Housing: The LCC Architects and Their Work, 1893–1914*, London 1980

A.L. Beier and R. Finlay, *The Making of the Metropolis: London, 1500–1700*, London 1986

R. Beevers, *The Garden City Utopia*, 1988

E. Betham (ed.), *House Building, 1934–1936*, ca. 1936

W. Bonwitt, *Michael Searles: A Georgian Architect and Surveyor*, Society of Architectural Historians Monograph, III, London 1987

P. Brandon and B. Short, *The Regional History of England: The South East from AD 1000*, London 1990

M. Brisbane and J. Wood, *A Future for Our Past? An Introduction to Heritage Studies*, London (English Heritage) 1995

M. Brown, 'St. John's Wood: The Eyre Estate before 1830', *London Topographical Record*, XXVII, 1995, pp. 49–68

G.E. Cherry, *Town Planning in Britain Since 1900*, Oxford (Blackwell) 1996

M. Cosh, *The Squares of Islington*, I, London 1990

H. Creaton (ed.), *Bibliography of Works on London History to 1939*, London 1994

T.C. Cullingworth, *Town and Country Planning in England and Wales*, 3rd edn, 1970

Davies and Keate, *In the Public Interest: London's Civic Heritage at Risk*, London (English Heritage) 1995

J. Delanfons, *Politics and Preservation*, London (E. and F.N. Spon) 1997

P. Denton (ed.), *Betjeman's London*, London 1988

Department of the Environment, *Planning Policy Guidance: Planning and the Historic Environment (PPG15)*, London (HMSO) 1994

R. Durant, *Waiting: A Survey of Social Life on a New Housing Estate*, 1937

H.J. Dyos, 'The Growth of a Pre-Victorian Suburb: South London, 1580–1836', *Town Planning Review*, XXV, 1954, pp. 59–78

H.J. Dyos, *Victorian Suburb*, Leicester 1973

A.M. Edwards, *The Design of Suburbia*, 1981

D. Edwards and R. Pigram, *London's Underground Suburbs*, London 1986

C. Ellis, 'Lambeth, une politique urbaine', in Gwénaël Querrien, *Londres, portrait de ville*, Paris (Datar) 1991

English Heritage, *Conservation Areas in London and the South East*, London 1990

English Heritage, *Framing Opinions* (supplement to *Conservation Bulletin*, XIV), London 1991

English Heritage, *Conservation Area Practice*, London 1993, rev. 1995

English Heritage, *Street Improvements*, London 1993

English Heritage, *Conservation in London*, London 1995

English Heritage, *Conservation Area Appraisals*, London 1997

English Heritage, *Looking After Conservation Areas*, Conservation Leaflet, London 1998

English Heritage, *Listing Buildings*, Conservation Leaflet, London 1998

English Heritage, *Looking After Historic Buildings*, Conservation Leaflet, London 1998

English Heritage, *The London Streetscape Manual*, forthcoming

English Heritage and the London Planning Advisory Committee, *Conservation in London: A Study of Strategic Planning Policy in London*, London 1995

English Historic Towns Forum, *Townscape in Trouble*, 1992

English Historic Towns Forum, *Conservation Area Management*, 1998

L. Esher, *A Broken Wave: The Rebuilding of England, 1940–80*, London (Allen Lane) 1981

R. Fishman, *Bourgeois Utopias*, New York 1987

J.H. Forshaw and P. Abercrombie, *The County of London Plan*, London (Macmillan) 1943

R. Glass (ed.), *London: Aspects of Change*, London 1984

M. Glendinning and S. Muthesius, *Tower Block*, New Haven and London (Yale University Press) 1994

Greater London Council, *Home Sweet Home*, London (GLC) 1976

Greater London Council, *The West London Report*, London (GLC) [ca. 1984]

Haringey Council, *The Tower Gardens Estate Repair and Conservation Guide*, London 1997

E. Harwood and A. Saint, *Exploring England's Heritage: London*, Norwich (HMSO) 1991

C. Hibbert, *London: The Biography of a City*, Harmondsworth (Penguin Books) 1969, rev. 1977

S. Humphries and J. Taylor, *The Making of Modern London, 1945–85*, London (Sidgwick and Jackson) 1986

D. Insall, *Chester: A Study in Conservation*, London (HMSO) 1968

S. Inwood, *A History of London*, London (Macmillan) 1998

A.A. Jackson, *Semi-Detached London. Suburban Development, Life and Transport, 1900–1939*, Didcot 1973, rev. 1991

K.T. Jackson, *Crabgrass Frontier*, 1985

W. Kennet, *Preservation*, 1972

J.R. Kellett, *The Impact of Railways on Victorian Cities*, London 1969

D. Lessing, *London Observed*, 1992

S. Macdonald (ed.), *Modern Matters: Principles and Practice in Conserving Recent Architecture*, London (English Heritage) 1998

K. McDonnell, *Medieval London Suburbs*, Chichester 1978

Ministry of Housing and Local Government, *The Green Belt*, London (HMSO) 1962

Ministry of Housing and Local Government, *Historic Towns: Preservation and Change*, London (HMSO) 1967

Ministry of Housing and Local Government, *Family Houses at West Ham*, London (HMSO) 1969

H. Muthesius, *Das englische Haus,* 1904, trans. as *The English House*, Oxford 1979

S. Muthesius, *The English Terraced House*, London and New Haven, 1982

C. Mynors, *Listed Buildings and Conservation Areas*, 2nd edn, London 1995

I. Nairn, *Modern Buildings in London*, London (London Transport) 1964

A. Olechnowicz, *Working-Class Housing in England Between the Wars: The Becontree Estate*, Oxford 1997

P. Oliver et al., *Dunroamin: The Suburban Semi and Its Enemies*, London 1981, rev. 1984

L.F. Orbach, *Homes for Heroes. A Study of the Evolution of British Public Housing, 1915–1921,*1977

J.J. Palen, *The Suburbs*, 1995

S. Pepper, 'Housing at Roehampton', in *The Cambridge Guide to the Arts in Britain, IX: Since the Second World War*, ed. Boris Ford, Cambridge (Cambridge University Press) 1988

N. Pevsner, *The Buildings of England: Middlesex*, Harmondsworth (Penguin Books) 1951

Pevsner: B. Cherry and N. Pevsner, *The Buildings of England: London 2: South*, Harmondsworth (Penguin Books) 1983

Pevsner: B. Cherry and N. Pevsner, *The Buildings of England: London 3: North West*, Harmondsworth (Penguin Books) 1991

Pevsner: S. Bradley and N. Pevsner, *The Buildings of England: London 1: The City of London*, Harmondsworth (Penguin Books) 1997

Pevsner: B. Cherry and N. Pevsner, *The Buildings of England: London 4: North*, Harmondsworth (Penguin Books) 1998

Pevsner: E. Williamson and N. Pevsner, *The Buildings of England: London Docklands*, Harmondsworth (Penguin Books) 1998

J. Phillips and H. Barrett, *Suburban Style: The British Home 1840–1960*, London 1987

Planning (Listed Buildings and Conservation Areas) Act, London (HMSO) 1990

R. Porter, *London: A Social History*, Harmondsworth (Penguin Books) 1994

S. Porter, *Exploring Urban History: Sources for Local Historians,* London 1990

M.J. Power, 'Shadwell: The Development of a London Suburban Community in the Seventeenth Century', *London Journal*, IV, 1978, pp. 29–48

A. Ravetz, *Remaking Cities: Contradiction of the Recent Urban Environment*, 1981

J.M. Richards, *The Castles on the Ground: The Anatomy of Suburbia*, London 1946

H.W. Richardson and D.H. Aldcroft, *Building in the British Economy between the Wars*, 1968

M. Robbins, 'Transport and Suburban Development in Middlesex down to 1914', *Transactions of the London and Middlesex Archaeological Society*, XXIX, 1978, pp. 129–36

R. Rogers, *Cities for a Small Planet*, 1997

P.G. Rowe, *Making a Middle Landscape*, 1991

Royal Town Planning Institute, *The Character of Conservation Areas*, 1992

Royal Town Planning Institute, *Conservation: A Good Practice Guide*, forthcoming

J. Ruskin, *The Seven Lamps of Architecture*, London 1849

A. Saint (ed.), *Politics and the People of London*, London (Hambledon Press) 1989

M. Saunders, 'Metroland: Half Timbering and Other Souvenirs in the Outer London Suburbs', in *Our Past Before Us*, edd. D. Lowenthal and M. Binney, 1981, pp. 165–74

G. Smith, *Ernest George Trobridge, 1884–1942: Architect Extraordinary*, exhib. cat., Oxford, Oxford Polytechnic, 1982

R. Speer and M. Dade, *How to Stop and Influence Planning Permission*, 1994

G. Stamp (ed.), *Britain in the Thirties*, Architectural Digest, [ca. 1980]

R.A.M. Stern and J.M. Massengale (edd.), *The Anglo-American Suburb*, special edn of *Architectural Design*, LI, London (Academy Editions) 1981

J.R. Stilgee, *Borderland*, 1988

R. Suddards, *Listed Buildings*, London 1988

D. Sudjic, *The 100 Mile City*, 1992

J. Summerson, review of J.M. Richards, *The Castles on the Ground: The Anatomy of Suburbia*, *Architectural Review*, May 1947, p. 187

J. Summerson, 'The Beginnings of an Early Victorian Suburb', *London Topographical Record*, XXVII, 1995, pp. 1–48

J. Summerson, *Georgian London*, London 1942 (revised edition 1988)

J. Summerson, 'The London Suburban Villa, 1850–1880', *Architectural Review*, CIV, August 1948, pp. 63–72; reprinted in *The Unromantic Castle and Other Essays*, London 1990

Survey of London, London (Athlone Press) (all volumes)

M. Swenarton, *Homes Fit for Heroes*, London 1980

D. Thomas, *London's Green Belt*, London (Faber and Faber) 1970

F.M.L. Thompson, *Hampstead: Building a Borough, 1650–1964*, London 1974

F.M.L. Thompson (ed.), *The Rise of Suburbia*, Leicester 1982

S. Thrupp, *The Merchant Class of Medieval London*, Ann Arbor MI 1948, rev. 1962

J. Treuherz, *Victorian Painting*, London 1993

Tudor Walters Report: Report of the Committee on Questions of Building Construction in Connection with the Provision of Dwellings for the Working Classes, London (HMSO) 1918

R. Unwin, *Town Planning in Practice*, 1909

S. Vere Pearson, *London's Overgrowth and the Causes of Swollen Towns*, ca. 1939

The Victoria County History (all volumes for Middlesex and volumes V–VII for Essex)

Wandsworth Borough Council, *Do it in Style*, London 1992

S.B. Warner jnr, *Streetcar Suburbs*, 1962

G. Weightman and S. Humphries, *The Making of Modern London, 1914–39*, London 1984

V. Wigfall, *Thamesmead: Back to the Future*, London (Greenwich Community College Press) 1997

F.C. Willats, *The Land of Britain, Part 9: Middlesex and the London Region*, London 1939

G. Wright, *Building the Dream*, 1981

M. Young and P. Willmott, *Family and Kinship in East London*, London (Routledge and Kegan Paul) 1957

Index

The index is to places, persons, architectural practices and important organizations and events mentioned in the chapters only. The Gazetteer has been arranged borough by borough and chronologically within each borough for ease of reference.

References in italic are to figure numbers.